The Daisy Chain

Muril Hart

authorHOUSE®

AuthorHouse™
1663 Liberty Drive, Suite 200
Bloomington, IN 47403
www.authorhouse.com
Phone: 1-800-839-8640

First published by AuthorHouse 11/13/2009

ISBN: 978-1-4490-3682-9 (e)
ISBN: 978-1-4490-3681-2 (sc)
ISBN: 978-1-4490-3680-5 (hc)

Library of Congress Control Number: 2009910732

Printed in the United States of America
Bloomington, Indiana

This book is printed on acid-free paper.

Contents

Dedicated to the memory of

My mother Lillian "Bill" McIntyre Knight

This Book:

Intro: This book is a collection of stories from the Knight/ McIntyre family as told to Muril Knight Hart by older generations of the families. Its writing is an effort to bring the ancestors of Troy and Muril Hart closer to an understanding of their forebears and give them a better grasp on the roots from which they stem.

Research on this book started years ago but the actual writing of it only began the morning of July 24, 2008.Material for the Dazerine section came directly from Lillian McIntyre Knight in conversations with her and from notes that she wrote, at my request, over the later years of her life. To my surprise, Lillian, my mother, not only did not object to the time and effort it took to record her marvelous stories of the young McIntyre family, to the contrary, she seemed pleased and proud of the opportunity to pass on her stories, the memories of her family growing up, and her mother's tenacious dedication to her family.

I heard these stories many times over the years, and in the back of my mind, I long believed that I would one day put them in book form for the younger generations of our family. However, something else always took precedence, and there was the fear that I wasn't competent to accomplish such a formidable task as actually writing a book. Now, at the age of 82 years, I think it is long overdue to attempt it.

The fact that when I awoke in the pre-dawn hours of this day to a foggy view of the world and noticed that my vision has worsened, I realized that time waits for no one, and the frailties of aging might preclude my ever completing this work that I had set out for myself years ago. The fear that I may be going blind threatened to overwhelm me, but it also goaded me to begin the writing of these family stories.

Doctors diagnosed and began treating the macular degeneration that hampers my vision several months ago. So, taking fear in hand, I begin this book.

This book is named "The Daisy Chain" in honor of my grandmother, Dazerine McIntyre, known as Daisy. The name originated about 1987, after a family reunion of Daisy's descendents gathered in Texas. Shirley Knight Collins suggested the Daisy Chain name. She explained that we were all links in a family chain that came from our grandmother Daisy, thus we were the "Daisy Chain". It made sense to us and we adopted the name.

Acknowledgements

It has been more than a year since I started this book. Now, it is finished and it is with some anxiety that I, being such an amateur at this book-writing game, send it off to be printed. Many thanks to those family members, you know who you are, who kept encouraging me to finish the book when I became discouraged to the point of quitting. Thank you for that kind word at just the right moment.

Thanks to P.J. Burton, Jenny Schubert, and Sarah Bliss for your help in reviewing an editing.

Credits are due to my sister, Jean for her earlier genealogy book, which I referred to for fact-finding details.

Thanks to, Jonell Hart, T.C. Bliss, David Hart, and Ryan Bliss, for their "how to" help to do this and that on the computer. Thank you to Rivers and Maggie for your interest in seeing the book done.

Thank you Troy M. "Tim" Hart for your thoughtful and well-appreciated comment on my "literary style".

To other members of my family, who are not mentioned here, I also thank you for your support and hope you will all enjoy reading this less than perfect book that is written especially for you.

PART 1
THEY CALLED HER

D
A
I
S
Y

PROLOGUE: DAZERINE (RHYMES WITH JAZZ)
THEY CALLED HER DAISY OR DAZ.

Daisy McIntyre was rarely called by her full given name, Louisa Dazerine. Her friends called her Daisy or Daz, depending on who was speaking.

Daisy was my maternal grandmother, born March 17, 1880, a courageous widow, she raised her children under adverse conditions, sacrificing her own comfort and well being to the needs of her family and she did so with great heart. She died before I was born but through the stories of her second daughter, my mother, Lillian, Daisy lived more vibrantly for her grandchildren than the paternal grandmother who was alive but absent for the most part of our lives.

Daisy was a charismatic woman, but like most strong people, a complex personality, both highly moralistic and naughty at the same time. Loyalty to family was high on her priority list as well as commonly good manners. The term, "commonly", is used to describe down to earth courtesy, not the fine manners of high society.

Daisy's husband, Jay, died when she was 32, leaving her with four young children to raise, alone. As a young widowed mother, Daisy's life was one hardship after another but her children never saw the fears or the doubts she felt, because she put forth an air of assurance that the bad times would be dealt with, and everything would be all right.

McIntyre Family 1907: Daisy, Lillian, Ira, Eva, Jay

The olden days

"I was born in 1905 in Arkansas on a farm called the old Ethican place," she began. It was my mother, Lillian McIntyre Knight speaking. She was about to tell my sister, Jean and me, a story about the "olden days." She wanted to share with us the life she had known as a child but more than that, she wanted us to know her mother, Dazerine Petty McIntyre and the family history.

Jean and I loved to hear the stories and we would sit quietly listening to her family tales even though we had heard them many times before.

"My mother said I was the ugliest baby she ever saw," Lillian continued. "She said I had long black hair that lay on my shoulders and I cried all the time for several days. She said no wonder that I cried so much with that face. My father was Elijah Jackson McIntyre but everyone called him Jay. He had wanted another boy to help with the work. He said girls just ain't much help with farm work. My brother, Ira, was nearly 3 years-old when I was born and my sister, Eva was almost 10. My brother Clell, the baby of our family, was born after me in January 1911" Lillian said.

"I didn't have much in common with Eva. She was a grown-up to me, more like a mother than a sister. She took care of Ira and me a lot when Mama was out working. Ira and I thought Eva could do no wrong. She was so good to us kids. She didn't hit me or even get cross with me, but she was sometimes a bossy kid. Ira teased her a lot and that caused trouble sometimes.

I remember when Papa sent away for some little cherry trees. Papa had just bought the Tillery place and we moved there. He put everything he had into it. He bought the two cherry trees and put them in the side yard. Money was always so scarce that it was a burden for him to buy the trees. They were growing real good and Papa was proud of his trees.

Mama had left us with Eva that day and Ira got one of his bad teasing spells. He was really aggravating Eva, and Eva finally got mad. She went out, and broke off one of the cherry trees and whipped Ira real good with it. When Papa got home and found out about his tree, he hit the ceiling. He was so mad, he cussed and reared and stomped. He even threatened to whip Eva but instead he just blew off and cussed more than anything. Mama wouldn't let him whip Eva. She just kept saying 'now Jay, now Jay' she would say, 'she's just a kid.' I can remember just standing there waiting for something to happen, he was terrible mad but he didn't hit Eva. Mama wouldn't have let him.

The Story Begins

It was a cold day early in 1912 and there was no heat in the house when the authorities showed up at the door of the two-room, tarpaper shack that was Daisy's new home in northeast Kansas City, Missouri.

This dreary house was far different from the modest but cozy home she had left in Arkansas after her husband Elijah Jackson "Jay" McIntyre died. Daisy, a young widow of only a few months, was at home alone with her children. Laid off from her job at the meat packing plant, living far away from family and friends in Arkansas, she was desperate with worry about where the family's next meal was coming from.

Work at the meat packing plant was grueling hard, meager pay, and deplorable working conditions. There were labor unions at that time but they were in their infancy and "sweatshop" labor prevailed. An employee might give his employer a good steady, seven days of work a week for months, but have one sick day off and be fired, no matter how well they worked or how dependably they performed in the past. Employers didn't worry about replacing an employee because times were hard and other workers waited in line to take the low-paying jobs.

As a grown woman, Daisy's daughter, Lillian, described to her children, events that occurred during that time.

"Mama was working in the meat packing house and Eva kept house and took care of us kids, and she also went out to look for a job," said Lillian.

"Ira and I always walked to the streetcar line to meet Mama when she got off work. I know now that Mama was sick herself that night …that evening", she corrected herself.

"We went to meet her," Lillian said. "It was nearly dark and Mama hadn't come. We waited at the streetcar line quite a long time, long past the time she should have been there. So, we decided to look for her.

We walked up one street and down another. We went back home to see if we had missed her but she wasn't home so we went back to the carline. She wasn't there so we started looking everywhere but we kept coming back to where she should get off the streetcar.

We had decided to go back to the carline when we saw her. She was real sick. She didn't know where she was. But, when we found her she said, 'what in the world are you children doing out in the streets so late?'

She was hugging us, and half crying. I guess she was so sick and worn out she just had a lapse of memory, but I guess she felt like she had to keep going," said Lillian.

Eventually, the long hours and heavy work took its toll on Daisy and she lost her job. She managed to get work housecleaning here and there or temporary work of some sort but it was not enough and hunger became an everyday companion to the family.

Finding work that paid living wages was difficult enough for a man in 1912 and almost impossible for a woman. There were always more people looking for jobs than there were jobs available.

Not rising from her chair, Daisy glanced out the window as three strangers emerged from the car and slammed the doors. Were they coming to her house? She wasn't sure but something about them made Daisy uneasy. What did they want, she wondered.

A combination of circumstances had prompted Daisy to sell out and move from the Ozark hills to Kansas City after Jay died. It was Bob Scott, her stepfather, who suggested the plan. Daisy was wary of Scott's offer that he would provide a home and buy groceries if she would keep house, do the laundry and cook for Scott and his grown son, Alonzo. She had good reasons not to trust his offer. Her childhood history with Scott was not good.

After Scott and her mother, Amanda Petty, married, when Daisy was ten, Scott had been an uncaring bully to both Daisy and her sister, Sophronia. (*Pronounced So- fron- yah.*) Daisy had two younger brothers, Will, three and Isaac, two. Amanda married three times; first to James Huffman, second to Daisy's father, Caleb Petty and third to Scott. Both James Huffman and Caleb Petty died as young men. Scott was married prior to marrying Amanda and had at least one grown son, possibly more children, that didn't live with him. Amanda had two older sons and a daughter from her first marriage, and two daughters and two sons by Caleb. The Huffman sons were young men at the time Amanda married Scott. George, 21, and John, 16, were outspoken in their objections to the marriage. They believed Scott to be lazy and an opportunist. They swore never to speak to Amanda again if she married him.

Daisy's father, Caleb, was known among his family and neighbors to be "an exceptionally good man." Before he died in 1855, he homesteaded 160 acres in the Missouri Ozarks and built a good home for the family.

Unfortunately, Caleb died in his 30s from pneumonia. George and John Huffman had been good and honorable sons to their mother after their father died and showed great respect for Caleb Petty but they wanted none of Bob Scott. They predicted that Scott would not work and provide for the family properly and that he would squander the assets that Amanda and Caleb had built up over their years of marriage. Amanda ignored her older sons' warnings and married Scott anyway. True to their words, her sons disowned her. As it turned out, George and John were correct in their assessment of Scott. After Scott and Amanda married, he did not work and he sold off Caleb's land, piece by piece, not for the saving or investing of it, but he used it to live on and for whatever he wanted.

Never far from Daisy's memories of life with Scott was one particularly bitter event. A heavy snowstorm had blown in covering the Ozark country in huge drifts of snow and biting cold winds. Scott in his usual overbearing manner ordered Dazerine, 15, and Sophronia, 16, out into the storm to bring in the stock and to do other outdoor chores. Daisy was not worried about herself but Sophronia was at puberty, a frail girl who experienced difficult menstrual periods. For whatever reason, Scott chose to ignore the fact that the girl was having a difficult time. Amanda didn't want Sophronia to go out and voiced her objections but, swearing insults about spoiled girls and other nasty remarks, Scott ordered both girls out into the cold and told them not to come in until they were finished. Amanda's pleas fell on deaf ears and Scott had his way.

Daisy took on the heavier chores and tried to shield Sophronia from the hard work as much as she could, but she felt a growing alarm as she watched Sophronia trying to get the work done. Sophronia was weak and she was leaving a heavy trail of blood in the new fallen snow as she worked. By the time they finished the chores and got back to the house, Sophronia collapsed at the door. Daisy helped her sister into the house and then lost her temper. She told Bob Scott she hated him and then turning on Amanda, she told her mother she would never forgive her for letting that happen. Sophronia was never the same after that night. She suffered nervous spells and convulsions; she died about five years later.

Daisy remembered all these things but possibly, due to her husband's recent death, plus two other life-altering events in close sequence, she let her desire for a better life influence her decision. Jay's death was difficult, but the family might have managed to scrape by where they were. However, shortly after Jay died, Daisy's oldest daughter, Eva, became deathly ill with typhoid fever and at this point in her life was not yet well. She had in fact gone in to what the doctor called a decline, sitting around listlessly, not interested in anything and staring into space. Secondly, Dazerine learned that her home was about to be foreclosed. The decision to move away from her family and friends, plus the stress and grief of the past few months had exacted a heavy toll on her and overwhelmed her better judgment.

Facing fear

The noise of car doors slamming and the murmur of voices, coming from the street once again caught Daisy's attention. She rose from her chair to look more closely out the window as three strangers, two men and a woman, approached her porch and walked to her door. They were all well dressed, but total strangers to Daisy. Over the years, Daisy had developed a keen instinct for trouble and for some reason not clear to her; the sight of these three strangers caused a sense of dread to seep into her bones. These people, she decided, looked like government people in their dark clothes and grim faces and Daisy was cautious of government people.

Her four children sat near Daisy on this dreary morning. Only the baby, Clell, whimpered he was hungry, even though the other three felt the gnawing pangs of an empty stomach.

Though these strangers seemed like trouble, Daisy decided to reserve her opinion. She was a country woman. Experience had made her cautious in her judgments and careful in her decisions. She would not jump to conclusions, she decided. She would bide her time.

The children sensed Daisy's wariness and they too became anxious. As she walked to the door, they clustered close around her skirt, matching their steps to hers. Daisy hesitated at the door, reluctant to open it.

A loud second knock sounded, but before she cautiously opened the door, Dazerine stooped and in low tones said something to Ira. Ira said nothing but nodded and quickly moved to a position by the back of the door as Dazerine opened it. Behind the door, a loaded shotgun sat, butt side down, against the wall.

She opened the door only as wide as necessary to hear their intentions and said "good day" to the strangers politely enough but with guarded restraint.

The visitors showed her their credentials establishing their authority with the city, then wasted little time stating their mission.

"Mrs. McIntyre," the woman began, "we are with the city relief bureau. It has been brought to our attention that you and your children are in need of help. Mrs. McIntyre, we are prepared to find work for you." the woman said in a condescending manner and waited for Dazerine's reaction to her words. Dazerine was a proud woman and not brought up to accept charity, but at this time in their lives, she would have welcomed help of almost any kind for her children's sake. However, the next words out of the woman's mouth shattered any illusions that Daisy might have had of getting the kind of help she needed.

The woman drew herself up tall, and pursed her mouth downward. She arched her eyebrows, then, clasped her hands in front of her. "Mrs. McIntyre," the woman said with exaggerated precision, "We will take your children and put them in an orphan's home where they will be properly clothed and fed. When you are financially able to care for them, you may get them back."

The woman stopped again to gauge Dazerine's reaction.

For a moment, Daisy was stunned, not able to speak or to take in the hateful words she had just heard. She stood as though frozen. Take her children! It was unthinkable! Her children in an orphanage; no, her children had a mother! They would not be taken from her!

Daisy's children had never seen their mother so angry. Lillian liked to remember her mother at that time. She recalled that Daisy was a tall woman, about 5ft.7 and thin.

"She was taller than I am," said the 5ft.4 Lillian. "She walked like she had a rod up her back and her chin slightly tilted up."

"Posture," Daisy often said, "is akin to good character and self respect."

A deep cleft in her chin softened Daisy's overall austere look and her clearly playful side was normally reflected in pale, Irish blue eyes that would brighten and sparkle to give away a quick if sometimes questionable sense of humor. Her overall look gave Daisy an appearance of confidence but at this moment, she was feeling anything but confident and there was no sparkle in her eyes. Her eyes were like ice.

"No one is taking my children," she hissed at the authorities and stepped back to slam the door shut. One of the men had stuck his foot in the door, and the other two surged forward into the room. A white rage came over Daisy and she drew herself up to her full height, glaring, tight lipped at the social workers. A combination of anger and fear threatened her reasoning and she trembled visibly.

Dazerine Petty McIntyre was a woman of pioneer blood, born and bred of five generations of frontier families in the Ozark hills of western Arkansas and southern Missouri; settlers who had learned to shift for themselves in hard circumstances. She grew up in the notorious Bald Knob Country near the Arkansas-Missouri state line called the lap land. For some time after the Civil War, the Bald Knob country was a wild and lawless area frequented by bandits and ruled by vigilante justice. Daisy often told her children true stories about road agents who committed crimes in one state and jumped over the state line to the other state to avoid the law.

Under vigilante law, these offenders were hung quickly in the public square or under a tree, sometimes unjustly, without due legal process for crimes they did, or appeared to have done. Eventually, the vigilante justice itself was corrupted to the point that it was difficult to tell which was worse, the law-breakers or the vigilantes. Some of Daisy's relatives and friends were Bald Knobbers in its early stages but left the group when the vigilante justice got out of control.

Daisy learned at a young age to look out for herself and her own people. In her Ozark home, she was known as a "woman to be reckoned with." These officious intruders would not intimidate her.

Daisy also had insight as to how orphans of that time fared. She had personally taken runaway orphans into her Arkansas home when they came begging to her door. She had listened to the stories of their dreary, institutionalized lives in the orphanages; how they were cut-off from relatives and living in crowded conditions subject to the whims and moods of low paid and poorly trained caregivers.

"We may need help, but no one is taking my children," Dazerine informed her unwanted visitors.

As they saw her anger building the men kept repeating, "Now, now, Mrs. McIntyre, Mrs. McIntyre settle down."

"Be reasonable Mrs. McIntyre. You don't understand Mrs. McIntyre," the woman spoke condescendingly to Daisy as though Daisy was an ignorant child. "It's obvious you can not properly care for your children."

She looked around the room with distaste. "Just look at this place," she said. "It's cold and bare. There's no food in the house."

Dazerine's response was an icy stare.

Then in a reversal of attitude, the woman social worker's voice became strident. She set her jaw. In a no nonsense manner, she spit out her next words, "Now stand back Mrs. McIntyre. This is the best thing for your children, and for you. We are authorized to take these children into custody and that's what we intend to do." She moved toward the children.

Daisy did not step back. To the contrary, she knew she must now take the steps she had hoped to avoid. Her children except for Ira clung to her skirt. Ira stood alert by the door, as his mother had told him to do.

Determination had erased any visible fear from Dazerine's face. Angry beyond thinking, she now put her earlier plan in action. Arms at her side, she made a twisting motion with her arm, turning her open palm toward Ira. Ira, quietly ready by the door, saw the signal and knew what it meant. He grabbed the gun from behind the door and shoved it firmly into his mother's hand.

Dazerine was no stranger to guns. She could shoot as well or better than most men. She had a steady hand and had often hunted with her two brothers, Will and Ike, in the Ozarks while growing up. With the shotgun resting on her hip, she cocked the hammer back. The three strangers saw the gun and heard the loud clack of the hammer. They let out a collective gasp and froze in their tracks.

"Now Mrs. McIntyre, now Mrs. McIntyre," they repeated, "you don't want to do this," and turning quickly, they stumbled over each other in their haste to get out the door and off the porch. According to Lillian, the authorities left never to return. After that, Daisy managed to get work cleaning homes and Lillian and Ira went out on the streets after school and picked up rags and pieces of iron and old whiskey bottles and sold them to rag pickers.

"We would get maybe a dime and that would buy a loaf of bread and if we were lucky we would get enough to buy a little can of Pet milk.

"We scrapped coal along the railroad tracks for the heating and cook stove," said Lillian.

"I remember once Mama got a whole dollar for cleaning someone's house and she was so happy, and I said I wish we could have some Post Toasties."

For the McIntyre children Post Toasties cereal was a rare treat. Before they moved to Kansas City, they had never seen prepared cereals.

"Well," Daisy told her children, "we will just celebrate." and she handed Lillian a dime.

"Run to the store and get a box of Post Toasties," she said as if they were about to have a party.

"Boy, I had never tasted anything like those Post Toasties. We would take them over candy anytime," said Lillian.

Lillian Looks back

Lillian remembered well the night her father died. The family lived in Denver, Arkansas. It had been a marvelous Christmas in 1911. Even Jay, who was normally dour and disliked holidays, got into a holiday mood. He seemed to enjoy the celebration as much as the rest of the family. Daisy had put great effort into promoting a happy holiday. She and Jay had their difficult times during the last few years of their marriage and she wanted very much to bring some joy back into their lives. Before Christmas, after swearing the children to secrecy, she had worked extra hours in the town's dry goods store while Jay was working away from home in the mines or some distant farm. She managed to get enough money to buy a Christmas gift for all the children. She got Eva and Lillian a doll, Ira a cork gun and some rattles for Clell. Both Ira and Lillian got new shoes. She also purchased some beautiful black satin fabric and carefully hand stitched Jay a satin shirt with white pearl buttons. He had shown great pleasure with all her skillful holiday preparations.

"It had been the best Christmas for Papa that I can remember," Lillian said. One of our neighbors, the Rooks, went out of town for Christmas that year and they ask us to stay in their house while they were gone. So, we went to stay over Christmas. It was just up the road a piece from our house, a nice big house, about like a city house. The Rooks weren't rich but they had more money than most folks around Denver did. We were there for about a week.

"Before Christmas, Papa had been especially cross. He hadn't been able to get much work that winter and he didn't want Mama to work away from home. He was probably thinking there would be very little for Christmas that year But, while Papa was off working all he could, Mama had gone down to Ellis Beck's dry goods store and got Ellis to let her work. He was glad to have her so she worked and unbeknownst to Papa she bought Christmas presents for him and us kids. She cautioned us not to tell and spoil her surprise. Papa was cross to us kids but Mama was real nice to him and acted real happy. Once he said to her. 'Daisy you acts like you swallered a caneery bird.' He was saying canary bird but he pronounced the "a" like an "e" so it sounded like neery.

He was a very stern man. Ira and I were afraid of him. Later, as I grew older I realized he wasn't mean but probably worried most of the time over the shortage of money. I know now that Papa was a good man and loved us kids but he was so stern that we kids thought he was mean, and he had a short temper and would cuss a blue streak over nothing," Lillian said.

"After Christmas Papa acted like a changed man. He was happy. He took care of our stock and the Rook's stock. He had to go down to our house every evening to feed our stock. He went to feed, I think it was New Year's Eve and he was gone longer than usual. Mama began to worry. She went to the door and Papa was coming but he wasn't acting right. I remember looking out in the yard and seeing Papa coming down the road. He would stop and stand sort of humped over.

Mama said, 'There's something wrong with Papa,' and she ran to him.

'I've got a terrible pain in my chest' Papa told her. Mama helped him up the road and into the house, and then she got him right in bed. She got Doc Price and he came out right away but Papa just got worse. They put Denver mud on his chest but it done no good. (*There was a medical theory about that time that certain types of mud, such as clay, contained healing minerals, and other properties that promoted healing. Denver mud may have been one of them.*) We got Papa on home and even called Dr. Scott (no relation to Bob Scott)out from Omaha, Ark. but he couldn't do anything either. It went on several days.

"Eva didn't sleep at all. She cooked, brought in wood, and kept the fires going all night. Ira, who was eight, and I were too small to mess with fire. Mama stayed with Papa all the time. That left Eva, who was 15, to do

14

almost everything that needed done around the house. I can't remember who took care of Clell, he was just a baby, but I'm sure Eva did that too. During all this, us kids just went around like zombies. We didn't know what was happening but we knew it was a terrible thing.

Papa is gone

"One morning I woke up to a terrible sound. It was Mama crying. I had never seen her cry before. And now, she made this long wailing cry like it came from somewhere deep inside her. Papa had died in spite of all they did. When our doctor gave up, Mama got Dr. Scott out of Omaha and they even used Denver mud but it did no good," Lillian said.

Following Jay's death, Daisy handled the funeral preparations herself preparing the body for the final viewing with neighbors help.

"They didn't have an undertaker or nice coffin. He was laid out in a pine box right there in the family living room and all the family and friends filed somberly past the coffin," said Lillian.

"He was wearing his black satin shirt with the white pearl buttons. We kids were standing around not knowing what had happened.

Friends and family came and they all passed by the coffin for a last look and I went up and looked at Papa lying there so pale and still. I guess at that minute, there was a breeze in the house that caused it, but I saw his shirt move across his chest, sort of like a person breathing, and I throwed a fit," said Lillian.

"People used to tell such terrible stories of people being buried alive. I remember one being told about a young woman who had lots of money. She was buried with her valuable rings on her fingers and a grave robber had dug her up. He cut off one of her fingers to get her rings and her finger bled. The thief was scared so bad he run off without taking anything.

And, there was another story told that for some reason they opened a coffin and found the woman on her face. She had pulled all her hair out. Being too young to understand all that talk, Ira and I believed the stories were true so when the wind blew Papa's shirt, I nearly went into hysterics. People told those old stories not thinking what effect it would have on a kid." Lillian said.

"Well", Lillian continued, "Papa was buried January 17, 1912 the day after he died. He died, I think, from what was called the black lung or pneumonia. He had come to Arkansas from New York and his lungs were bad from working in New York mines with dynamite. He was what was called, an expert powder man. When crops were laid by in the fall, he went all over the county digging water wells for people. He also worked in some of the mines around there. I don't know how, but he used dynamite to blow water wells. He was a dynamite man for the railroad when he first came to Arkansas in 1900,' Lillian said.

"After the burying was all over, Eva walked in her sleep. She got up three nights in a row and built a big fire in the middle of the night. Mama heard her and she got up too. She just watched Eva until the fire burned down, and then Mama would take Eva very carefully back to bed. She was afraid to wake Eva up. She worried it would throw her into shock." said Lillian.

Sometime in 1911 before Jay became ill, he mortgaged their debt free home to buy a fine horse and buggy. The purchase would have been a good investment for him if he had lived, even though it was a huge expense for the family's tight budget at the time. The horse was out of the famous Morgan breed.

"It was such a fine horse. It could pull a buggy or haul heavy timber. It was also a fine riding horse," Lillian said. "Papa figured he could earn the money the horse cost back in a short time," Lillian said.

Jay was confident that with the additional work plus the high dollar stud fees the animal would bring, he would quickly pay off his debt and be money ahead. Jay knew the horse was famous for its stamina and versatility .Unfortunately, he never got the chance to prove his theory.

Making the hard decisions

"We might have made it if Eva hadn't gotten sick," Lillian reflected. "Sometime after Papa died, Aunt Delia sent word asking for Eva to come to her and Uncle Will's place to help out during hog killing time."

Delia Petty was Daisy's brother Will's wife. Delia and Daisy were good friends as well as sisters-in-law. At the age of 15, Eva was considered a young woman who could take over the household chores, childcare and whatever household help was needed. Daisy didn't want to let Eva go. She needed Eva's help herself. Eva was a big help, in not only managing the household and looking after the younger children, but she and Daisy together had been operating the only phone service in Denver. However, Daisy knew that Delia would not have sent for Eva if she didn't really need her, so she let Eva go. While she was at Will and Delia's home, Eva became ill.

"Mama had Uncle Will bring her home. I remember that time so well," Lillian said.

"Eva had typhoid fever. She was so sick Mama had to quit work to take care of her. The doctor came every day. He had Eva take big doses of castor oil. Eva didn't like it at all and because she was so sick, she didn't know what she was doing and she would fight off the medicine and beg them not to give her the castor oil. Sometimes, Mama had neighbors help her give Eva the castor oil. When they did, I always ran out in the yard to a big swing. I'd get in the swing, and put my fingers in my ears and try not to hear Eva crying. I often wondered how she managed to live at all.

"At one point Eva almost died. She had been in a sort of coma for a while. Then she heaved a big sigh and went limp. The doctor took her pulse and pronounced her dead, and pulled the sheet up over her face. Mama got sort of hysterical I guess. She tore that sheet away, grabbed a bottle of whiskey, used for medical purposes, and began rubbing Eva's body in the whiskey with both hands and talking to her.

The doctor took the sheet from her and tried to put it back over Eva's face. Neighbors attempted to calm Mama and pull her away but Mama was like a wild woman. She pushed them away and kept on rubbing Eva. The doctor told everyone to leave Mama alone," Lillian said.

"Then Eva said, 'What's the matter Mama?' Everyone stopped what they were doing and just stared at Eva in surprise. Dr. Price said, 'It wasn't me that done it Daz, it was your will for her to live that did it."

Moving On

"Sometime after Eva got better but was still sick, the doctor warned Mama that she wasn't to have any solid food," said Lillian.

"Typhoid fever causes the victim to run very high fevers that cause internal organs to be very tender," Lillian said.

She said the patient's stomach and intestines are in such a vulnerable condition that they cannot tolerate solid food.

"One day Mama had to be out of the house for some reason and Eva asked me to get her a piece of bacon from the kitchen," said Lillian.

"I told her, Mama said she couldn't have it but Eva kept begging me and started to cry. 'Just a little piece' she said. It had been a very long time since Eva had any solid food, just weak soup. I knew she was hungry. Finally, she got me to get it for her. And, I had just got to her bed when Mama came in. Mama saw what I was doing but she didn't say anything, she just looked at me, took the meat and put it back. Then she said, 'You don't want your sister to die do you? Of course you don't. Now remember what you almost did' and, I sure never did forget it," Lillian said.

"Eva was sick for a long time. She seemed like she couldn't get well. She would sit listless in the chair and didn't take interest in anything. The doctor called it a decline and thought a change might be good for her. Then, Grandpa Bob Scott came down there and convinced Mama she could get work in the big city and he thought it would help Eva. Aunt Vick, Mama's sister in Kansas City, wrote Mama and urged her to come. She also said Mama could get a job and could probably do much better there than in Arkansas," Lillian said.

Daisy reflected on all her options. Eva's health was uppermost in her mind... The doctor had said a change might be the best thing for Eva. Dazerine's ability to provide for her now fatherless children had to be considered. However, the final straw was the fact that they were about to lose their home. Finally, after much deliberation, Dazerine made her reluctant decision to sell out what little she had in her Arkansas farm and move to Kansas City.

"So Mama sold what she could and just left everything else sitting," said Lillian.

It was Daisy's brother, Will, who handled the estate sale, and he did his best to bring in as much money as possible for Daisy, but results of the sale were disappointing. It was, after all, a poor farming community. Much of the local commerce in Denver was the trading of farm goods and homemade items. Very little actual cash money exchanged hands. Daisy took what money she had and packed what few things she could carry on the train and traveled to Kansas City.

"She packed our clothes and some things and left the rest of the stuff sitting in the floor," said Lillian. "I guess the neighbors got it. We had a cord bed and a cradle and a whole pile of quilts and braided rugs, and at least a hundred quarts of vegetables and quite a lot of meat," said Lillian. "Mama was so upset about the whole thing. I don't think she knew what she was doing. She was really sick herself," Lillian said.

Leaving all her cherished belongings to go to some unknown place was painful for Daisy. She knew she would miss her old friends and neighbors. Her children were even more reluctant to leave the only home they had known. Lillian, even at the young age of six felt a keen sense of loss.

Lillian Remembers Happier Times

"The same year Papa died, the thrashers came to cut Aunt Cal Young's meadow," Lillian remembered. "Ira and I sat on the fence watching the big thrashing machine go through the meadow. We had never seen such a big piece of machinery."

"Denver was more a village than a town. It had no central government but there were several stores and other businesses. .

"The Avery place is the first home that I remember," Lillian recalled. "I don't know why it was called Avery place unless that's who originally built it. It was about a 3-acre place. It was a hewed log house with here and there some bark still on the logs. I loved that place. To me, it was the most beautiful place in the world. We had the prettiest yard with flowers everywhere, and on the front porch, there was a marble vine. I never saw another one like it. It had what looked like little marbles on it," she said.

"We lived up the hill from the crick (creek) and Ira and I spent a lot of our time sitting on the fence of our front yard watching everything go by. We seen several cattle drives, just short ones, but we loved to watch them. We saw some sheep drives and once we saw a turkey drive. I remember what a lot of noise they made. We did not miss hardly anything that went down the road.

The house was built as one big room and a side room was built for a bedroom. That room was very small and dark. It was a bedroom but I can't remember ever being in it. But, if I acted up, Mama would threaten to put me in there. That's all she would have to do," said Lillian.

"We had a lean-to kitchen. The fireplace was big and had a hearth you could sit on. There was no glass in any of the house windows. The windows had slide-boards to open them and were only open in warm weather. There was a braided rug, on the floor, that nearly covered the whole room. The nicest bed in our house was in the front room.

Eva, Ira, Lillian, Clell, 1911

We had an upstairs and the steps went up on the outside to the second floor. That's where Eva and her girlfriends would sleep when she had company," said Lillian.

Daisy took great delight in teasing and she would go to elaborate lengths to play a joke on someone. On one occasion, she knew her brother, Ike, would be coming to her house along a wooded path after dark. She also knew that Ike was afraid of the dark. About the time she thought he would be on his way, Daisy went out of the house and hid by a tree. She waited an hour for Ike to come by. When he finally came down the trail, she jumped out at him and growled, "Put up your hands." Ike was properly startled and Daisy's efforts rewarded. Eva may have caught the brunt of Dazerine's pranks possibly because her reactions were so rewarding. On this occasion, Eva had girlfriends overnight.

Lillian said, "Mama got all dressed up in men's clothing and blacked her face. After dark, when the girls had settled in for the night, she went outside, climbed up a ladder to the upstairs window, stuck her head through the window and in a loud gruff voice said 'what are you doing up here.' Boy, those girls came down that staircase like a cattle stampede," Lillian said.

"Mama had a pet horse. His name was Prince and she really loved that horse. He learned to come to the kitchen window and nudge it open. He would put his head in and beg for sugar. Mama would give him a lump of brown sugar and he would whinny like he was thanking her.

"We had a wood burning cook stove and I can still remember that hickory wood smell when the fire was burning. The roof had homemade wood shake shingles. I can remember Papa making wood shingles and putting them on the roof. That place always felt like home to me. The side door opened toward a crick bank. It was clear blue, swift water. I guess we lived about a city block from the crick bank. Ira and I loved to play along the bank.

"There were two Maple trees in our front yard and it seemed like they were always full of birds.

"The barn was a wooden barn and the path from the house sloped up the hill to the barn lot. When we went to Denver, we went up through the barn lot. In the spring, the whole pathway was covered in blue flax flowers.

"I can remember going to Denver on Saturday. It was a sort of get together day there and seems like nearly everyone would be in town. We would stop and talk to everyone.

" Mama worked a lot for Uncle Henry Youngblood. She did a lot of wallpapering for him. I remember one pattern was great clusters of grapes. All good friends were called uncle or aunt but the Youngbloods were related to Mama through marriage. Aunt Martha Huffman and Aunt Delia Petty were sisters. Delia had married Daisy's brother, Will Petty, and Martha married Daisy's half brother, James Huffman. The Youngblood sisters were half Cherokee Indian.

"Uncle Henry was quite a colorful person. He was studying to be a lawyer so he started having what he called a kangaroo court. He would watch everyone in town and try to catch them breaking some rule of behavior, such as a young man kissing a girl or someone cutting wood or any kind of work on Sunday or some other minor infraction. He would then issue them a summons to appear in the Kangaroo court. Then, he would hold a mock trial at the schoolhouse, and call witnesses and go through everything like a real court with all sorts of shenanigans. The schoolhouse would be full. Everyone would come and have a good time teasing and poking fun," said Lillian.

"I remember going to Aunt Jane Youngblood's. That was Uncle Henry's mother and his brother Gar. But, their place was very different from Uncle Henry's. It was a one-room house. They had a place to cook outside and there were hound dogs laying around in the yard. Aunt Jane would cook up two or three pans of corn bread and cut it up in squares to feed the hounds. All Uncle Gar Youngblood did was hunt. I liked Uncle Henry real well, but I didn't like Uncle Gar because he teased me so much," Lillian said.

Daisy was a generally well-liked and respected woman around town, but one woman, Nola Rooks, who was a busybody, did not like her. Nola was a tall, thin woman and always seemed to have her nose in the air. She took it upon herself to tell people how to behave, the right and wrong way to live, what was proper, and what was not proper. There seemed to be some bad blood between Daisy and Nola, according to Lillian. Nola may have been jealous of Daisy.

Daisy had a friendly, winning way about her that drew people to her with little effort, often confiding their hard luck stories and secrets to her and frequently seeking her out for advice. She loved to laugh and though somewhat straight laced in many matters she could not resist a good joke or a funny story. Her daughter, Lillian, was a favorite with Nola's parents. They doted on the child, pampering her with lumps of brown sugar and rock candy. Nola and Dazerine were both excellent equestrians and often rode horses in town.

One day Dazerine started to town on her horse. A skilled seamstress, she was dressed in a new riding habit that she had made herself. Her outfit was the latest fashion and she felt good in it. It was made of dark material and had a split skirt similar to culottes but ankle length so that she could comfortably ride her horse astride. Dazerine was riding her horse down the road to Denver, and perhaps being dressed in her new outfit, she rode a little prouder than usual. She met Nola coming from the opposite direction. Nola rode sidesaddle, as she considered it the proper way for a lady to ride, and she carried a long switch for her horse. She always carried a long switch. Some people said she often swung the switch at children and dogs.

When Nola saw Daisy, she moved her horse to the middle of the road to block her path. Daisy reined her horse out to go around Nola, and Nola once again reined her horse to block Daisy. All the while, Nola was scolding at Daisy, something about women who wore split skirts and rode their horse astride instead of decently sidesaddle as she did, and in proper skirts, she emphasized.

Daisy told Nola bluntly to "get out of her way" and tried to get past her but Nola was not through talking and once again moved to block Daisy. Daisy said not a word but looked squarely at Nola then reached out, grabbed her shirtfront and jerked Nola off her horse. Nola went down with a thud taking a hard seat on the rocky road.

"She made a real scene yelling and screaming after Mama," said Lillian.

However, Daisy never looked back; she just rode on down the road as if nothing had happened," Lillian said.

"Mama was not a pretty woman but she was a handsome woman," said Lillian.

"A slightly hooked, English nose kept her from being pretty," said Lillian.

Long exposure to outdoor elements had also weathered the fair skin of the country woman.

"She had freckles and her skin was wind burned but her hair was beautiful, like a thick copper coil. Mama was an indescribable person," said Lillian.

"She had all the personality in the world and she was a nut besides. She would do anything in the world for a joke," said Lillian.

A lot of her jokes were played on Eva. Daisy herself had little or no apparent fear of anything. Therefore, she may have been a little insensitive to the trauma her playful antics caused her eldest daughter.

One of the more questionable jokes Daisy played on Eva was when Eva was sitting with Clell, who was just a few months old, on the outside stair steps.

"Mama had been out in the garden and she killed a little green garden snake. Eva was sitting about halfway up the outside stairway," said Lillian.

"Mama came walking up with the little garden snake and said 'Sister, look here,' and then threw the snake in Eva's lap. Eva screamed and jumped with Clell in her arms clear to the ground and Mama just belly laughed.

Daisy knew the garden snake was harmless but failed to understand the depth of Eva's terror of snakes.

"Mama was what you might call a character. She had a mischievous nature. She didn't mean to be mean," said Lillian

"None of us kids took after her in that way, but we worshiped the ground she walked on. She loved all of us kids but Ira was her special kid. Most country women of that time favored their first son."

Daisy, looking back

Daisy, as a child, spent much of her time in her grandparents, Sol and Liz Petty's, care. Both were recognized country doctors and well respected for their healing abilities. Dr. Sol, as he was called, was an herb doctor, and his wife, Liz, Dazerine's step-grandmother, was an herb doctor and a faith healer. They reportedly healed some skin cancer with an herbal mixture, and saved many premature babies by putting them in a warm oven with the door open.

Sol and Liz Petty

While in their care, Sol and Liz took the time to teach Daisy much of what they knew about healing. She learned to identify healing herbs growing in the wild, how to gather and store herbs, and their general use. They taught Daisy how to deliver babies and as an adult, she was well known in her own right as a mid-wife and healer. She often roamed over the countryside assisting local doctors as they tended the sick.

Daisy had a strict upbringing. Her step-grandmother was a spiritual person and held strict, prim values. It was probably due to Liz Petty's influence that Daisy never rolled her sleeves above her wrist or wore her skirt above her ankles. Daisy herself was a combination of strict parent and mischievous friend to her children.

There was no place in Daisy's life for vanity but Lillian always believed her mother took secret, but well deserved pride in her hair.

"I think she was proud of it but she never bragged on herself," said Lillian.

Lillian recalled one evening as her mother sat by the big rock fireplace in the center of the family's log home.

"After supper Mama would comb her hair when she was fixin to go to bed. I loved to watch her. The flames would catch the light in her auburn hair and it was beautiful, real thick and long. This one time, I remember she had sent off to a mail order catalogue for some combs for her hair. On this evening, she sat down by the fireplace and took down her hair. She took the new combs out of her hair and laid them down at the edge of the hearth. All of a sudden, there was a spurt of flame and the combs were gone. No trace of them was left. It's one of the things I never forgot," said Lillian.

"I remember really living it up when I had pneumonia. I was about five. I must have been real sick for both doctors to come to Denver to see me everyday there for a while. Dr. Price was our regular doctor and he called Dr. Scott in and ever time they came they would bring me a pear or an apple and chocolate turtles and rabbits and I wanted to save ever one. I thought I could keep them, I guess. I can't remember just what became of them.

"While I was sick Mama sent off to someplace and got a Bible story book. It was a beautiful book. The book was all embossed in pretty colors and the pictures were all in color. It was the most wondrous book I ever saw. Every evening after supper, Eva would read a Bible story to us. That is one of my best memories and I have a great many good memories," said Lillian

"Denver had its characters," Lillian said, "and one of them was Uncle Billy Head," Billy Head was what Lillian called "shirttail kin." She knew they were related but she wasn't sure exactly how.

"We all loved Uncle Billy", she said as she recalled one particularly amusing story about him.

"Everybody went to church in Denver. That was the only place there was to go. Every summer there was a baptizing down by the crick. People brought their old clothes to church to be baptized in. When it was time to be baptized, they changed out of their good Sunday clothes and put on their old clothes. No one had a swimsuit. The preacher would walk them out into the water about waist high, go through the ceremony, say the prayer, and then dunk them backwards into the crick.

" On this particular Sunday, the preacher had talked Uncle Billy into getting baptized. It was a big day and just about everybody in town attended. Everyone lined up along the crick bank to watch. You could tell who was to be baptized because they were wearing their old clothes and waiting their turn," said Lillian.

"Out they went, one by one. Then it was Uncle Billy's turn. The preacher started walking him out into the water when Uncle Billy saw a snake swim out into the crick. No one else saw the snake, no one but us kids and Uncle Billy. There was that snake swimming along. Now, Uncle Billy was tongue-tied and he said, ' there's a nake in the water.'

"No one paid any attention to him and, the preacher was so engrossed in his sermon he must not have heard him.

" Uncle Billy pointed and said again a little louder, 'there's a nake.'

" The preacher droned on and Uncle Billie was looking around, kind of wild eyed and scared to death, and the preacher walked him another step out into the water.

" Uncle Billy jerked away from the preacher and yelled 'there's a 'Dod dammed nake in the water and I'm getting out of here', and he did too. Of course that ended the baptizin," Lillian said

Buffalo Bill comes to Denver

"It must have been about 1910, when I met Buffalo Bill Cody, the famous showman, buffalo hunter and frontiersman. We knew the Cody family ever since I could remember. His sister was one of our neighbors and lived just around the corner from us," said Lillian.

"One of Buffalo Bill's nephews who lived near us died, and Buffalo Bill came to his funeral.

"The Codys, who lived near us, were well mannered, hard working people," Lillian said. "They were albino people, and Buffalo Bill had pink eyes and long white hair. He had a sister named Orville. She was at our house a lot. Mama put sage tea in Orville's hair and it made her hair light brown. She was thrilled with her light brown hair.

"Orville liked to tease Ira by bugging her pink eyes at him. When she did it, he would run away from her.

"Every one liked the Codys. I can see Buffalo Bill just the way he sat on his big white horse and all that silky white hair down over his shoulders." Lillian at this point got a far-away look in her eyes and a tiny smile played across her lips. "He looked then like the statue of him I saw later in Colorado where he was buried," she said.

Life's lesson learned

Jay McIntyre was not Daisy's first husband. She was just 15 when she left her mother and stepfather, Bob Scott's, home to get married. Ironically, it was Bob Scott's son, Charlie, with whom she chose to elope. After the fight she had with her step father and Amanda over their mistreatment of her sister, Sophronia, Daisy desperately wanted to be away from them.

Charlie was 25, a gambler and man about town, a man of experience, widely traveled and sophisticated. He knew how to treat a girl and was a glib conversationalist.

Did he sweep Daisy, a naïve, country girl off her feet with his free wheeling smooth talk or was she looking for a way out of her unhappy life under Scott's heavy-handed discipline?

Perhaps it was one or both, but things around the Scott household had deteriorated sharply after Sophronia collapsed at the kitchen door. Whatever motivated the young Daisy to elope, she and Charlie were married June 4, 1895. In May 1896, the couple had one child, a girl named Eva.

By the time Eva was a year old, Dazerine was weary of the wildly uncertain life she had with her gambler husband. It seemed they were either rich, spending money like there was no tomorrow or they were starving with creditors nipping at their heels. She hated the constant moves his gambling required and the unsavory and coarse company of Charlie's associates. Finally, Daisy could tolerate his lifestyle no longer and she left him, taking Eva with her. However, Charlie had other ideas. He came begging her to return to him. Daisy succumbed to his pleading and returned to her husband. She did it for Eva's sake, she said.

As it turned out, Charlie had actually duped Dazerine in to coming back to him because he wanted to steal Eva away from her. With the help of his sister, May, he took Eva away and across the state line to another sister, Ann's, home.

When Daisy realized what had happened, she was devastated and Charlie thought he had succeeded with his baby-snatching scheme. However, what Charlie didn't realize was that both his sister, Ann, and his brother, Lee, were fond of Daisy. Ann took the baby, Eva, in and cared for her, but she immediately sent word to Daisy, through Lee that she had the child. Lee was not only a friend; he was in love with Daisy and wanted to marry her. Lee drove Dazerine to Ann's home to retrieve Eva.

Once she had Eva back in her possession, Daisy never returned to Charlie and eventually divorced him. She and Lee remained friends but that was all it could be for Daisy. Although she admired and was fond of Lee, she was not in love with him.

Soon after that, Daisy found work at a Carroll County, Arkansas, boarding house. It was located in Cedar Township. Wilson Beaver, 67, and his wife Martha, 61, owned the establishment, and it was strategically located near the area where a new railroad line was under construction through Arkansas. The boarding house was a large family-style structure that had five regular boarders. It had a homelike atmosphere and was a popular place to eat for both the railroad men who boarded there and the township's residents.

This was the boarding house where Dazerine, then a young divorcee, met Elija Jackson "Jay" McIntyre. Daisy was a waitress, a cook and did whatever job needed doing around the boarding house. She and Eva also lived there.

Eva was four. She was a bright friendly child and because she was tiny for her age, she looked even younger than her four years. The tiny girl was a favorite attraction with the boarders who were railroad workers, mostly family men working away from home and lonely. She became a charming little distraction for the lonely railroad workers. She would mix and mingle with the boarders who pampered and spoiled her with attention. Daisy was always nearby.

Eva would climb on the empty tables and dance for the boarders who applauded and gave her pennies. Eva loved the attention.

Jay joined the railroad company in New York. He had worked his way across the country as a dynamite man when he arrived in Carroll County. Upon arrival, at the boarding house, it was the tiny Eva who caught his eye, but he was soon attracted to Daisy. The attraction must have been mutual because they quickly became more than friends and were married in 1900.

Jay McIntyre, a man of mystery

Jay McIntyre, who is to this day somewhat of a mystery man to his descendants, came to the boarding house with a white baby shoe in his pocket. He had no family in the area and never talked about his past. The baby shoe was never explained.

Jay was a complex man, on one hand he was a good, hardworking man, honest to a fault, but on the other hand he could be obstinate, overly controlling and jealous. The fact that he was 20 plus years older than Daisy might account for some of his controlling behavior, but when it came to matching his will against Daisy's, Jay sometimes met his match.

He didn't like for Dazerine or the children to go many places. Eva being of an age to go out with other young people, double date or go to parties would ask Jay if she could go to a chaperoned party or a dance in town. He would tell her she could go, but, when it was time to leave and Eva was dressed and ready to go, he would arbitrarily tell her she couldn't go for one reason or another.

Lillian said, he treated her mother in much the same way, saying the family would go on a church outing or a social gathering in town and then at the last minute say something like, "where do you think you're going?" Then, Lillian said, "He would say, 'You're not going anywhere.'" The family would be disappointed and Jay would be satisfied to do nothing the rest of the day.

However, Lillian remembered one time when Dazerine had enough of Jay's obstinate behavior. She had spent the morning frying chicken and preparing the picnic basket for a town picnic. She got the children dressed, and loaded the basket and the children in the wagon.

"Where do you think you're going," Jay asked?

Dazerine answered, "To the picnic."

Jay said, "You're not going anywhere. Now get down off that wagon"

"Then Mama said, 'Oh yes, we are,'" Lillian quoted her mother.

Jay reached up and pulled Daisy off the wagon. He then told the children to get down.

Daisy just reached down, picked up a rock and threw it at Jay. The rock caught him right in the head. Jay went down and he didn't get up.

"Mama got back on the wagon and drove off with him laying there in the yard. We went to the picnic and had a good time," said Lillian.

When the family got home, they were not sure what to expect from Jay. However, Jay had little to say and the subject was never mentioned again, Lillian said.

Although he was often overly strict and controlling, Jay did have a gentle side to him. Lillian said. Rare though the tender moments with her father were, Lillian did recall one particular time. It was raining and her father was sitting by the window reading and watching the rainfall.

"He reached out and picked me up and set me on his lap," said Lillian. "I felt so odd and didn't know what to say or do. He started talking about his little sister in New York.

"Her name was Lillian and he told me she would always say the rain rhyme. Then he taught me how to say it, 'Rain, rain, go away come again another day. Little Lillian wants to play.' I said it and sure enough it quit raining and for years I thought he really caused it to stop."

Another time, her father was working outside near the house but beyond the yard fence.

"I went out to watch Papa. Mama opened the gate so I could walk close to where Papa was working. I was getting near to him, talking all the while but Papa didn't seem to see me. He didn't answer me or move. He stopped working but he kept staring at something past me. As I got closer, all of a sudden, he grabbed me, ran to the fenced-in yard and threw me over the fence with himself over the fence right behind me. As I hit the ground, I let out a loud angry howl of indignation. But, when I looked around, I saw the biggest, meanest looking hog I had ever seen. I stopped crying and stared at a wild Arkansas Razorback hog, one of the most vicious wild animals in that country.

"Papa had done everything right. He had saved my life. That Razorback would have killed me for sure if Papa hadn't grabbed me and ran," said Lillian.

Endearing as those moments were, they would be obscured by one of Jay's outbursts of controlling, out of place anger. One particular Sunday evening after church services concluded was one of those occasions.

Jay was always overly strict with Eva, but when she came of dating age, he got even more arbitrary about what she could and could not do.

"Mama attended church regularly but Papa never went with us," Lillian recalled.

"Back then, when church was over the young boys lined up at the church door and would ask the girl of their choice if they could walk her home. This Sunday night Papa had come down to the church unannounced about the time it was letting out and the boys were all lined up at the door. When Eva walked out ,a boy named Nolan Wells ask Eva if he could walk her home.

"She said yes and when he took her arm and walked her out the door, Papa grabbed Nolan and kicked him down on the ground. He gave Nolan a good cussin. Mama was terribly embarrassed and upset. Eva started crying and ran home. I felt so sorry for Eva. What for her had started out to be an innocent and fun time was turned ugly and embarrassing by Papa's actions," Lillian Said.

"Eva could hardly bear the humiliation. Papa had a quick temper and was too proud to ever admit he was wrong or sorry. But back then, it seems some grown ups thought they had to set a serious example for us kids. Except Mama, she was a great hand to cut up and have fun. I never heard her complain or wish she had nice things."

Remembering Denver, Arkansas

"It was 1911 when the circus came to our town. The news about it coming was all over town before it got there.

"The circus man got there first so he could find a place to set up and wonder of wonders our big field down on Long Creek was the place the man wanted.

"In exchange for letting him use our field, we could go see everything for free. It was only a small circus I'm sure, but it was very large to my eyes.

"We got to see everything, the pretty girls riding on the big horses, standing on the horses' backs and doing all kinds of balancing acts, the calliope playing their music. It was wonderful.

"Everyday they drove the elephants down to the creek and walked them out into the middle of the creek. Elephants would get their trunks full of water and then blow it on the other elephants. They really would do a lot of bellering and it was quite a sound and also quite a sight.

"We got to see every show every night or day that they were there. They had some big white horses and the pretty girls rode them around in a ring. They stood on their hands then they would do a flip and then they were standing on their heads. They would swing down almost under the horse's feet. I've seen bigger circuses since then but none better than that one, as far as I'm concerned," said Lillian.

"The Miles family lived down the road from us, and Ira and I didn't like the Miles kids at all. They had runny noses and their clothes were dirty and we just didn't like them but they wanted to play with us. We would do anything to get rid of them. At that time a fellow came there putting on a hypnotizing show at the schoolhouse, and of course we all went.

"It was quite a show. The fellow would go through the act of hypnotizing this girl, and she would go to sleep and nothing could wake her up until the hypnotizer went through his act and snapped his fingers and then the girl would come out of the trance.

"From watching that show, Ira and I got an idea of how to get rid of the Miles kids. We got a bottle and put dirt in it and some water and when the kids came down to our house we put on our act of rubbing medicine on their heads and mumbling magic words. We put on such a good act that the kids got scared and went running home and told their mother on us.

"And, here came Mrs. Miles and told Mama on us. Well, Mama wanted to laugh so bad, she could hardly hold her face straight. She sent Mrs. Miles packing, then started scolding us and in spite of herself, she got tickled and just broke down laughing and went into the house. She never said another word about it and we were relieved because we thought sure we would get a whipping," said Lillian.

"Mama worked out a lot because Papa was a well digger, a dynamite man, and he would be gone for days or weeks at a time when he was on a job," Lillian said. "In addition to other odd jobs, Mama also worked as a nurse for Dr. Price."

"I went with Mama when she went to work for Aunt Cal Young. Aunt Cal ran a hotel and had peacocks. Mama sometimes worked for her when drummers (traveling salesmen) were in town.

"Mama was a cook, a waitress, and dishwasher. I would play with her daughter, Virgie, who was a little younger than me. Virgie had lots of toys but she wouldn't let me play with them. She would sit on them and spread her skirt out to cover them. She had some "tidily winks" the first I had ever seen.

"The hotel was like a big house. Aunt Cal boarded the drummers who sold harness and other farm supplies. Sometimes when there were more drummers than she could house, she would farm them out to neighbors.

"In town, on Saturday, the women would be in a bunch talking about their garden and quilting bees and the like. The men would be playing mumbly peg, pitchin pennies on a crack in the porch, and talking about their crops. Jim Griffin, the storekeeper would give all the kids a peppermint stick. I can see it like yesterday," said Lillian

"And another thing I remember was how proud the women were of their butter molds. Mama's was round and carved in the wood, right on top, was an acorn. It was kind of like a brand. That's how the women identified their butter. The women took pride in having the cleanest butter. All the town women would try to get Mama's butter."

Telephone service comes to Denver

"Mr. Elrod, Henry Youngblood and Dr. Price got the idea to bring the telephone system into Denver about 1910 or so. They worked long and hard to bring in a phone system that could reach out to places beyond Denver," said Lillian.

"They were all prominent men in the town who owned most of the business and they wanted Denver to prosper and grow," said Lillian. "Dr. Price thought it would be helpful to his patients when they got sick if there was a good phone service."

Daisy was an important link in the town's efforts to promote the phone service because she was chosen as the best person to operate the new switchboard once it was installed.

"All that was well and good, and after Papa died, both Mama and Eva got jobs at the switchboard as operators," said Lillian." Eva took the day shift and Mama took the night shift. The switchboard was in Griffin's store, so Jim Griffin and whoever was able to, took over the rest of the time.

"To celebrate the new phone system, Jim Griffin and Uncle Henry got a dance going. Jim Griffin came down to our house and insisted that Mama should come to the dance," said Lillian.

" It was less than a month since Papa died so Mama didn't plan on going but Jim insisted Mama must come and of course Eva, being of young courting age, wanted to go. Mama finally decided to go, but she wasn't going to dance.

The party was the talk of the town. "There wasn't supposed to be any liquor because Arkansas was a dry state but someone managed to bring some in," said Lillian

There was, however, one overriding concern about the dance. "One of the families around there had a feud going with another family. When the notice went up at Griffin's store that a dance was going to be held to celebrate the establishment of the new telephone service, two young fellows from these families served notice on each other not to come to the dance, or to come shooting. They called it a feud. However, the dance was held anyway, Lillian said

"Sure enough when the dance was going right good and everyone was having a good time, we heard shots. We went outside, there was one of these boys laying on the ground, and the other was getting on his horse and headin out of town. These two fellows had rode up, squared off and shot at each other. Of course, that was the end of the dance."

A terrible night in 1908

While most of the McIntyre children's lives in Arkansas were homey and safe, there was a time back in 1908 that struck terror into the very being of then 3-year-old-Lillian.

Although the Civil War (The *War Between the States*) was long over by the time Lillian was born, the lingering emotions and bigotry that had caused the war still flamed high in Arkansas for generations later. Some people, even those who had never known a black person harbored a grudge against the entire black race. Black people took their lives in their hands when they ventured in to some areas of Arkansas.

"I remember a terrible night. It was 1908."said Lillian. "At the time I hardly understood it at all. There were men with guns and lanterns and bloodhounds baying. I didn't know what it was all about at the time, but as I got older and looked back, I found out that a Negro man had got off the train at Cricket (Arkansas) and at that time seems nearly all white people hated Negroes. I had never seen a colored person, in fact I never seen a colored person for years afterwards either. The first Negro I ever seen was the porter on the train we traveled on to Kansas City. That was 1912.

"But, back to the time. We lived 10 miles from Cricket where this Negro man had got off a freight train at. I don't know where he was going or why he got off the train but I remember the big bunch of men out carrying torches and they had their hounds on leashes and men carrying lanterns and beating the brush all along the creek.

"The men came to our door and wanted Papa to go out with them but he refused. The men didn't like that too much but they left," said Lillian.

What the men didn't know was that Jay was from New York and, that his father, Stephen, had fought and died in the Civil War trying to free the slaves.

"Mama shut the doors up and bolted them shut and we sat in the dark. I could hear all the hounds baying, and men hollering at the sounds of the dogs when they thought they were close to their quarry. Ira and I were scared to death. We didn't know what was going on until years later. Mama told us what it was all about. She said she thought the feller got away but no one ever knew. That's as much as we knew.

"When I was 14 years old, about 1920, I lived near a railroad in Cricket, Ark. again, and I lived close to the tracks. When the train stopped, the porter just reached out and set the steps down, and got back on the train.

He stood way back so no one had to touch him. I never really knew what happened or whether that other Negro man got away or not but I can hear those hounds baying to this very day and when Ira and I asked questions about that night, Mama would just say 'You just forget all about that.' That's the first I ever knew there was such a thing as a Negro and I never seen a Negro until we came to K.C. and I was scared to death of the Negro porters," said Lillian.

Arkansas, a last frontier

Arkansas maintained a frontier lifestyle many years after other states modernized and became more cosmopolitan. Traveling by covered wagon in Arkansas in the early to mid 1900s was a common form of travel. The Whitlow family traveled in this manner. The Whitlows were a young family. They had one son and two small girls.

"It was about 1910 when the Whitlows came through Denver in a covered wagon. They were a musical group and camped down on Long Creek, near our house," Lillian said.

"Mama saw them setting up camp and went down to invite them to supper but 'No, they had plenty,' they said."

During the night, it started to rain. Daisy was familiar with Long Creek. She knew that a heavy rain would soon push the creek well out of its banks and the Whitlows camp would be flooded. She got out of bed and dressed, lit the lantern and went down to the camp to warn the Whitlows. "Now this crick gets mean when it gets a hard rain," she told them. "You better get your horses and wagon up in the yard until the storm passes."

"Sure enough the crick got up, and it rained and rained and the crick got higher and higher until it was almost in our yard, and of course the travelers stayed until the crick went down. The storm was not expected to last long but it did. It was probably a week or more. They had no choice but to stay," said Lillian.

"Every night we'd congregate in the living room and the Whitlows would play their music and sing. They had guitars, a banjo and accordion. I remember that banjo so well. We loved to hear it. The woman and the girls sang in harmony really pretty.

"Papa would get mad and go to the barn but not Mama. She was a kid all her life. Ira took up with the boy and he taught us to make whistles from slippery elm; and boy if you think we didn't have a lot fun with them," said Lillian.

"It was a wonderful time but Papa didn't like it at all. He hardly spoke. He had been raised under the rule that life was a hard row to hoe and he was going to hoe it right. We had to go to bed at dark to save on the coal oil lamp fuel. His day started about 4:30 a.m. and ended at dusk. He was up and had the feeding done and breakfast ate and was in the fields by sun up in the summer time, and when the crops was laid by he went all over the country digging wells and any other work there was to do."

Leaving home in the Ozarks

That rustic, close-knit, country life was the life that the McIntyre children were born to, but all that changed when Jay died. Lillian, only six years old at the time, remembered well the trip north aboard the slow, swaying train. "I got sick on the train. I guess it was the motion of the train," she said.

"Mama's step-father, Bob Scott, came to Arkansas to help her move to K.C. We had a big basket of food and we ate out of that basket the whole way. That is all but me. I was sick all the way," said Lillian.

"We got off the train at Kansas City Union Station. Grandpa Bob got us on a streetcar and saw us on our way to Aunt Vick's house. I remember that so clearly. Mama was carrying Clell and she kept telling me and Ira to help Eva. She was so pale and weak she could hardly walk. We didn't know where Aunt Vick lived."

Getting off the train earlier that day, at what was to the children the "larger than life" downtown Kansas City train terminal was a bewildering experience for them. They had never been outside of the Ozark hills, and their heads were swimming with the noisy hustle and bustle of activity at the train terminal. Crowds of passengers milled around the terminal, some boarding the train to leave and other passengers disembarking. Loading areas were packed with people picking up luggage. Businessmen rushed by, suitcase in hand. Mothers scolded and herded their children to their destination. The loud constant hum of voices echoed throughout the terminal and booming loud speakers announced train arrivals and departures in unintelligible voices.

"After Grandpa Bob helped us get on the street car to go to Aunt Vicks, he left and went on to somewhere else," said Lillian.

"We were a pathetic looking little group," Lillian described her weary little family as they began to search for the home of Dazerine's sister, Vick.

"We made quite a sight straggling down the street looking for Aunt Vick's house. Eva was so weak from the typhoid fever she could hardly walk and Clell was only a baby and too little to walk. We were so very tired and Mama was so worried about Eva. We walked a very long way," said Lillian.

Daisy, exhausted and sleepless after an all night ride on the train, held Clell in her arms and looked for street addresses. Ira, her oldest son, who was eight, and Lillian did what they could to help.

"We were standing across the street from a small grocery store, trying to get our bearings, when the store door flew open and the biggest woman I ever saw came out and across the street, going on like an old mother hen and she herded us all into the back of her store where she lived. She got us all sat down and eating while she called on the phone to Aunt Vick's home. She acted like she had known us all her life.

"The big lady was Mrs. Whiteside and she was by far the biggest woman I ever saw. She wasn't just fat, she was tall; she weighed about 300 pounds.

"After we finished eating, we went to Aunt Vicks. She lived in a nice, three-story, house about a block from the store."

Vick's home was an attractive house in a good neighborhood but Dazerine's reception was less than warm when they finally arrived. What Dazerine didn't know at the time was that Vick's husband had experienced a recent business reversal but even so, he required his family to keep up a prosperous front. Although they were not poor, Vick's family was in dour financial straits. Vick had always been somewhat prideful and she never let on that her family was also feeling financial hardships. However, while she didn't admit it, she made it clear that there was no place for Daisy's family in her home.

"But she took us in for a couple of days until we found the little 2-room house at 1022 Ewing and Mama set out to get a job."

Daisy's premonition of false promises from Scott proved true sooner then she expected. After she arrived, their arrangement quickly fell apart.

"We moved in to a small tarpaper covered house. There was a water faucet in the yard. I was just six and I just couldn't understand how the water came out by just twisting the little handle," Lillian recalled.

Lillian's experience with water in Arkansas was only with wells or cisterns where the water was pulled up with buckets, or taken from a nearby creek.

"Grandpa Bob Scott and Uncle Lon moved in with us. They were supposed to work and pay the rent and buy groceries. Mama was supposed to do the cooking, laundry and that sort of thing," said Lillian.

However, it did not work out that way. Bob Scott failed to keep his part of the bargain. He and his son worked, but the rent wasn't paid and the groceries didn't come in.

"One day, both Eva and Mama were gone. Mama was at work and Eva had gone out to look for a job. Ira, Clell and I were at home. None of us had anything to eat that day when Grandpa Bob and Lon came in with some milk and pie. They went in to the kitchen and set the milk and pie on the table. Ira and I didn't say anything but Clell was little and I knew he was hungry. He asked for something and Uncle Lon told him to get away.

Clell started to cry and I asked Grandpa Bob to give Clell some of the pie. He told me to shut my mouth, and get out of there and leave him alone. I said 'please just give him a bite.' He said he would slap me down if I didn't shut up.

I got really mad then and grabbed the pie and threw it out in the yard and I just dared him to do anything about it. After I did it, I was scared but I never let on and they just got up cussin and left the house. I don't know if they knew how hungry we were.

After that, Mama told them they would have to go somewhere else to stay. Mama had gone to work at a meat packinghouse. She worked ten hours a day, six days a week for one dollar a day. Eva's health had gotten better. She took care of us kids and also went out to hunt work. We didn't know what it was not to be hungry," said Lillian.

When Dazerine moved her family from Arkansas after Jay's death, it had seemed a reasonable solution to her problems. She thought the move to Kansas City would bring more job opportunities with the chance of higher wages but the promise of a better life had fallen far short of the realities, and the job skills that had served Daisy well in Arkansas proved of little marketable value here in this new location. She now faced the most desperate time in her life. She had no money, her children were hungry and no job opportunities were in sight. True, her life after Jay's death had seemed bleak there in Denver and she had hoped the move might somehow dispel the decline that Eva had fallen into after being ill with typhoid fever. Now, she remembered her Arkansas home fondly. There, she was surrounded by family and friends. Here in Kansas City there was no one. Her stepfather had broken his promise of help and her sister's bright promises had faded.

Cora Leedom was the first neighbor the family met when they moved into the little two-room house on Ewing and it was Cora who kept them from starving on more than one occasion. It was a long time before they met her husband Charlie but "Cora came over to see us when we first moved in," said Lillian.

"She was so nice. She fed us many a meal when things got so bad," said Lillian.

While Cora was a good hearted, generous woman, her husband Charlie was less than generous. He had forbidden Cora to give away food that he had paid for. Charlie was not inclined to spend his hard-earned money on anyone but his own family, and not too much for them.

"Cora had to sneak food out behind Charlie's back but she did it and I don't know how we would have got by if she hadn't helped us," said Lillian.

Cora was indeed good-hearted, but she also liked the nightlife and parties and that eventually caused the little McIntyre family grief.

A Question Of Friendship

The next few months in Kansas City drug by slowly for Daisy and her family. Each day brought uncertainty and hard work that exacted a deeper toll on Daisy's health and energy.

Eva's health gradually improved to the point that she could get a job. By working together, and each person contributing to the family's welfare, they were able to scrape through the dreary winter without further outside help.

Now, Daisy faced a new problem. Eva, recovered from her long illness, a pretty 16-year-old, full of life and yearning for gaiety and excitement, had started sneaking out with Cora Leedom to nightclubs, parties and other places while Daisy was at work.

Daisy found herself in the awkward position of reproaching someone she knew she should be grateful to. Daisy knew well that Cora had kept her family from starving many times. She brought food to Daisy's table when there was nothing for Daisy's children to eat. Cora had done it with a free heart, going against her husband Charlie's orders not to help them.

Daisy felt a deep sense of gratitude to Cora for her generosity and encouragement during her family's hardships. She liked Cora as a friend, but now Cora was, Dazerine believed, leading Eva astray, taking her naive young daughter to places Daisy did not approve of, where liquor was served, and encouraging Eva to meet men of unknown character.

Cora did this knowing that it caused a conflict between Eva and Daisy. She did it knowing that Daisy was angry, and worried about Eva. Cora was a generous and good- natured, woman. Cora was a pleasant person.

She kept a clean house and her children were well fed. She played the piano and sang a lot around the house.

Nevertheless, Cora's behavior with Eva caused Daisy to question her friend's moral values. Above all else, Daisy worried about Eva's welfare.

Cora's desire for beautiful clothes, music, dancing and fun began to overshadow her good qualities for Daisy.

"Cora had a good heart and our family probably would have starved if she hadn't helped us out, but she liked men," Lillian added. "That's what worried Mama."

Eva was a pretty girl. Even at 16 she was tiny, barely five foot tall but very much a young woman easily entertained with an infectious laugh that drew people to her.

Eva had grown up in a protected atmosphere among close friends and family. She was an innocent to the worldly ways of city life and knew nothing of the guiles of men. She was a perfect pawn for the more sophisticated Cora, and Daisy was well aware of that.

"Cora first tried to get Eva lined up for a man to make money," Lillian said. "She would come get Eva to go with her to Dreamland, a local open-air dance pavilion. Sometimes, Eva took me along. It sounded pretty but it was just a place to meet men. It was a big dance pavilion with row boats on the Blue River," said Lillian.

"Before all the industries were built there and their operations fouled the water with their industrial waste, the water was bright and clean and sparkled in the sun. Young girls carried parasols to keep the sun off, and there was a low hum of music all the time with people dancing. It was like a fairyland to me. I didn't know it was a bad place.

Eva was only 16 and I was six but she seemed like a grown-up. She had to slip off when Mama was at work or doing something else. Sometimes, some of the bigger girls and boys at Dreamland would put me in a boat with them but mostly I sat on the bank. Eva and Mama used to argue a lot about it. Mama liked to have fun but not at taverns and beer joints. She was straight-laced and she didn't approve of places like Dreamland. When Mama caught Eva there at Dreamland, she would jerk her home so fast it would make her head swim." said Lillian.

This state of affairs went on for several months with Daisy and Eva arguing many times into the night.

"Cory finally got Eva married to that John Wheelen because she thought he had a lot of money. I guess he did at the time," said Lillian. "He was a well spoken, good looking, debonair sort of man and was always well dressed. Before Daisy realized what was happening, Eva was married to him and moved in to her own apartment with him."

Grandpa Knapp and security

Sometime between the authorities visit and June of 1912, Dazerine went to work as a housekeeper for a jeweler named Knapp. She also cleaned his jewelry shop. It was only six months since Jay died but it had been an eternity of hardships for Daisy. The jeweler was aware of Dazerine's plight and recognized her as a good honest worker. One day he approached Dazerine with a job offer. His brother, Francis Knapp, in Ottawa, Kansas, a veteran of the Civil War was seriously ill. The old veteran was a widower and needed nursing care and a housekeeper. His brother was not only ill, the jeweler said, he was also blind.

Francis Knapp was a corporal when he was discharged from the United States Army on August 30, 1865 at the age of 20. He had served three years as a Union infantryman. During that time, he had contracted erysipelas and it had caused him to go blind. (*Erysipelas is an acute streptococcus bacterial skin infection that can lead to other health complications.*)

The jeweler thought the move to Ottowa would be a good job opportunity for Daisy and a blessing to his brother if Daisy would accept the position. It would relieve him of a tremendous worry, said the jeweler, if he knew his brother was being well cared for.

Dazerine accepted the job offer and moved to Ottowa but considering the stricter social standards of that day, everyone involved believed that the two should be married. Even though it would be a marriage of convenience and in name only, it would protect Daisy's good name. She was, after all, a young widow. Even though he was older and ill, she would be living in the same house with him, and marriage would not only protect Daisy's reputation it would protect the good name of Francis Knapp, a decent church going man, from gossip. The move turned out to be one of the happier and more secure periods for Lillian and her siblings, Ira and Clell, since their father's death.

"Grandpa Knapp was real good to us kids," said Lillian. Because of his advanced age, he asked the children to call him grandpa and they happily obliged. "I felt like he was really my grandpa," said Lillian. Her own grand-parents had died before Lillian knew the pleasure of doting grandparents. Lillian must have filled a special place for the ailing Francis Knapp also, because he seemed never to tire of her company, and she was delighted to be his constant companion, serving as his eyes to the world. Lillian had never had so much attention in her life and she blossomed under the warmth of it. The neighbors began calling her Francis's little girl and Lillian accepted

Lillian, Clell, and Ira in Ottowa, Kansas

the title with pride. "He went to church every Sunday morning and evening and he took me with him because I liked to go. Ira went to Sunday school most of the time but not as much as I did. Grandpa went for long walks everyday and I went with him there too. I would tell him everything

I saw. He would stop and talk to his friends and ask them what they thought of his little girl. He would talk like I really belonged to him. He was some kind of an officer in the church. He and some other old men would have communion at each other's house ever so often, and he would take me with him. And he acted like he was real proud of me.

I was in a play of some kind either for school or for church and Grandpa took me. When the play was over and I came down in the audience where he was sitting, he hugged me and said I was so pretty and that I sang so sweet. I didn't even think about it at the time that he couldn't see me at all. He always talked like he could see the same as anyone else."

"I remember how Ira and I kept an eye on the well there in Ottowa. Mama didn't whip us ever, but she would threaten to get her bonnet and go off. Ira and I thought she really would do it so we would do nearly anything to see that she didn't leave. Mama was getting letters from Eva and I think there may have been something about them that worried her. Then one time she got mad at something and said she felt like jumping in the well. I sometimes wondered if it might have been that Eva had written and told Mama some bad news or that she was in a bad way and needed help.

Grandpa said, 'Now Daisy you don't mean that.' But Mama said, 'Oh, yes I do.' And from then on, Ira and I kept close watch on the well. I'd make an excuse to play where I could watch the well. And if I couldn't, Ira would. One of us kept an eye on the well all the time. Years later, I told Mama about that and she almost cried. She said she wouldn't have done that for anything in the world if she had known we took her seriously".

Daisy and the children had been in Ottowa a couple of years when Francis Knapp died. "I don't remember who told me that Grandpa was gone but I'm sure it must have been Mama," said Lillian.

"I felt so bad when Grandpa died. I liked him so much and he died in his sleep. I knew he was old and sick but it bothered me for a long time. I kept wondering if he tried to call anyone, or if he hurt and many other things. Mama noticed that something seemed to be wrong with me and she said, 'Sister, are you all right? You don't act like you feel good.'

Then I told her I wished Grandpa hadn't died and that I didn't know he was sick. She explained to me that he just died of old age and that he wasn't in any pain. That he just went to sleep and slipped away," said Lillian.

"Grandpa Knapp's funeral was a grand, somber affair. He was placed in a beautiful coffin, and put in a black carriage. Four black horses were hitched to the hearse and a long line of people all dressed in black walked behind the hearse. They moved in a procession down the street to the cemetery. And they drove so very slow," said Lillian.

Leaving Ottowa

"Grandpa's sons were real nice men. They came when he died and they told Mama she could stay on there as long as she wanted to," Lillian said, "but, Mama wouldn't stay. I often wondered why she didn't stay. A neighbor lady that made light bread to sell came over and offered Mama her bread business if she would stay but Mama could never take anything from anyone unless she paid for it. After the funeral, Mama packed up and came back to Kansas City, Missouri and that's when things got really bad," Lillian said.

When Daisy and the children arrived back in Kansas City they found Eva living in deplorable living conditions. Her marriage to John Wheelen had been dreadful. If, as Cora had believed, Wheelen had money, he did not spend it for Eva. "We discovered that he had treated Eva so bad that she was real sick. Mama packed Eva's things and took her home with us. And the hardships started all over again," Lillian said.

"Mama would get a job and work a week or two and then lose her job because she would be too sick to work. Eva finally got a job at a children's hospital and she worked there for quite a while. Ira and I changed schools at least four times a season during that time. When we were not in school we were junkin (collecting junk) and taking the stuff to the junk yard and hoping we would get enough money for supper and breakfast. The odd thing about it was, I don't remember being hungry myself at all," said Lillian

"I don't know how long we had been in Kansas City when it was getting close to Christmas. Mama didn't know how she was going to handle Christmas. We kids knew it was close to Christmas and were talking about Santa Claus. Mama put off telling us as long as she could. It was Christmas Eve, and Mama was telling us that she was afraid Santa wouldn't be able to find us because he didn't know where we were since we had moved so far away from our home. We didn't make any fuss but I can remember feeling pretty sad when a loud knock came at our door.

Mama got up and opened the door. There stood Santa Claus and another man, and there was a truck down in the road with some coal on the truck. The men carried in a bunch of boxes. We had all kinds of good thing to eat. I got a Rollie Pollie doll, some Christmas candy, and some clothes. Ira got a cork gun and Clell got some toys. I can't remember what all we got but I know it was the most wonderful Christmas we ever had. It was the Goodfellers who did it," said Lillian, (*The Goodfellows Lodge is a charitable organization*) "We never knew who turned us in but I have always thought Mrs. Whiteside had turned in our name to the organization."

Hanging On

"Sometime later, a road grading crew came in our neighborhood. Mama went to where the men were working and asked for the boss. A big man came out and asked what he could do for us and she asked him where they ate. Mama and the big man talked awhile and Mama got the job of cooking for the graders. They had tents and all but, they didn't cook. So, for a while, Mama cooked for the road graders. When they would move to another area to repair or build roads she would pack us up and follow them. We moved when the graders moved."

Daisy was an excellent cook and that may have been one of her easier jobs but the children were constantly uprooted to different schools and new neighborhoods. As a result they grew up with few close friends and a limited social life.

Lillian and Ira didn't seem to miss having a lot of friends outside the family. In fact, the trials and hardships of their young lives seem to draw them closer and build a stronger fraternal bond between the two of them. They were inseparable as children and when times got hard, they became, without doubt, a team. They worked together, played together and, got in trouble together and they argued. Sometimes they quarreled fiercely but at the same time supported each other in all their childish pursuits.

"Ira and I got a paper route with the Kansas City Journal Post," said Lillian.

"The route was really Ira's, of course, but I always went with him. We got up about three a.m. We had a good-sized route and most of the people were really nice except for this one woman. She lived on a fairly high bank and she wanted her paper in a certain spot on her steps. We tried to throw it up there right where she wanted it and we always got it in her yard but not right on her steps. She never gave us a good word but the other people were nice."

Lillian and Ira picked up the newspapers for their deliveries at the 15th Street Fire Station. "We really liked those guys," Lillian said referring to the firefighters. "They were so good to us. The fellows there would give us a hot cup of coffee when we came in to pick up the papers. It sure tasted good and warmed us up on cold days. Several times, we would be there when the fire alarm sounded. Those were exciting times. It was quite a sight to see the firemen go into action and to see those horses perform. The firemen would back the horses right up under where the gear was hanging. In no time at all the gear dropped over them and the horses were harnessed and the fire wagons were on their way; the bells on the fire wagon ringing to warn people they were coming and to stay out of their way," said Lillian.

"One particularly cold morning, Ira woke up sick with the croup. I had to go deliver the papers by myself. I remember I was a little scared. When I got to the fire station all the boys there were a welcome sight. It was so very cold. My feet felt like they were frozen. The firemen rubbed my feet and got them warm again. Then they wrapped pieces of newspaper around my shoes and then wrapped a piece of burlap tow sack over that.

I left there and I went on down 15th street to the railroad yards to deliver the paper to the guard at the railroad shanty. It was quite a distance. I was cold again and the railroad shanty was a welcome sight. I ran a little faster for the hot cup of coffee Ira and I always got there. When the guard seen only me, he asked 'Where is your brother'?

"I told him Ira was sick. He poured me a cup of coffee and said, 'Get on over here close to the stove.' And I did, but then he pulled me close to him and started to kiss me and he put his hand inside my coat. I jerked back, hit him, and ran away as fast as I could. He called me to come back but I kept right on going and crying. I was so scared. But, I throwed all the papers and I think I was more disappointed than scared. The man had been so nice to Ira and me and we both liked him so much. We never stopped there to get warm anymore. We just got close enough to throw the paper and that was all."

In those days, a number of children that Ira and Lillian knew frequented areas around the railroad tracks. They salvaged one thing or another from freight trains that passed through the area. Being of similar circumstances from poor families, they formed a casual fellowship and passed the time of day with one another.

"Ira and I scrapped coal all the time. As soon as we got home from school we changed out of our school clothes and put on some older clothes and took our sacks and went to the railroad track so we could get enough coal for the next day.," said Lillian.

"One evening, one of the railroad bulls caught us and he started getting on to Ira for letting his little sister do such hard work," said Lillian. Railroad bulls was a slang term used to describe a patrol guard division of the railroad company.

According to Lillian, Ira didn't say anything but she was outraged. She did not appreciate a stranger presuming to criticize her brother. "I turned on the railroad bull and just got all over him," she said. "He laughed and said 'you sure are a sweet tempered child.' Then he showed Ira and me how to carry the coal easier and he rolled some good big chunks off for us.

We also got in the empty grain cars, and took our sacks and an old piece of broom and swept the cars. We would usually get a half gallon of grain. There was this nice lady, Mrs. Morgan, there in Sheffield. She would give us 30 cents for a half gallon of grain. I doubt she had any chickens but we never thought about that at the time.

"About 1916, a boy I went to school with was killed. His name was Carl Watson. He was about 12 or so years old," said Lillian. "Carl jumped out of one of the box cars and fell, and the fast, through train ran over him," said Lillian. "It killed him. Every one along the street knew Carl and liked him and we all felt real bad.

"There never seemed to be any rest for Mama. She would get a job, work a week or two and then lose her job because she was too sick to work. She probably wasn't eating right and just wore herself down. We were always having to move. I guess Mama couldn't pay the rent so we would find some place where the rent was cheaper. Eva finally got a job at the children's hospital and she worked there quite a while. Ira and I changed schools at least 4 times a school season. When we were not in school, we were junking and taking the junk to the junk yards hoping for enough money for food. We moved so much I never went to the same school a second term. But, I always managed to get fairly good grades except in handwriting. I remember that Ira and I always had something to play on.

"We were always looking in the dump for things to make something to play on. We found enough boards and wheels and iron rods to make us a 3-wheeled jig and we sure had a lot of fun on that thing. Once when we were out junking we found a big barrel so we started figuring how to use it. Ira said we could roll it down the hill then he said to me. ' I bet you're afraid to roll down the hill in it. You are a fraidy cat... I'll dare you, fraidy cat.' So, of course, I couldn't not take a dare and I crawled in the barrel. Ira gave it a push and down the hill I went. I thought I was going to be beat to death before I reached the bottom of the hill. As the barrel rolled down the hill, I bounced from one side to the other. Needless to say I never did that again."

Recalling the old days

It was their earlier days in Arkansas that Lillian liked best to remember, as she grew older. She and Ira were constant playmates. When Ira was about seven years old, she said, he got angry about something. In a Tom Sawyer like move, he decided to run away from home. "Mama told him if he really wanted to go, why... just go. She went and fixed him a lunch and tied some clothes in a bundle and put a stick through the bundle so he could carry it easy. She told him goodbye and hoped he would be OK," said Lillian.

"I remember he started out so cocky and brave and I was so upset, I started to cry. But, Mama shook her head and told me to tell Ira goodbye. Ira went on out the gate. We lived off the road quite a ways and at first he marched right along and, then he went a little slower then, he stopped and looked back and that was it. He came running back saying, 'I don't want to go Mama,' over and over. Mama said, 'Well son, we will take you back this time but the next time you decide you don't like your home remember how you feel now,'" Lillian said.

"One time Ira and I got into a fuss, and I guess Ira was in the wrong. Mama sent me out to get a switch to whip him with," said Lillian. " I got a long green switch but I broke it every so often. Mama didn't notice it was broke that way and she brought it down across his bottom and it flew all to pieces. She got a funny look on her face and she looked at us. I think she was about to laugh and she turned right quick and went into the house."

Lillian recalled a time when she was about five and Ira was eight. Daisy took the two of them with her to wash clothes in the creek down by an old sawmill. The weather was warm and Eva stayed at the house taking care of the housework and watching the baby, Clell. "Mama probably took us with her to keep us from aggravating Eva," Lillian said.

Daisy built her fire to heat the water in a big iron wash pot and went about her clothes washing. Lillian and Ira went to play on the big sawdust pile by the mill. "It was a real big sawdust pile and a lot of fun to run and jump in," said Lillian

"We were having a big time," Lillian said, "when Ira decided to play a little rough. He ran up and gave me a big push but he caught me off guard and down the sawdust pile I went. Of course I yelled when he pushed me and got my mouth full of sawdust, and then I rolled on out into the crick. I had sawdust and water in my mouth and I choked and nearly strangled to death," said Lillian.

"Mama stopped the washing and came after us. She scolded both of us, me for squallin' and Ira for pushing me down. Later, after we were home and things had settled down, Ira came around where I was playing and said, 'Sister, I wished I didn't push you.' I acted all tough and said, 'You didn't hurt me at all.'"

Ira, being the older by three years often felt a certain amount of responsibility for Lillian's safety. That sense of responsibility was encouraged by Daisy. Many times, Ira was admonished to watch over her when they were away from the house alone on errands or just playing. In those early days, people around Denver worried about gypsies traveling through the Ozarks stealing children. Rumors abounded about dark skinned gypsies traveling through the forested hills of Arkansas in covered wagons stealing small white children and selling them to wealthy foreigners in far away, large towns.

The gypsies, reportedly, especially liked little blond or light skinned, blue-eyed girls with curly hair. Lillian at four or five was a pretty child with curly red hair bound up in long braids that hung to her waist. She had big Irish blue eyes and a sprinkling of freckles across her nose. Daisy, always a protective mother, was afraid the gypsies might steal her pretty little daughter and sell her to someone who wanted a little girl with curly red hair. She sometimes spoke of this worry to the children and warned them to be wary of strangers while away from her.

"Mama had told us to watch out for the gypsies. We really believed it and Ira watched me like a stern Daddy to make sure it didn't happen," said Lillian.

Whenever they were away from the house alone, Ira, still a child himself practiced certain precautions to keep his little sister safe from the dreaded gypsies. "Neighbors used to swap favors a lot," Lillian said, "One time Mama's milk cow was dry. She needed some milk so she gave Ira and me a bucket and sent us over to Aunt Darhooley's for milk.

"We had to go down a hill through the woods and cross over a road. We did a lot of playing on our way through the woods but when we got to the road Ira would put his ear down to the ground and listen. If a wagon or a rider was coming, he could hear it from a long way off. If he heard something close, Ira would grab my hand and run into the woods, and hide me. He always thought he had to look out for me."

Although they were generally well behaved for the most part, Ira and Lillian were far from perfect and often found themselves deeply involved in a bit of mischief that seemed to evolve out of nowhere with little effort. It just happened. Ira, who was a good and protective brother in most instances, had a serious problem with teasing, and often promoted mischief, especially for his sisters.

"One time we got in trouble, or I did. I was a kind of a smart aleck kid, I guess, or a dumb kid, don't know which," said Lillian. "Mama had a hen nest at the side of the house, and Ira and I were playing there. Ira dared me to throw a rock in the hen nest. There were a couple of eggs in it. At that time, I thought it was a disgrace to not take a dare so I grabbed up a rock and threw it in the hen's nest. I don't know if Ira went and told on me or if Mama just came out to see what was going on. I told her I did it.

She said, ' Well you like eggs so much, you can eat it so she dipped the broken eggs out of the nest and put them in a dish and said now eat the eggs just as they are. Boy, I sure didn't like that but I started in to eat and Ira begged Mama not to make me eat them and he said it was his fault. I don't know if Mama was about to laugh or cry anyway she turned and went into the house real fast," Lillian said.

On another occasion, Ira dared Lillian to shoot out the church window with a slingshot. Again, she couldn't stand not to take a dare and again, she was in trouble. It was about this time that Ira decided she was such a tomboy that he would call Lillian, "Billy." The name stuck and was later shortened to Bill, and she was called that for the rest of her adult life.

Daisy had never allowed anyone to shorten Lillian's name to Lillie or any other nickname, so the name Bill was not used around her. Later on when everyone else was calling her Bill, Ira began calling Lillian, Sis.

Dangerous practices

In the early 1900s, it was a common practice for sales companies to have samples of their products thrown into the yards of people's homes. It was quite simply a way to advertise the products and promote sales. The salesmen who threw products into the yards were called drummers because they were often accompanied by the beating of a drum to announce their arrival..

Lillian remembered one childhood story involving drummer' samples, that never failed to bring a smile to her lips. Ira and Lillian had finished their morning chores and were sitting on the doorsteps when a drummer came through Denver in a one-horse hack. He was throwing sample plugs of chewing tobacco into all the yards.

"The tobacco was peachy plug and it was sort of sweet smelling. Ira and I ran out to see what the man had tossed in the yard. Mama came out too and stood on the porch," said Lillian. "She wanted to know what we had. Ira kept smelling of the tobacco plug and I guess Mama thought she would cure him of liking tobacco before he ever got started chewing on it so she said, 'Son, go ahead and chew it if you want to.' So, I wanted some too. Mama said, 'Go ahead.

"We both bit off a big chew of the tobacco and sat there on the porch as proud as punch to get a chew of that tobacco. Mama let Ira set there for a while then she sent him to the wood lot to cut some wood. He was chopping that wood and chewing. Pretty soon, Ira turned as white as a sheet and started getting sick. He really got sick.

"When she saw how sick he was Mama got scared and then she looked at me. I was sitting there smart aleck as you please. The tobacco hadn't made me sick at all and I think the fact that I was not at all sick and actin' pretty smug about it aggravated Mama and she got cross with me. Ira was sick the whole evening," said Lillian.

While the tobacco-chewing incident was comical, there were times when throwing sample products out into homeowner's yards proved serious, and sometimes fatal. Another questionable practice of that day was the door-to-door sales of unproven and untested medicines by traveling salesmen. There were apparently no controls of this practice, or if there were, few people were aware of them, and they were apparently largely unknown rules and not enforced. Many of these sales products were of doubtful origin as to purity or quality, and as a result, many people were sickened or died from using them.

Such was the fate of one of Dazerine's dear friends in Arkansas. A salesman came through town on horseback selling a chill tonic. Daisy's nearby neighbor, Sarah Elrod, was not feeling well and decided to try the new remedy.

Daisy and Sarah were both young mothers. They shared many common interests, cooked in each other's kitchens, traded recipes, and gossiped over coffee in each other's kitchens. They watched over each other's children and shared family confidences.

"We all loved Aunt Sarah Elrod," said Lillian. "She wasn't our aunt but us kids called all close older friends either aunt or uncle because little kids weren't allowed to call grown-ups by their given names. Aunt Sarah was expecting a baby and a drummer came through there selling chill tonic."

Lillian remembered the morning after Sarah bought the tonic. Sammie Elrod, Sarah's young son, came to their house early, before breakfast. "Just before he came, Mama said, 'Someone is surely coming with a hole in his britches because my nose was itchin'." Lillian remembered. "That was an old timer saying," said Lillian.

"When I saw Sammie coming up the hill I remember thinking Sammie didn't act right. When he walked in Mama started to joke with Sammie, 'Sammie have you got a hole in your britches because my nose was itchin.' I remember the way Sammie looked and how sad he looked," Lillian recalled.

He said, 'Aunt Daz, our Mama is dead.' Mama was shocked. She stared, confused, at him for a second and said, 'Sammie that just can't be.' He said, 'Yes she is. Will you come?'"

Of course, she would come, Daisy assured the young boy and she went immediately to the Elrod home. She stayed through the funeral. As it turned out, something in the chill tonic caused Sarah's death.

"We heard that there were several other women who died the same way," said Lillian. I guess there was something in the medicine that caused the women to lose their babies and their lives too." said Lillian. "Mr. Elrod packed up his family and moved to Texas. We didn't hear from them again." Lillian said she often wondered, "where they all got off to."

Earning a living:

While trying to earn a living as a housekeeper in Kansas City, Dazerine met with a variety of personalities from her various employers. There were those, such as Judge Latshaw, who treated her with respect and kindness, while others showed little regard for her hard work and house-cleaning skill, or her honesty. . "Mama worked for Judge Latshaw and I remember how he bought peanut butter in little wooden buckets and he would give Mama the buckets for us kids to play with .Every bucket he gave us would have about two inches or more of peanut butter in it," said Lillian. "One time he gave us one with almost a half bucket left in it. I remember thinking how wasteful they were. As I got older I realized it was his way of helping us and letting us keep our pride," Lillian recalled.

However, not all of her customers were so gracious. In contrast to Judge Latshaw's kindness, one of Daisy's female employers showed Daisy little regard, and slyly watched her while she worked, as though she thought Daisy would steal from her. "She lived in a fine, large house. I never seen her but Mama would tell us about the people she worked for." Lillian explained.

"This one lady was of the so-called better class of people. Mama cleaned her house and cooked the evening meals. The lady kept a glass of peppermint candy sticks on the table in a glass vase. Mama would serve the evening meal and immediately when the family had eaten, the lady would quickly remove all the nice foods, like jelly or desserts and the candy sticks, from the table. Mama couldn't help noticing but she didn't care. She couldn't afford to care, she needed the job. She thought the lady was kind of chintzy," said Lillian.

The Boarding House

Her many years of experience working in boarding houses and house-keeping jobs, became useful resources to Daisy about 1915. At that time, she had the opportunity to rent a large, two-story house and establish a boarding house of her own. With her background experience to guide her, success came quickly to her new business. Here was work that Daisy knew well. She was an excellent cook, housekeeper and skilled homemaker. Her boardinghouse became a comfortable home away from home for her boarders. She served good hearty meals and kept the place clean. The business thrived and Daisy finally, after many years of struggling, had a steady income.

"The boarding house was down on Washington Park Boulevard.," said Lillian. "That's all done away with long ago. Sheffield Steel took the whole thing and it later became Armco. The house had 15 rooms and only men boarded there. Mama had two employees, Hannah Rosen and her brother Gustav. They were immigrants from Sweden. They were both hard workers and eager to please. Hannah cooked for us and Gus took care of such things as the furnace and handyman stuff. We all got to be good friends.

"There were lots of manufacturing places around there. Some boarders worked at the K.C. Nut and Bolt, that eventually turned into Sheffield Steel Corp., and then into Armco. Others were employed at Butler Manufacturing, the feed and grain tanks and other manufacturing places. There were little dry goods stores, J.B. Lanes Grocery Store, Lumberyards, coal yards, and a drug store. Sheffield was like a little town inside the Kansas City limits. It also had six saloons.

"J.B.Lane's Grocery Store was a wooden building with sawdust on the floor. The grocery counter was about 30 feet long. It had a cash register and a coffee grinder with a big wheel about 24 inches in diameter on the counter. You ordered your coffee beans by the pound, not coarse or fine, just ground. Later on, we had a choice. They put the coffee beans in a funnel on top of the grinder. Mr. Long turned the handle and the ground coffee came out of the bottom into a metal pan. Mr. Long would then put the ground coffee into a brown paper sack. The coffee aroma filled the whole store," Lillian said.

"Mr. Long was big man about 5'11 or 6 ft. and weighed about 200 pounds. He moved slowly and walked loose-jointed with his hands swung out from his body in a kind of lope. He dressed in khaki pants and a blue chambray shirt and he always wore a white bibbed apron. He was a quiet but good-natured man," Lillian said, and went on to describer the store further.

"Store merchandise, such as canned goods, was stored on ceiling high shelves behind the counter. The ceiling must have been about 10 feet high. This was no self-serve store; customers told the storekeeper what they wanted and he got it for them. Canned goods, stored on high shelves, were retrieved with a long wooden rod utensil outfitted with a mechanical metal attachment that clamped down over the cans by squeezing the rod's handle. There was some canned goods but a lot of the store merchandise was fresh produce brought in by local farmers. Poultry was purchased live from coops. Customers picked out the chicken they wanted and Mr. Long removed it and weighed it feathers and all.

The scales inside the store sat on the counter. They were a fancy metal with a plate glass surface to weigh things like meat and cheese and small items. There was another larger floor scales outside on the store porch to weigh sacks of potatoes, flour and other large volume sales. Many of the women customers liked to save the sacks for sewing projects. Most customers charged their groceries then. Mr. Long kept little tablets with each family's name on the tablets under the counter. He would carefully jot down each item and mark the price in the little tablets at the time of purchase. When the customers came in to pay the bill, their children were often with them and Mr. Long would hand out free candy such as peppermint sticks, marshmallow animals, chocolate turtles and little sugar hearts with words on them. Horehound candy was a favorite," said Lillian.

Getting to know the boarders:

The boarding house was doing well and Dazerine had a steady income. Fortune was smiling on her at last. One of her boarders was Jason Moreland Knight. He, his 19-year-old son, John and 15-year-old son Okla lived at the boarding house. Mr. Knight was a divorced carpenter/contractor. His estranged wife, Lillie, had left him for another man. Mr. Knight worked nearby in one of the mills, so he and his two older sons, had moved with him to the boarding house. Mr. Knight also had two younger sons and a grown daughter.

When Eva divorced John Wheelen, she moved back home with her mother to the boarding house. When she met Mr. Knight's oldest son, John, she was immediately attracted to him. John Knight was a tall, outgoing, and handsome young man. the attraction between the two young people was mutual and John began courting the diminutive Eva right away. He went out of his way to be nice to her, showering her with attention. Eva fell head over heels in love with John, and by 1916, the two were married. The marriage was a union that pleased Daisy. After Eva's unhappy marriage to John Wheeling and the mistreatment Eva had endured at his hands, Daisy thought Eva's future was now secure with her new husband. John was a steady worker. He was always pleasant to Daisy. She was sure Eva had made a good match this time.

Eva Knight John Knight

One evening, not long after Mr. Knight moved into the boarding house, he arrived home from work with his two younger sons, Homer, 11, and Noel, 9, in tow. The boy's mother, Lillie, had turned them out of her house telling them to go find their father and live with him. They set out on the streetcar to find where Mr. Knight worked and he brought them home to the boarding house.

Homer did not make a good first impression on Lillian. When he came in, he immediately began teasing her brother, 4-year-old Clell. With little adieu, he grabbed the boy up in a bear hug, and promptly gave him a "Dutch rub". The so-called Dutch rub consisted of rolling the knuckles of one hand into a half fist and rubbing the knuckles hard across another person's head.

What Homer didn't know was that just prior to Daisy opening the boarding house she had been to Arkansas where Clell had contracted typhoid fever. He was three years old and had possibly drank water from a contaminated well or creek. Although no one else became ill, Clell ran high fevers and was very sick. When he recovered, he had forgotten how to walk. Lillian spent hours everyday encouraging her little brother to first take tiny steps while holding her hands and finally to walk and play in a normal fashion. During that time, she had become very protective of Clell.

When Homer gave Clell the "Dutch rub", the little boy let out a loud yowl and started crying. Nine- year-old, Lillian, was enraged. She gave Homer a hard push away from her little brother, grabbed Clell up in her arms and gave Homer a tongue lashing he never forgot. Homer, a brash and undisciplined 11year-old jumped nimbly out of her reach. He was just having some fun with the "big baby", he told her, and laughed loudly at the indignant Lillian.

Even at the age of eleven, Homer was a fighter. He and Noel had a paper route that required them to catch a trolley car, fetch the papers, and sell them on the streets of downtown Kansas City. He learned early on that if a boy was to survive on the streets at that time he had best know how to fight. Some of the street corners offered a far better potential for income than other corners. Homer and Noel had one of the good corners and Homer intended to keep it.

Since the only way to keep a good sale corner was to fight for it, Homer did. The boys were challenged by some of the bigger newspaper boys for their corner on a daily basis. When Homer fought an intruder for his corner, it was not to punch him in the face, or to bloody his nose. Selling newspapers was a serious business for him. It put food on his table and clothes on his back. Homer was not playing. He used hard blows to the body knocking the wind out of his opponent and bruising his ribs to get rid of the competition fast.

Eventually, Homer and Noel had the opportunity to move into better paying, less stressful jobs and Homer became a water boy at the Railroad Round House where trains turned around. He took pride in this menial labor and glowed with pleasure when the older workers told him he was the best water boy they ever had.

Homer 11, Noel 9

Mr. Knight and his sons lived upstairs at the boarding house. All four boys were noticeably lacking in good manners and careless in their behavior. Homer and Noel were brash young boys, but they were good-hearted. They became genuinely fond of Daisy and she of them. During their stay at the boarding house, she saw to it that they were well fed. She kept their clothes clean and took an interest in their activities, and did what she could to provide a wholesome home life for them, and at the same time, encourage a few good manners and a more gentle behavior. Homer and Noel appreciated her kindness and responded warmly to Daisy's attention. They were good workers and Daisy was careful to acknowledge their help. She complimented their work and let them know when she was pleased with their behavior. As time went on a real bond of friendship and respect grew between them, and the boys, especially Homer, would do anything she asked of them.

Okla Knight

However, Okla was different. At 15, he was an angry boy with a chip on his shoulder, selfish and indifferent to other people's feelings. Sometimes he would go upstairs and deliberately start a fight with Daisy's son, Ira. During his youthful years of poor, to totally lacking, parental guidance, he had developed a belligerent attitude that caused hard feelings for himself and others around him. Okla wanted to get his parents back together, an unlikely goal at best, but he seemed to think that as long as Mr. Knight and the other boys were comfortable at the boarding house, that Daisy was an obstacle to his goal of reuniting his parents.

"One particular time we were having the noon meal," said Lillian. "Okla. was eating some beans. He found a rock in the beans, and said he had found 'one of Mrs. Knapp's old snaggled teeth' in them. (Daisy had retained the last name of her husband, Francis Knapp after he died)

Daisy had tried to be patient with Okla up to this point. She knew about his lack of guidance and she put up with a lot of his nonsense. "But, this time she lost her temper and blew up all over the place," said Lillian.

Though she was not a vain woman, Dazerine was embarrassed that her teeth were no longer pretty. She had been too poor in the past few years to consider dental care. More importantly, Dazerine was a southern, country woman, brought up with the unshakable belief that unprovoked rudeness in anyone was an unacceptable breach in manners. For a young man to belittle an older woman was an insult, not to be tolerated. Mr. Knight apparently agreed.

Jason Knight 1915

"He took Okla out of there as quick as he could and whipped him," said Lillian

Unfortunately, Daisy's lifestyle as a boarding house keeper was to be short lived because, during this time, serious rumblings of war began to resonate in Europe. Newspapers carried bold front-page stories of Germany's military aggression into small bordering countries in Europe.

World War I

Americans in general tried to look away from what they considered the European conflict. They wanted nothing to do with war. However, one small country after another crumpled and fell before German troops in Europe. The German Chancellor, Kaiser Wilhelm, was rattling swords at France and England. Russia was also involved and by 1916, all Europe was involved in war with Germany. Eventually, the German Emperor was inflicting atrocities that impinged on Americans. With the sinking of the British ship Lusitanian, about 100 American tourists lost their lives. Other atrocities followed and threatened the safety of Americans traveling abroad. There were attacks on American commercial interest as well. Finally, United States President, Woodrow Wilson decided the United States had had enough and Congress declared War on Germany in 1917. The United States joined forces with France and England to bring down the militant German dictator.

During World War 1, Germany not only conducted a military war, but they also practiced germ warfare. The influenza and small pox germs were their choice of weapons. As it turned out, those two diseases of WW1 accounted for more casualties in civilians and military troops than battlefield fatalities.

"We was very much aware of World War 1," said Lillian.

"A lot of boarders left to go to war. Mr. Treece was one of them. He dated one of my cousins. He was as wide as he was tall until the Army got a hold of him. He slimmed down and he was thin. When he got out of the Army, he changed that around and got fat again. Mr. Treece was jolly and just like one of the family," Lillian recalled.

"Uncle Lon (Alonzo Scott) died in the war," she said. "He must have been about 18. I remember seeing him leave for war after he was drafted. I don't actually remember seeing him leave but I saw him in his uniform. I was pretty small but I remember seeing him when he went to camp. He was dressed in his uniform and he was kind of struttin' around and he looked kind of handsome." Lillian said.

Actually, Alonzo Scott didn't die in combat; he died in an army camp of the flu while he was waiting to be deployed.

"Flu and small pox were epidemic in the whole country," said Lillian.

"Aunt Vick went out to see after things after he died and to claim his body," said Lillian.

"Aunt Vick came back from camp a broken woman. She doted on Lon. He was her baby brother, Mama's too. Aunt Vick helped raise him after Grandma Amanda died in January 1906," said Lillian.

Amanda died during a bad winter storm. A deep snow had covered the Ozark hills followed by ice. Daisy heard that her mother was very sick with pneumonia. Eva was still a child, Ira a small boy at the time, and Lillian was a baby but Dazerine bundled them up and went to her mother. The day Amanda died there was a sheet of ice over everything. No one would come out to take Amanda to the churchyard to be buried so her son, Isaac and her nephew, Jim Sisney put spike shoes on Jim's small mule so it would be able to walk on the ice. Jim made a sled out of some pinewood he had in his barn. They hitched the sled to the mule and placed Amanda on the sled, then walked beside her all the way to the churchyard, about four miles, so she could be buried.

Lon was 20 years younger than Vick and 10 years younger than Dazerine. He would have been about 16 when Amanda died. He was more like Aunt Vick's kid than her brother," Lillian said. "He had been spoiled rotten. Aunt Vick like to have never got over his death. Uncle Lon had a military funeral. Mama went to the funeral but she didn't let us kids go.

The flu and small pox epidemics were so bad Mama kept us soaked down in sulphur to keep us from getting sick. People were dying like flies. The doctors were so busy you couldn't get one and if you did, there wasn't anything they could do. There were no shots or anything like that. Two thirds of the people in the boarding house got sick but no one died," said Lillian.

"Some people said it was some kind of germ warfare. It was terrible. We worked all the time. Men lived upstairs in the boarding house and I had to carry water all the time. Everybody worked as long as they could stand to take care of the sick and bring the food," said Lillian.

"I can't remember the details too much but I remember Hannah and Eva jumped sideways to keep from flying during the epidemic. I don't think they ever slept. All that couldn't happen nowadays but it happened then.

"I remember those big old heavy water pitchers I carried up and down those stairs. I drew water from the well on the back porch with a rope and pulley and took them to the boarder's rooms.

The rooms were about 12 by 14 and had two boarders per room. There was a bed on each side of the room. I made beds and filled water pitchers. The beds were big feather beds and pillows. I pushed and punched the feather beds, put sheets on each bed and quilts.

"I had to empty slop jars. Take them out to the privy and dump them. Only sick people used slop jars. I remember sulfur burning on the stove. Mama believed that burning sulfur helped kill any airborne germs. She would sprinkle it over the cook stove and if you weren't careful, you would choke on the fumes. A coal furnace heated the house with ventilators in the floors. People lost their jobs when they got sick. Some left the boarding house but some stayed. The rooms were full when the sickness hit. I slept with Mama, me and Clell both," said Lillian.

Lillian continued her story. "After so much exposure to it, Mama got the flu; but she was getting over it. The Knight boys were sick too, when their mother, Lillie, Mr. Knight's ex-wife, now Mrs. Gaines, came in and went upstairs. She gave Noel, Homer and Okla a dose of the drug Laudanum to ease their cough and make them feel better, she said.

"Mama knew Laudanum to be an addictive narcotic. When she heard what Lillie had done she really lost her temper, and ordered her out of the house," said Lillian.

Laudanum is derived from opium. It is a recognized addictive narcotic now, but in that day and time, it was accessible over the counter without a prescription. It was used to treat a variety of ills.

"About that same time we learned that Dr. Dargatz was a spy," said Lillian. "Dr. Dargatz and his family was neighbors a few blocks away. Their family home was on the corner of Bennington St. and Winter Road. Dr. Dargatz had his medical office in the home. A lot of people thought Dr. Dargatz was a little odd and, there got to be too much talk around there. When the government finally found him out, and came out to get him, I remember, Dr. Dargatz climbed up on the porch roof of his house. We saw him scrambling around up there," said Lillian

"There were no loud sirens or a big hullabaloo. But, a great big crowd gathered around and we heard the ruckus. Most police walked and some rode horses in those days. We heard that the police came after him and he tried to shoot it out with them. They finally got him down off the roof and the police took him away. After they got him to jail, the police told the crowd 'That's all now,' and they sent the crowd away. They didn't tell us anything. Before they picked him up, everyone knew there was something wrong with Dargatz. Then we found out that Dr. and Mrs. Dargatz were helping old Kaiser Bill (the *German Emperor, Kaiser Wilhelm*) and a lot of people died from it. I don't know why they didn't pick her up too," said Lillian.

"Dr. Dargatz was sent to prison and the rest of the family stayed there on Bennington for many years later. Dr. Dargatz was a short chunky German. He spoke with an accent, and had emigrated from Germany, a long time before the war broke out. The family had lived there on Bennington and Winter Road for a long time. The house was big two-story, stucco house and his office was in the house. It was a pretty nice house for them times.

"Mrs. Dargatz was a courteous person but very reserved. We never did doctor with Dr. Dargatz. After they took him away, we never heard anymore about him. I knew and liked his son, Emil, and his daughter Matilda was a sweet and friendly girl. "We was very much aware of the end of the war. Everyone went haywire, bells ringing, horns blowing. Downtown Kansas City was just pushing and shoving through town. In the fringe areas, everyone was marching with flags ands singing, "Kaiser Bill went over the hill and Kaiser Bill is dead."

"I get the two wars mixed up now. World War 1 didn't seem to last very long. The Americans got in about 1916 and about 18 months it was over," Lillian said years later.

Back to the Ozarks

The combination of the war and the flu epidemic, seriously impacted Daisy's boarding house business. The times were unsettled. Factories that had produced military goods either closed or cut back production. Many people lost their jobs and moved away. As former boarders came back from the war, they soon married and found homes of their own. Most of the boarding house rooms were empty and Dazerine knew it would take some time to build up a new clientele. She was once again in a position of transition trying to decide what she should do.

Ira, then 17 and assuming many responsibilities of a grown man had grown weary of city life. He had always considered Arkansas his real home and he wanted the family to try their luck once again in the Ozarks. The boarding house was a rental, so there would be no worry about selling the place. Dazerine's brothers, Will, Ike and her half brother, James Huffman had stayed in the Ozarks and were doing well. Dazerine decided that perhaps this was a good time to look at her home state.

"We moved to Arkansas in the spring of 1919. The First World War was over and my brother Ira wanted to go back to Arkansas. So, we moved to Myrtle Ark," said Lillian. It was a beautiful place and I really loved living there. We lived on a hill and there was a big field in back of the house. I was always out roaming the fields seeing what I could find. Mama and I slept in the front room and Ira and Clell slept in the bedroom in the attic.

"There was a very small store and a little post office there also. The post office was about 8-feet-square. There was a railroad a short ways from Myrtle. Mama had a big garden and a strawberry patch. A rancher let us milk one of his cows so we had plenty of strawberries and cream.

" We didn't have much money except when I picked strawberries and took them down to the railroad cook cars. They were real happy to get berries and any fresh vegetables too. We got to know all the kids around there.

" One neighbor was named Hodge and the other was Dobbs. They were real nice and we went to visit them several times. Some people lived across the creek from us and people lived back in the woods but we didn't see much of them. We had a one-room house and a lean-to kitchen but we wasn't in the house that much anyway except at night.

"There was a road ran right by our house but it wasn't much traveled, just farmers going to their fields. It was early spring and our house sat on a hill that sloped down to the creek. It was a wonderful place for a kid to play. We were in the water every day. We didn't have any swimsuits we just wore old clothes. There wasn't many people living close. There was only one store and it was very small and only had a few staples like coffee, sugar and salt and salt pork. We got our water from a spring that was down the hill from the house. There was a big sycamore tree right at the top of the hill and there was a big bobcat that sat there and watched like he thought he owned the whole hill and could hardly tolerate mere humans. I would always stop and pass the time of day with him. We kept our food like milk and butter in the springhouse where it was cool and the food stayed fresh so I saw the bobcat pretty regular," said Lillian.

"There was a farmer that lived back in the hills there and he sometimes drove right by our house with a plow in his wagon. Mama needed a garden plowed so she had me watch for the man with the plow. One day the farmer drove by with his family. Mama had me stop him and asked if he would plow our garden. He said he would, and right then and there, he got out of his wagon, took down the plow, and started to plow.

"There was a woman and a girl, and two little boys in the wagon. The woman came in and set down and Mama just couldn't get a word out of her. I did manage to get the girl to talk a little. When the man got the plowing done, Mama asked him how much she owed him. He said 'nothing.'

Mama told him she didn't intend for him to do all that work for nothing, but all he said to his wife was, 'Woman get the kids in the wagon.' Then he said 'get up' to his horse and drove away. The next day, we heard that he had drove straight to a man's house that had done something to him, shot the man, and killed him. Seems it was a grudge killing.

"We moved from Arkansas to Pine Top, Missouri to a small place with mountains all around us. Mama had met someone who knew the owner of the place and he needed a housekeeper and someone to help him with his vineyards. The house was only two rooms. Ira and Clell slept in the attic and Mama and I slept in the front room. The owner, Mr. Hutton, had a bedroom right off the kitchen. It was hardly enough room but we had fun there and we were always outside anyway," said Lillian.

"It was a wild, sort of remote place. The only close neighbor was a bachelor named Mr. McAlester. He was a very odd man. He didn't approve of Mr. Hutton because Mr. Hutton made wine and he also occasionally gave us kids a very small sip of it. And it was good, too. Mr. Hutton was also the mail carrier there," said Lillian.

"Ira and I liked to roam around the mountains. I liked to go in the caves. One time I crawled into a cave and it was full of snakes. I sure did not stay long in there.

"We had to carry water from the spring, which was the only water we had. It was about a quarter of a mile from the house. When Mr. Hutton came from his mail route and after I got acquainted with his mules, he would let me take them to the spring to drink. He always told me to never get on the mules but after I got to know the mules real good, I decided I might as well ride as walk. So, I did get on the mules and they never seemed to mind at all. Mr. Hutton was always warning me about the mules but we got along just fine.

"There was one time when I had a scare going to the spring. We had been hearing about some wolves. There was a warning about a wolf pack that had been seen around there and there was a bounty set on the wolves' heads. Some men called "wolfers" were out hunting the wolves and they were telling everyone to be on the lookout for them.

"That evening Ira had gone somewhere with Mr. Hutton and Mama and I and Clell were busy when Mama noticed it was getting dark. She said 'Sister you better get to the spring right quick before it gets dark'. So, I grabbed my bucket and started for the water.

"As I got started out I could hear the wolves and for a little while I just didn't know what to do but I decided I'd better get the water so I went on to the spring. When I got to the spring I looked around and there I was, as close to the wolves as a good-sized room. Those wolves just stood there quiet as could be with their heads lowered and sort of staring at me. Boy, I sure got that water fast and got out of there. There was at least three wolves probably more. The next day we heard the wolfers had run them down and killed the whole pack. If I remember there were six or seven in the pack," Lillian said.

One afternoon, during their stay in Arkansas, Lillian was out walking with a girl friend. She was 13 or 14 years old. It started to cloud up so the girls decided they should start home before it started to rain.

A farmer who lived down the road from them had borrowed a horse from a neighbor to go with his horse and make a team to pull a wagonload of logs.

There was a fork in the road where the men had placed a high stack of logs. The two girls were approaching the fork in the road about the same time that the farmer was nearing the same location with a load of logs.

"We were by this fork in the road when the lightning flashed and scared the horses. They reared up in the air and came down running," said Lillian.

"One horse went down one road toward its home and the other horse went down the other road toward its home. We were right in front of them. I started to run to the edge of the road, but my friend yelled 'climb the logs.' Then she turned and ran to the edge of the road," said Lillian.

"I was about half way up the logs when the wagon tongue hit me right in the back. All the logs rolled down on top of me. I was unconscious for a while. After the man, who was driving the wagon, dug me out I couldn't move for some time, and I couldn't see. I didn't want Mama to worry about me so I didn't tell her I was blind. I was so sore I didn't want to walk around anyway. I was afraid I would always be blind and I worried about how I was going to tell Mama. After a few days, my sight began to come back. I guess I had damaged a nerve. It took a long time for my back to heal," said Lillian.

"I remember one time while we still lived in Arkansas, I felt real good about myself. This was about 1919. Mama left me and Ira with Aunt Delia in Omaha, Arkansas and she went back to K.C.

"Eva was married to John Knight by then and she was expecting her second baby. She wanted Mama to come and be with her when the baby was born. So, Mama went to be with Eva and Ira and I went to school in Omaha.

"They were having a reading class at school and the way the kids was reading was awful they would put an 'anda' between each word When the teacher called on me I got up and read my part off almost like I was just talking. When I got through reading, I started back to my seat," said Lillian.

"Mr. Powers, the teacher, said, 'Just a minute Lillian. Would you mind reading another page' and of course I did. When I finished he said 'Now that is the way to read. Who taught you to read?'

"I felt good at the time but it was the beginning of more trouble because I out read everyone in school, boys and girls. My cousin, Vada, (Vay-dah) didn't like me much anyway and after I got the praise for reading better than the rest of the class, I had more enemies than friends. It ended up in my cousin Vada quitting school and me and my other cousin Edna getting a whipping. Seems like there was some friction between us all and somehow it ended up in a fight. Even my aunt Martha, Vada's mother, got into it.

"Mr. Powers gave us the choice of taking a whipping or quitting school. Vada quit but Uncle Will wouldn't let Edna quit. I didn't really have a choice to quit. My mother was up in Kansas City so there was really no one to say whether I should quit or not.

"So, when Mr. Powers asked me if I was quitting or taking a whipping. I took it out in being a smart Alec. He made a regular Kangaroo court out of it. He called on witnesses to the fight and all that stuff.

When he asked me what my part in it was, I answered him real nice and real polite and overly nice. I bowed and said yes sir and no sir and all the kids were snickering.

I was really showing out and I even offered to go out and cut the switches. I don't think I would have done it if the teacher hadn't belittled me and said I didn't really have a right to go to school there because my parents didn't live there and pay taxes," Lillian said.

"The day of the whipping Mr. Powers wasn't at school when we got there but he came in soon afterwards with a couple of big switches. Edna and I had dressed for the occasion. We put on two or three petticoats so it wouldn't hurt so much but he was wise to that. He whipped us across the legs and he really hit hard too I could hardly keep a straight face. After he quit, I looked him right in the face and smiled all the time. He was mad as fire I guess. He brought the switch down a couple of extra hard licks on me, and my boy friend, Dewey, just raised up in his seat and started toward Mr. Powers. Mr. Powers threw down the switch and said 'Go back to your seat'. Mr. Powers dismissed class. After that he was real nice to me," said Lillian.

Back To Kansas City

When school in Arkansas was out for the summer Lillian and Ira went back to Kansas City. Ira was 18, and Lillian, 15. Both were now considered of working age and further schooling was not of significant importance. If they could read and write and had a good understanding of elementary arithmetic, that was all they really needed to do well in that time.

Ira was soon working full time and not long after that, Lillian got a job working for a mail order firm named the National Cloak and Suit Company. Before long, they were both bringing in regular paychecks. They had watched their mother working long and hard, sacrificing herself to their needs for many years. The two of them got together one day and talked it over and together they decided their mother had worked long enough for them. Now it was their turn to do for her. They rented a house at 500 FullerAve. It was a large house with nice roomy upstairs, sleeping rooms. Lillian gave her entire paycheck to her mother and Daisy gave Lillian back an allowance for spending money. Ira turned a part of his paycheck over to Daisy, but kept most of it. This seemed to be a fair arrangement because Ira was a young bachelor of courting age and he needed money to squire the eligible young women. Additionally, he earned higher wages than Lillian, being a woman, could earn. Therefore, he was able to contribute a fair share to the arrangement and still keep a good portion of his wages.

Ira Jay McIntyre, 1920

Mr. Knight was still a bachelor at this time. He didn't really like being alone but, neither was he looking for a wife. Even so, he enjoyed the comfort of a home cooked meal and a homey atmosphere. His two younger sons had remained in contact with Daisy's family. Their adult children, Eva and John Knight, were married with two children, so it was natural for Jason and Daisy to be friends. They had many common interests, so at some point before 1923 he was once again renting a sleeping room and boarding at Daisy's home. He had one of the upstairs bedrooms. The extra money that came from his room and board allowed the family a comfortable income.

Daisy took care of all the housekeeping. She did the laundry and cooking and handled all household affairs. This arrangement allowed time for Daisy to help Eva with her growing family. It worked out to be an agreeable situation and for some time it worked well.

Lillian was thrilled with her new job. She was the youngest employee there. Her supervisors were well satisfied with this young, eager to learn, employee and took her under their wing. They spent extra effort to help her learn the business and went further to recommend that management send her to business school, at company expense, in order to further her education and improve her career opportunities. Lillian took pride in her work and was well pleased with her success on the job.

Even though Lillian gave her entire check to her mother, she managed to save money from her allowance to buy Daisy small gifts.

"Mama gave me money for car fare and lunch money," said Lillian. "I liked to walk and we lived only a mile from my work so I would save my carfare money and walk to work. Sometimes I skipped my lunch. When I had enough money, I would buy something pretty for Mama. She loved getting presents, and I'd get as much pleasure out of watching her open her presents as she did in getting them. Her face would light up and she got so excited. Homer liked to give her pretty things too."

Life altering blow:

It was an early spring day in 1922 when fate once more stepped in to deal the McIntyre family a life altering blow. The weather was still cool and the windows were not yet open. One day, some men came into the neighborhood throwing samples of a new insect repellent in all the yards. The insect repellent was guaranteed to rid homes of household insects. It killed any and all of them according to the package label.

Bed bugs were a particular household pest in those days and homemakers constantly battled the dreaded little red bug whose bite could turn their beds into a nightmare. Every spring and fall, it was a regular housekeeping chore for Daisy to take the mattresses off the beds and check all the little crevices for any signs of the pesky red bugs. She would then wipe down the wire bedsprings in kerosene and spot treat any suspicious areas.

Dazerine was a meticulous housekeeper with a high disgust for household vermin. It was about the time of year when she normally did her bed check, so when the samples landed in the yard, Daisy read the label and decided to give the insect killer an immediate trial on the upstairs bedrooms.

The new guaranteed insect killer was named Formaldehyde. Very few people of that time had ever heard of it.

Lillian was still working when Daisy began treating the beds. When she arrived home, Lillian didn't see her mother and went looking for her. As she entered the front door, she smelled pungent fumes that seemed to be coming from upstairs. She hurried upstairs and found Daisy there passed out on the floor. The room reeked of the formaldehyde fumes. Fumes so thick they threatened to overwhelm Lillian. She quickly threw open the windows. She knew she must get her mother out of that room quickly. She covered her mouth and nose as well as she could and dragged Daisy out and into the fresh air. That short period of time and the effort of dragging Daisy out, was almost too much for Lillian. She too was almost overcome by the fouled air. Once they were out in the fresh air, Daisy regained consciousness but she remained groggy and dizzy for some time. She was ill for several days and she developed a persistent hacking cough.

Several months passed and Daisy was still trying to throw off the racking cough that plagued her sleep and left her exhausted. However, the cough did not improve and if anything, it was getting worse. Daisy began losing weight and it seemed to her that she was always tired. Lillian was seriously concerned about her mother's condition but she did not connect Dazerine's poor health to the insecticide. "I was worried sick," Lillian said. "Mama began spitting up a little blood when she coughed."

Daisy McIntyre Knapp

Daisy eventually went to the doctor and he diagnosed her cough to be consumption. By November of that year, Daisy's health had worsened. Another doctor was called in and he diagnosed her illness as anemia.

Even as she faced the grim realities of her illness, Daisy put her family's needs above her own. Whether her ailment was from anemia or consumption, Daisy knew that while a person might ease the symptoms of the diseases, there was no known cure for either consumption or anemia.

Daisy now worried about what would become of her unmarried daughter, Lillian, if she (Daisy) should die. Men could take care of themselves she believed. However, Lillian was only 17. She was young and innocent. Without her mother to look out for her, what might she do? Daisy was convinced that Lillian would need the security of a husband and marriage. There were so many pitfalls and dangers for a pretty, young, unmarried woman like Lillian. Daisy wanted to know that Lillian would be well cared for when she was no longer there to look after her. She wanted to see her daughter settled and married before she died. One day Daisy called Lillian into her room to talk about her concerns.

Homer Knight was the man that Dazerine wanted Lillian to marry. She had watched him grow up for eight years from the time he was a ten-year-old to eighteen. She believed she knew him well and she believed him to be a good man. Homer had always been good to Daisy, and Daisy thought Homer loved Lillian. He was a hard worker, generous with his money.

"I think Homer loved Mama as much as I did," said Lillian.

"When he took me places he always asked if Mama wanted to go. He took her with us to the movies. Mama loved the movies."

Mr. Knight was solidly behind the marriage and he was quick to say so. Homer was more than ready to marry Lillian.

They all seemed determined to get her married. Lillian however was not ready to get married to Homer, or anyone else. She might marry him later perhaps, but not now. She was only seventeen and doors of opportunity were opening for her. She was

Lillian McIntyre, 1920

doing exceptionally well on her job. Her supervisors had told her she had the promise of a good career. She was not ready to settle down. Not yet!

She wanted to do so many things before tying herself down to marriage. No, Lillian's plans did not include marriage at this time.

However, Daisy and Mr. Knight were both persistent in their goal to see the two young people married. "If I married Homer, Mama told me, she would have peace of mind," said Lillian.

"I would do anything for Mama," Lillian said. So finally, she gave in to her mother's wishes and agreed to be married.

Lillian "Bill" and Homer Knight 1922

Homer and Lillian were married July 15, 1922. Lillian dressed in her best dress and Homer wore his only suit. They were married in Leavenworth, Kansas before a justice of the peace. Daisy and Jason Knight were their only witnesses. The marriage lasted for 60years until 1982 when the two died at the ages of 78 and 79.

Saying goodbye:

Several months had passed since the episode with the insect killer. Dazerine's cough persisted. She had her good days and her bad days but her health was not improving.

In January of 1923, Mr. Knight came down sick with the flu. Even though she herself was not well, Dazerine took care of Mr. Knight during his illness. He had been in bed sick for several days and was on the mend, but far from well when his daughter, Vera, came by for a visit. Vera had been working in a local hospital as a nurse's aide. She considered herself somewhat of an authority on medicine even though she had no formal medical training.

There was at that time a radical new theory circulating among some medical people concerning the best treatment for influenza. Some theorists declared fresh air was one of the better treatments for the flu. Vera had heard this theory discussed around the hospital and she, a young novice, concluded with her limited experience that this new unproven technique was the correct medical treatment for her father.

With great authority, she came into Mr. Knight's warm room, wearing her white nurses uniform, and threw open the windows. The cold, fresh January air flowed quickly into the room and chilled the warm air to icy cold. She pulled the blankets off the bed leaving Mr. Knight uncovered. Without warm cover, Mr. Knight still warm from fever began to shiver violently from the extreme cold.

Daisy stood aghast at Vera's treatment of her father. However, she could do little to stop it. Though she firmly disagreed with Vera's actions, Daisy reasoned that Vera worked in a hospital, and therefore Vera should know more than Daisy did. There was also the fact that Vera was, after all, Mr. Knight's daughter and, Daisy was just a friend. She had no real authority to override Vera's actions.

However, when Vera left, Daisy quickly replaced the blankets and closed the windows. She did what she could to get Mr. Knight warm again but the damage was done. Mr. Knight died of the influenza and pneumonia on January 29, 1923.

Several months passed since Dazerine first became ill. Some days were better than other days but she was still losing weight and her cough was worse.

"Ira thought a trip to the Ozarks might do her good," said Lillian.

Daisy agreed that she would like to take the trip to see her brother's families. It would be a little warmer there and, it might indeed make her feel better.

Daisy had been gone about a month when in December, Ira wrote her that he was thinking of moving back to Arkansas. About that same time Lillian went down to see Daisy. When Lillian stepped off the train, Daisy was there to meet her. Lillian was shocked at her mother's appearance." I almost fainted," said Lillian. She tried to put on a brave face. However, she could not hide her concern.

Daisy was a caricature of herself. She had lost even more weight. She was hollow eyed, dark circles lined her eyes, and her cheeks were sunken. Her skin was a gray color and stretched tight across her face.

Lillian brought Daisy home with her.

A year had passed since Daisy first became ill. As the colder weather approached, each day was worse than the last. A harsh steady cough racked her body leaving her weak and listless until she could hardly get out of bed.

Lillian was still working but she decided to quit her job so she could spend more time with her mother. Daisy had moved to Eva and John's home a few miles away. Lillian would get her work done and then walk to Eva's house to be with Daisy. When it was time for Homer to be home from work, she walked back home.

The day came when the doctor told the family that Daisy could not last much longer. They had known this day would come but it was almost more than they could face.

Daisy died January 15, 1924. It was a Tuesday evening She was 44 years old. She was buried January 17 on Clell's birthday. He was 13. She was grandmother to four of Eva's children. Lillian was expecting a baby in July. Ira, who had married Margureet Leedom, Cora's daughter, in December 1923, was also expecting a child in July.

There were eventually 21 grandchildren and thus the links of the family chain were added and the Daisy Chain began to grow. All the grandchildren grew up hearing stories about their Grandmother Daisy from their parents. Stories that never grew old to them. Her grandchildren verbally handed down Daisy's story, and down through the years it has been retold, until she has become a family legend in the eyes of her descendents.

Ina Mae Knight was Daisy's oldest grandchild. She was 7 years old and the only grandchild that really knew her Grandma Daisy. She remembered well the day Daisy died.

"Grandma watched after me a lot in those seven years," Ina told her younger cousins.

"She was a real nice lady, and when I wouldn't mind she would say, 'If you're not good, I'll leave." said Ina.

"We were living on Smaley St. when Aunt Lillian and Uncle Homer brought Grandma out to our house sick. She didn't live long after that. I remember there was ice and snow everywhere the night she died. "I could hear Clell crying."

Several date related, coincidences marked Clell's life. His father, Jay McIntyre, died in January of 1912. He was buried on January 17. It was Clell's first birthday. His mother, Daisy, died January 1924. She was buried January 17 on Clell's 13th. birthday. After his wife, Pearl, died, he married Genevieve on Oct.1, 1976. Twelve years later on their anniversary, Oct.1, 1990, Clell died.

"When I was told that Grandma had left us," Ina said, "I thought maybe if I promised to be real good she would come back. I ask Mama, (Eva) and she started to cry. I knew it had hurt her.

"When the hearse came after Grandma it couldn't get close to the house because of the ice and snow. My Daddy and Uncle Homer Knight had to carry her for a block to the hearse. She was buried at Mt. Washington Cemetery in Kansas City, Missouri," Ina said.

It would be more than 30 years later, after information about the dangers of insecticides became more evident, indeed, after the world in general became more aware of their environment that Daisy's family would begin to make a connection between the formaldehyde poison and Daisy's sudden onset of illness. No one could prove it or actually knew, but family members, after reading the symptoms of the poison, began to see similarities to the symptoms of consumption. Finally, they came to believe that exposure to the formaldehyde fumes had burned Daisy's lungs and caused her death, not consumption, nor the anemia that doctors had diagnosed.

Daisy had been well before the exposure to the formaldehyde fumes, they reasoned. The onset of illness began almost immediately after the fumes overcame her. Was the cause of her death ever proven? No. Time had eliminated the possibility of proving it.

Elijah Jackson McIntyre, the mystery man.

Elijah Jackson McIntyre was known as Jay by most of the people who knew him. He came into Daisy's life when she was 23 and he was 46. There was always a bit of mystery about him. Daisy knew he was from New York and that he had worked in the mines there. She remembered that Jay carried a white baby shoe in his pocket, which he never explained. She also knew that he received mail from his family in New York but she never read it. Beyond that, she knew very little about his background.

It was many years before Jay's second family knew much more than that about him, but as time went by, his grandchildren became curious, and eventually they launched a family search to see what they could find out about their mysterious grandfather. Fortunately, Daisy, and later her daughter, Lillian had kept the old letters sent to Jay about 1902 from his family in New York and they offered clues to his former life. Daisy's grandchildren found the old letters stored away in a box of Lillian's memorabilia. Daisy had, according to Lillian, written Jay's family in 1912 to inform them of his death but their answer to her letter had apparently been cool and dismissive and she never contacted them again, Lillian said.

Research into Jay's family, done about 1950, by his grandchildren revealed that he had another family in New York that included a wife and four children, as well as an extended family of brothers and other relatives. What caused Jay to **le**ave his New York family, hire onto Railroad construction across country, and settle in Arkansas? Why did he then remarry, start a second family and apparently never tell his family in New York about his second marriage? Those questions were never answered, and probably will never be answered. Even so, much has been learned about his family ancestry and ours, since those earlier times. That record is shown in Part 3, of this book, titled "Ancestors."

The following is part of the information that research revealed about Jay's life.

Jay was Dazerine Petty Scott's second husband and the father to three of her children. They were married in 1900 and again in 1903. Why two marriages? No one seemed to know. The couple's oldest child, was a son, Ira Jay, born in 1903, second was a daughter, Iva Lillian, born in 1905, also known by her nick name, "Bill", in her adult life. Their third child was a son, Clell born in 1911.

In family letters dated 1902, Jay's brother, John. and niece Eva, speak fondly of their feelings for Jay as a brother and uncle. They beg him to come home, that things will be worked out, and all is forgiven. Eva's letters speak of Ira, a champion swimmer, who drowned while swimming in the Great Lakes. Excerpted phrases from John's letters mention that, "We have a father who gave his life for the Union...our mother has gone to meet our father. Brother, I like to call you brother.

It does me good for you have always been a good brother to me."

Research of 1892 records in New York showed Jackson McIntyre, age 36, in the town of Schroeppel, Oswego County, New York with a wife, Carrie, age 34, and children, Ella, 14; Alma, 12; Charlie, 8 and Stephen, 3.

A woman named Eva McIntyre, 23, is also in that census, also Hiram, Louise and Elmer McIntyre. These people are believed to be part of Jay's extended family

Jean Fisher, about 1980, checked census records in Ontario County, Victor, New York State, She found that in 1880, a Jackson Elijah McIntyre, age 23, born in New York, parents born in New York lived in Dwelling #50, and had one daughter, Ella. Even though 1880 census shows him as Jackson Elija and not Elijah Jackson, there is little doubt that the two are the same man.

Listed in dwelling 29-30 is Ira C. McIntyre, a farmer age 70, born in New York, his parents were born in Massachusetts, his wife Florence age 45 born in New York.

In another dwelling number 48-50 was John A .McIntyre, farmer, age 25, born in New York, wife Emmet, born in New York, and daughter, Eva L., age 5, Lillian C., age 2 and Ira V. age 4 months. There is little doubt that the John in the census is the brother who wrote so eloquently to Jay in 1902 and John's daughter Eva is almost certainly the niece who wrote the other letters. Jay obviously named his Arkansas children for his family in New York because their names are the same as some of those folks listed in the New York census.

The census lists both John and Ira C. as farmers. An occupation is not listed for Jackson Elijah. This census ties together with letters written to Jay McIntyre by John and Eva McIntyre.

The 1902 letters are as follows: There are ellipses where the handwritten letters were damage over time making a few words unreadable.

(In the following letter John McIntyre writes to Elijah Jackson McIntyre in Arkansas Feb. 1902 from John's home in New York)

Feb.6, 1902

My Dear Brother,

We received your letter by the 6:18 mail P.M. yesterday. We were getting quite uneasy about you, but when we got your letter it explained all, but when we learned the contents we were very disappointed for we all had our minds made up that you would surely come to make your home with us, that is until you got well anyway, and now they think it is all over with but I'm not agoing to have it that way. I wish it was so that I could come out there, then I would see and talk to you. I can talk better than I can write, but I cannot do what I would like to do if I could...........see you in a short time and I would bring you back with me. But seeing I cannot come out there and talk to you I am agoing to do some talking on this paper. Now I am going to begin. I have quit writing so now you can see I am talking. Brother, brother, brother.............

What a word that is. Did you ever stop to think of that word? Brother or sister, did you ever think of the tie that bound them together. Of course you have.

You answer me that we are born of the same mother and the same father. Well that is true, but I tell you we are more than that. Did you ever think of the difference, I think you have not? My dear brother it is all that I can do to talk now but I set my teeth together and go on......... going to tell you what.........it is for it seems to me that our minds are blended together. This very moment it is 15 minets to 9 p.m. of course it will be different there. No you have not thought of the difference, for as you no all that are born of the same man and woman, same mother and father, are brother and sister by birth and some it ends right there, for they grow up wild, they care nothing for them and their parents care nothing for them and again their parent are situated that they cannot care, their little ones they have to separate......here the other. The.... Never to see each other again. Just think of that. They are brother and sister, yes by being born of the same parents, and that is all the tie, just think of it. But it is not so with all. It is not so with us. We had a father that gave his life for the Union. He gave his life for us. A true and loving father. He did all he could for us. When he was with us who could do more? No one. We had a mother who stayed here with us until we were fathers. But she looked after us she loved us just the same and more if such a thing is possible when she held us on her nee. Now brother you know what I say is true. She tried to keep us together. She taught us to love and help each other. Who could do more? Now brother as our mother is gone to meet our father and brother I do not think we ought to disobey her wishes. We both know what her wishes would be. She would say Johny, you and Jimy ought to help your brother all you can. Now is that tie stronger than the mere chance of being born brothers bound by a loving father a loving mother till their death. She loved us when boys and when men and we loved each other when boys and when men. And now Brother, I like to call you brother it does me good for you have a always been a good brother to me. Do you think I'm going to sit down and not try to help you? I guess not. I can't rest night from thinking of you. Worrying about you. You say don't worry, I tell you that is not human nature. Now I want you to put ...... excuses under your feet and come to my home, shame on you for thinking you would be a load on me. I guess you don't no me. I haven't been sick for what you could call 7 years. Think of that now. Do you think you would be a load? I guess not. Howard McGann, my son in law, I think you know him, I am not sure but I will say to you that he is a good man that uses everyone well. A good man of good reasoning powers. Well, we had a talk about you today I told him you could not think of living on me because I had poor health He says I guess your brother don't know what shape you are in. Now he says you write him and tell him how you are and I guess he will come. We want you to come here and have your foot treated as it should be. We think you have been obliged to neglect it. If that is true it should be stopped. You say you work some, but you couldn't hold a job. You will not have to hold a job. But if you can be your boss, that is work as you please. You can earn something. If that is the case then we can fix that all rite but I will not talk about that now, you and the rest of us will talk about that when you get here. So you can see it is all settled. That you are coming and coming now as I said you have no excuses to make, put them under your feet and keep them there. Or if you can't do that send them down here ahead of you and maybe we can take care of them better than you can there is no way of noing what we can do until we have a chance. We did think you might have some debts that would bother you, but as you think of leaving there in the spring we thought we must be wrong because if you could go to one place you could go another, so come here. If you do owe you see them and tell them how it is. Tell them you would have a better chance to pay them by coming here than by staying there. For we could help you little by little until your accounts were settled. Show them this if you think it would do any good. Tell them just how it is and I don't think they will say no. For they must be good people or you would be out in the streets. Now brother I must stop talking, for I have talked a long time just 5 hours and 15 minutes it is 1: oclock Saturday morning. I began Friday eve.15 minute it is 1: oclock Saturday morning. I began Friday eve 15 minutes to eight so I will bid your good by. I want you to answer this as soon as you can. If you have anything to look after before you can come write us first and look afterwards,

> We will see that you get here
> Good by J, A, to J. McIntyre
> Phoenx, Oswego County N.Y

Jay's niece, Eva L. McIntyre in New York

On Feb. 8, 1902, Eva L. McIntyre wrote to Jay from Phoenix, N.Y

Feb 8, 1902

My Dear Uncle,

I have received your letter a Thursday night was pleased to hear from you. But was disappointed in your answer. We had our minds made up to have you with us in a short time. And hope that we will still have the pleasure of having you with us. Papa has written you a letter so I will only write a few lines. I know that you will excuse this short letter. When you come we will have a nice long talk. Won't we? I want you here to help me celebrate my birthday, which is the 18. I will be 27. Ira got up a party for me last year. I shall never forget it. But he is gone. (Ira, her brother, was a championship swimmer. He drowned swimming in one of the big lakes nearby) We wanted you to come, don't say no. We have worried over you.. Papa won't be contented until you come. You have done so much for him and we know you would again---------
----Papa wants to help, if you will give him a chance. It seems as though you

ought to come. Well dear uncle I am---------must hurry. Please excuse paper. Hoping this will find you well. Hoping it won't be long before we can see you. I will say goodby.

From Your Loving Niece,
Eva L. McIntyre

Answer as soon as possible

One letter from Jay's niece, Eva L. has a missing first page. There is no date on the remaining pages but the letter appears to have been written near the same t time.

----------came back the same night. We had a nice time. I took a long streetcar ride. Enjoyed it very much. I had an invitation to spend decoration in Syracuse, but I expect company from Fulton. A lady friend will probably spend the day here. I hope that will be a nice day. Papa and Mama have been up to the cemetery to work this afternoon. We have a beautiful lot. Poor Ira it hardly seems possible that he has been dead nearly a year, and then sometimes it seems that he has been gone so long. Lillian received her-------all right. They are all well. Aunt Nellie is well and this leaves us all well and hoping your foot is improving. We only wish that it was well. I received a letter from Charlie a few days ago. He said Steve was working in the farm for Uncle Lin. Well dear Uncle J we are not going to get discouraged about your coming. I think that things will turn out all right so that you can come. We want to see you keep your mind on coming. I wish you was here now. Uncle James is in San Francisco now, or was a week ago. I received a letter from Florence today. They are all well. Uncle J. do you remember Nick Pendergast? (farm across the river up past Steve Pendergast farm) Mr. Gates lived on the farm when you was here Johnny Williams lives in the farm now. He went there this spring. We have been over there several times. Well Uncle what have you been doing since you wrote me? I don't like to think of you working in the mines. Well, we have company this evening. A gentleman called in to see Papa-so he, Papa, and Mama are talking and I am trying to write. It will be a great wonder if I don't get some of their conversation in my letter. Well Uncle, you remember Will Baker, John Baker-------- days the weather has seemed like spring. We have had a long winter. Well Uncle J., I started this letter yesterday, but I didn't finish it so I will try and finish it this morning. I have to go

downtown and want to mail it when I go down. Roland, Lillian's little boy, is here teasing to go down town with me. We went to the donation last night. It was for the benefit of our pastor. When I came home they had taken in $120.15. This leaves us all well and hoping it will find you the same. Uncle J. I guess I haven't told you that I have heard from Uncle Jim. I have received two or three letters from him. He was in Cripple Creek, Col. But I got a letter from him yesterday telling me not to write him until I heard from him again. I presume he is going to leave there. He has been traveling since he left here. I will------ Papa is working. Good Bye.

Hoping to hear from you soon. From your Loving niece.
Eva L. McIntyre
With love and many kisses
Hoping it won't be long before we can have a good visit.

Lillian "Bill" Knight and brother Ira Jay, McIntyre in their 70s

Part II
Growing Up In The Great Depression

Introduction: A few words about changing times

I have recently heard my generation referred to as the "Greatest Generation". I was born in 1926 and the statement is somewhat humorous to me because when I was growing up, I thought my generation had missed all the real stuff of history. Inventions such as the automobile, airplanes, the discovery of electricity, the telephone, pioneering the country, we had them all. Everything that could be invented was invented, and everything worth discovering had been discovered. The country was settled from sea to shining sea. What more could my generation possibly contribute? Surely, it had all been done, or so I thought.

Little did I realize then, that I would be living in a time that would create some even greater milestones in history. I never knew what a terrible time the Great Depression was because I was born into it. I never knew anything different. There was also the fact that my father, Homer Knight, was the type of man who, if need be, would have turned the world upside down to take care of his family. He and my mother, Lillian, never let us know we were poor. I did recognize, even at the time, that World War 2, 1941 to1945, would be significant in history. Medicine made phenomenal progress in my lifetime; and two new states, Hawaii and Alaska, joined this great nation. There were monumental achievements in the space program and in July 1969 Neil Armstrong and E.E. Buzz Aldrin Jr. walked on the moon. Something that I was told in school would never happen.

In the 5th Grade, my teacher told the students that man could not possibly reach the moon. The idea was ridiculous, she said, no one had yet broken the sound barrier. She pointed out that man could not possibly survive in the rarefied air of space. Nevertheless, they did, and a man on the moon is old history now. My generation saw the discovery of penicillin and other antibiotic "miracle drugs". With the "March of Dimes" initiated by President Franklin D. Roosevelt in the 30s, students at my school, and over the rest of the United States, brought their dimes to school each week and the money went toward research for a cure for polio, then known as infantile paralysis. That disease took the lives of, and crippled millions of children in the 30s and 40s and before. It took awhile to find the cure but eventually the research paid off. We got the polio vaccine in the 1950s. You rarely hear of polio anymore.

Doctors now transplant hearts and all sorts of human body parts. Couples who couldn't have children on their own, are taking fertility drugs and using donor sperm to make babies. People are walking around talking on phones with no wires and sending e-mails all over the place from a little box in their homes. Yes, it has been a great generation.

With the introduction of newly invented miracle fabrics to produce wash and wear clothing, the advances in washing machines and dryers, and the improvements in laundry detergents that replaced the old fashioned soap, laundry day is not the same heavy drudgery it was prior to the 1940s. Dreft was the first mass produced laundry detergent that I remember.

Nylon was the first miracle fabric that I recall. It was the topic of the day when I worked, after school, at Montgomery Ward in K.C. Missouri. Women, of my day, will surely remember the early nylon hosiery. Those nylons (that's what we called the hosiery) were a real treasure in WW2. Oh yes, the girl's legs looked good in those sheer nylon hose, but they were hard to get. Nylon was needed for the war effort. Never had we seen such a fabric, or experienced such strength and durability as polyester. A strong, lightweight material, it was also used to produce parachutes for the Air Force as well as many other key military products. Silk had been the previously preferred material for stockings but silk too, was rationed. More often than not, those horrible rayon stockings were all we woman could get. A few hours of wear and rayon hose stretched and bagged to make what looked like blisters at the knees and ankles.

Innovations in kitchen equipment are too numerous to mention, the electric dishwasher, the electric, food mixer, microwave ovens, as well as with many other modern home conveniences.

Splitting the atom was little more than a "pipe dream" of science, our schoolteachers declared prior to the 1940s. Even though scientist talked of splitting the atom, it was not logical to think it would really happen, our teachers said. The atom was the smallest particle on earth, too small to see with the naked eye, so small you could see it only with a super-powered microscope, she reasoned. Could something that small be split, we were asked. Well, it did happen and science has gone far beyond those early expectations many times.

My generation witnessed the dropping of the first atomic bombs on Hiroshima and Nagasaki, Japan on August 6 and 9, 1945, a dubious distinction, but it brought WWII to an end; and splitting the atom has since been the catalyst for other scientific discoveries on all fronts of modern society such as medical equipment, space travel, etc.

Some of the major social changes that came about in Post WW II days were the changes in the status of women. We began to hear words such as, "women's lib," and "Feminist." The dramatic social changes for women after the war, may have been triggered by the necessity for women to assume the traditional roles of men when the majority of able-bodied men were called in to active military duty to fight the wars on two fronts. While the men were off fighting Germany and Japan, women, of necessity, stepped into the vacated male roles for four years. They discovered that they could not only handle most male jobs, they actually excelled at many of them. During the war, women took on positions of authority, and leadership usually reserved for men. They became accustomed to being in charge, independent and capable of earning a living wage. The result was that, after the war ended, many women were not content to return to only the domestic roles of homemakers and mothers. The merits of those changes are still being debated.

Television and air conditioning did as much as anything to change social habits of the 40s. Children of my era never heard of such a thing as TV or AC. The radio was new to us. We had wind up record players and crystal sets.

Shortly after WW II, television and air conditioning became standard household furnishings, and the habits of summer evenings spent on the front porch, visiting friends and neighbors, playing cards, dominoes, or other home entertainments came to an end, squeezed out to be replaced by quick news and televised entertainment.

Closing up the house for air conditioning and television, instead of opening up the windows, to catch a summer breeze, and look out on the neighborhood, went a long way to curtail neighbors socializing and interacting with one another. Back in the old front porch days, when mothers were usually home, if neighbors saw children misbehaving or getting into trouble, they would lend a hand, inform the responsible parents, or do whatever the situation demanded.

A bright hot day in the 1930s or 40s brought children outdoors to play instead of holing up in the living room under refrigerated air to watch TV.

I may have thought we missed all the great times of history but as it has turned out my generation was right in the middle of one of the greatest and most innovative generations.

The Daisy Chain: Growing up In The Great Depression

Daisy Chain Families
Eva and John Knight Family
Children:

Ina, 1917
Johnny, 1920
Eula, 1921
Shirley, 1923
Betty, 1926
Ruthie 1928

Ira and Margurette McIntyre Family
Children:

Ira Floyd, 1924
Thelma, 1926,
Charlene, 1928,
Margie, 1930
Billy, (William Clell), 1932,
Dorothy, 1934
Lloyd, 1938
Bobby, (Robert) 1940
Stanley.1946

Lillian (aka Bill) and Homer Knight Family
Children:

Jean, 1924
Muril, 1926
Audrey 1928
Judy, Adopted, born 1943

Clell and Pearl McIntyre children:

Roger, 1939
Sharon, 1940
Wanda, 1942

The Old Neighborhood, the way it was

Growing up in the 1930s I heard two oft repeated axioms: One; I should eat everything on my plate because the children in Europe were starving, and two; when I walked out of the house, I should remember that I represented my family, and if I did something bad it was a reflection on the entire family. Many children of my time grew up with similar philosophies. The odd thing is I accepted these adages as right and true. They made sense to me. Today these antiquated sayings, which I confess still make sense to me, produce tolerant smiles from many young parents and I am once again reminded of how times have changed.

The area of Kansas City, Missouri where I grew up was called the Sheffield District because of its close proximity to Sheffield Steel Mill where many fathers worked. The mill was close enough for my father to walk to and from our house to work each workday. That's how it was then; you lived close to your work.

Our house at 504 Fuller was a block down from Independence Ave. In the 1930s, Independence Ave. was a brick two-lane street. Some time in the 40s, it was widened, repaved, and later, widened again even more, and repaved to make a major highway. It finally became State Highway 24. In the 1930s, our homes were in a residential neighborhood of older homes, wide sidewalks and esplanades of grass between the sidewalk and the street curb.

The House at 504 Fuller Ave. Kansas City Missouri

The sidewalks provided us, not only a safe place to walk, but also a good place for neighbor children to congregate and ride scooters, coaster wagons and roller skates.

Our roller skates were not the shoe-like skates that children use now. They were steel skates. There was no need to worry about outgrowing our skates because they could be adjusted with a skate key to fit almost any shoe size. They had leather straps that came up around the heel to buckle across the foot and clamps came from each side of the skates to clamp on the sole of your shoes. The clamps of course put a lot of pressure on the shoe soles and I lost many a shoe sole to those type skates. The skates could also be adjusted with a slide to lengthen or shorten them.

Most of our neighbors knew each other well enough to make our neighborhood a safe place for children to play without constant supervision by parents. One adult or another looked out the window frequently enough to keep an eye on us.

During the 1930s and 40s, the McIntyre / Knight youngsters pretty much dominated the youth scene around the Fuller Ave. and Roberts Street. The reason was due simply to sheer numbers. There were more of us. We were a tight knit, clannish group of good friends as well as relatives. Uncle Ira and Margurette had nine children, Aunt Eva and Uncle John had six and my parents had three. Uncle Clell also had three but they came along later. Other children who wished to play with us were always welcome as long as they understood that it was our neighborhood.

Fuller Ave. and Roberts St. ended at the corner to form an L shaped block, so strangers had no reason to drive through. That street corner was our super playground, especially after dark when a bright corner street light illuminated a large portion of the neighborhood. Mama could stand on our porch on Fuller Ave. and look out to see that we kids were all safe, and Uncle Ira could do the same from his house on Roberts. I remember well, Mama standing on our porch and calling, "Jean and Muril, come to supper," or calling out to let us know one of our favorite radio shows, such as Jack Armstrong, the all-American boy, was on.

We frequently played hide and seek under that corner light, and as time went on, we learned to dance the "Big Apple" there. The Big Apple later became more popularly know as the "jitterbug."

There were of course those times as some of the boys got older when they would lead girls like Loretta S__ out to the darker edges of the street light and be gone for five or ten minutes while the rest of us pretended not to notice.

Marjorie Lea McIntyre was the fourth of Uncle Ira's children. She was born in 1930.She remembered the old neighborhood fondly. "Our children would never believe how we enjoyed living in our great little city neighborhood. The older cousins were always ready to play games we could all do until they wanted to rid themselves of the younger ones. Then, they would play hide and seek and the smaller cousins would go inside to keep from being scared out of our wits."

No description of the old neighborhood would be complete without a mention of Mrs. Weigstein and her corner grocery. Theresa Weigstein was a WWI German War bride. She was a widow by the time I was born, and seemed like an old woman from the first time I remember seeing her with her silver white hair pulled back tightly from her chubby face and her round clear metal-rimmed glasses perched over her nose. She had a small round body and always wore old-fashioned dresses well below her knees, sensible shoes and a big old apron with a bib top. Although she had been in this country for more than two decades, she still spoke with a heavy German accent.

Theresa Weigstein, 1945

She was a quiet woman and seemed to us to have no life outside the store. She had no children although there was a niece who came regularly to see her. Her niece was obviously wealthy. She drove up in a big black car and had a chauffeur. Her clothes were of the latest fashion, her dark hair neatly coiffed and she wore diamond rings on her manicured fingers which she liked to flutter about.

As we got older, we girls began to build imaginary stories about Mrs. Weigstein and one day we got brave enough to talk to her about her past life. We asked her about her silver and turquoise earrings that she wore in pierced ears. We knew no one else who had pierced ears. We wanted to know if getting her ears pierced hurt, and how she met her husband and what it was like to come to this country as a war bride. Mrs. Weigstein answered our nosy questions, only briefly, as though her life was of little consequence, and should be of no interest to us. After that, we built our own stories and imagined the young Theresa Weigstein as a beautiful German girl whisked away by the brave and handsome American soldier in the waning weeks of war.

Mrs. Weigsteins grocery was an old, two-story frame building. The store was downstairs and her living quarters upstairs. Even though most people at that time were getting indoor toilets, Mrs. Weigstein had an outdoor privy at the back of her lot that she continued to use until the early 1950s. She only got indoor toilets because her wealthy niece insisted on it. The store building had a wide front door that opened on Independence Ave., a busy thoroughfare. Her back door opened on the less traveled Fuller Ave. We always used the back door.

When you walked in the back door, there was an exposed water pipe and faucet against the back wall where Mrs. Weigstein washed her hands after getting coal oil (kerosene) for customers from her shed in the back yard. A wooden bench with an enameled wash pan and a large bar of soap sat along the wall under the faucet.

On the other side of the hall was her kitchen and business office. The kitchen door was always open and we could see her old-fashioned stove, table and chairs. Her office desk was an old baker cabinet. The most fascinating part of Mrs. Weigsteins kitchen, for us children, was a very large, very old cuckoo clock. It hung on her back 12 ft. high wall, next to the steps that went up to her living quarters. Mrs. Weigstein said the old clock was made in the Black Forrest of Germany, and even in the 1930's it was an antique. The clock monopolized one section of the wall. The clock itself was about 24 inches or so wide and at least 30 inches tall. It was made of dark wood shaped like a little chalet type house with a peaked roof. It was ornately trimmed with beautifully carved leaves, animals and birds. The clock pendulum was probably 16 or more inches long and the chains that wound the clock stretched from the bottom of the clock to about a foot from the floor with heavy pinecone shaped weights on the ends. On the hour, two tiny doors opened just above the clock dial. Out came a miniature carved boy and girl from small doors and they twirled around and danced while a cuckoo bird cuckooed merrily along with the chimes. Only the bird came out on the half hour to cuckoo one time.

About 1939, Mrs. Zahner, a middle-aged German woman, actually Mrs. Weigsteins sister-in- law, came to live with her at the grocery store. Mrs. Zahner was often unhappy about the way things were going in Germany. No one ever explained her unhappiness to us, but after a short time, it was obvious for all to see. At times, she was not cautious in her conversation when we children were in and about the store, which was often, because we usually picked up items several times a day, as we needed them. The average family still used ice boxes to store perishable foods, and ice boxes did not hold great quantities of food as they do today, making frequent grocery trips necessary. Like many adults, Mrs. Zahner didn't realize that children listen to adult conversations. For the most part, we heard Mrs. Zahner decrying a new report of Adolph Hitler's atrocities in Europe. She would be upset to tears, over what he was doing to the Jews in Germany and Poland. She wrung her hands in anguish and wept over the latest word of Hitler's new advances into the small countries bordering Germany and the atrocities that followed his incursions. Sometimes, she seemed to hover over Mrs. Weigstein, speaking furtively in her ear about something she read in the daily newspaper. She whispered but in tones that we could hear, she spoke of her fear of Adolph Hitler. It was as though she had to talk about it. We knew from her conversation that she still had family in Germany. Mrs. Weigstein with barely a change of expression would shush her, when we came in to the store, and urge her to be quiet while we were there. That's when we began to believe that Mrs. Weigstein, who attended a Catholic Church was actually Jewish. We had heard stories about Jewish immigrants who once they were in America, adopted the Catholic faith to avoid being labeled Jewish and experience the discrimination that being Jewish in the 1930s and '40s involved. We never questioned Mrs. Weigstein about that however. That would have been too personal.

Jake Zapaross, Mrs. Weigsteins produce man, was a Russian Jew, newly immigrated to America, and he was outspokenly delighted to be in the United States. Jake was forced from his home in Russia. He narrowly missed being murdered in an anti-Jewish movement in Russia. In contrast to Mrs. Weigsteins quiet demeanor, Jake was outspoken in his hatred of Hitler and the Russian regime. Although he was usually full of good humor and funny anecdotes, he hated the Russian government passionately, and at the mention of his homeland, his mood could turn from jovial to sour in seconds. Jake liked to stop by our house and talk to Daddy when he had an opportunity to do so. Then, he would shake his fist passionately and curse the Russian government that had forced him and his family out of their home in Russia.

Jake drove a horse and a long wooden wagon loaded with fresh fruits and vegetables to various stores over the city. You could hear the clip clop of his horse's hooves pounding the pavement, and the sound of rolling wagon wheels, from a block away as Jake came down Fuller Ave. Whether we saw him or not, we always knew when Jake had made his deliveries at Mrs. Weigsteins Grocery because his horse left pungent smelling droppings in the street by her back door.

Most of the neighbors on our street bought their groceries at Mrs. Weigsteins store or from the Company Store. Sheffield Steel Corporation sponsored the company store. Mill employees, who ran short of money before payday, could charge their groceries, some clothing, and other items that the store carried. The charges were then deducted from the employee's paycheck before the employee ever got it. Prices of items at the Company store were inflated and Daddy was adamantly opposed to using the company store so we shopped only at Mrs. Weigsteins.

"Most families in our neighborhood charged their groceries and paid the bills on the 8th and 23rd of each month. That was when Sheffield Steel Company regularly paid their employee's wages. We children liked to go along when Mama or Daddy when they paid the grocery bill because Mrs. Weigstein would fill a small brown sack with candy as a treat for us, allowing us children the choice of candy. We were always careful, as Mama had instructed us, to not appear greedy and be sure to say thank you.

The two Mrs. Fitches lived on the corner of Independence Ave. and Fuller. One was a widow and the other an "old maid." I could never remember which was which and didn't care. They were both gentle and friendly to the children who might stop in for a visit. They had a nice house and beautiful wicker porch furniture that sat on a wide veranda in the summer months and were carefully stored somewhere else in the winter. The two Miss Fitches always preferred to have Daddy come and make any home repairs to their house that they might need. When Daddy couldn't do it, Uncle Ira or Uncle Clell were called on.

Stella Cook, who was our age, was their niece. Stella was an only child. She and her parents lived next door to the Fitch women but she stayed with them much of the time. No one seemed to know what Mr. Cook did for a living, but the word around the neighborhood was that he was a lawyer for the Mafia. The Cooks had a nice home, and Stella, an overweight and spoiled child, always had the latest and most beautiful toys, and clothes that she liked to flaunt around the rest of the neighborhood children. We might not have minded that so much if she had been a pleasant child but she was not. For some reason she was jealous of Jean and me. One day she came down to our front sidewalk and wrote vulgar words and names in big white chalk letters on the walk. When Mama saw the words, she was shocked and angry. She paid a call on Mrs. Cook, and before it was over, Stella had to come clean all the dirty words off the sidewalk.

Mrs. Black was the widow of a railroad man. He was killed on the job in a work related accident. Rumor had it that Mrs. Black was wealthy from the settlement that the railroad company was forced to pay her due to her husband's accident.

Mrs. Black lived across Independence Ave. from the Fitches and the Cooks. The most notable thing I remember about Mrs. Black is that she rarely had a pleasant hello for children, and the most notable thing she said was "Don't pick my flowers, and stay out of my yard," even though no one picked her flowers or got in her yard, but we did have a few giggles at her expense. Mrs. Black, a woman of indeterminate age, wore dark, shapeless and unflattering dresses, which were always a little short and tight for her matronly figure. She had a broad rear, so that when she bent over to tend her flower garden, which bordered the street, you could see up her dress almost to the top of her long, brown cotton stockings. You couldn't see any skin since she also wore long legged underwear but it was a most unflattering view.

Mrs. Black was an opinionated woman who didn't mind speaking her mind whether anyone wanted to hear it or not. Early one morning, she went to Uncle Clell's house unannounced to see if she could hire him to do some home repairs to her house. When she knocked on the door, Uncle Clell still in his undershirt and pants was drinking his morning coffee. He answered the door just as he was with no shirt on. Instead of voicing her reason for calling on him so early, Mrs. Black proceeded to lecture him on the impropriety of answering the door to a lady caller without first putting on his shirt. Uncle Clell was not too keen on enduring such a lecture before he had finished his morning coffee and promptly told her if she didn't like the way he was dressed she should go back home and find someone else to do the work.

Most of the houses around Fuller Ave were situated on 50-foot lots so the houses were close together. Our house was on a gently sloping hill. The homes were modest but comfortable homes and most of them housed a number of children.

Jess and Clara Markwell lived across the street from us on Fuller Ave. They were wonderful neighbors. Clara, a cheerful matronly woman was a devout Christian. She had been married once before she married Jess and she had a tall, dark haired, athletic, and very handsome son, named Raymond Mitchell. He was much older than Jean or me but he was always mannerly and good to us. He was our idol and we thought he was wonderful. We were truly saddened when Raymond was severely injured in a WWII battle that left him in a wheel chair for the rest of his life.

Jess drove a City bus for the Kansas City mass transit company, and to Clara's chagrin Jess sometimes enjoyed his liquor a little too well. He was a dark haired, slightly overweight man but still a good-looking man. Where Clara was a quiet, retiring sort of person, Jess was outgoing and talkative. One warm summer evening, after dark I think it might have been July 4th., Jess was out in his side yard in his pants and undershirt, with his shotgun. Firecrackers were popping all over the neighborhood and Jess wanted to celebrate with some noise also. He didn't have any firecrackers or other noisemakers, so, he thought he would make some loud noises by shooting off his gun. I have no idea what kind of gun it was, but it was powerful.

Jess was cautious in his handling of the gun but, he had already put down a few mixed drinks, and that may have affected Jess judgment. For safety reasons, he decided to lie down on the terrace and shoot his gun straight up in the air. He stretched out flat on the ground, and rested the gun against his shoulder aimed straight up. He pulled the trigger. From across the street, the blast from the gun sounded like cannon burst quickly followed by a howl of pain and loud swearing. The gun kicked back so hard on Jess's shoulder that it broke his collarbone and injured his shoulder. It was a long time before Jess could raise his arm over his head, or drive his bus.

Harry Hawkinsmith lived down on the corner of Roberts St. and Bennington. Harry was married at one time but at the time of this story, he lived with his mother. He was a big man, in his twenties, probably 6 ft. 1 or so and he must have weighed more than 200 pounds. We girls, Thelma, Jean and I, met Harry one afternoon somewhere between 1935 or 1937 when we were passing his house and noticed this poor man sitting on the porch in a wheel chair. The porch was a veranda shape that covered two sides of the house so that it fronted on both Roberts Street and Bennington.

Harry looked depressed and lonely as he sat there in that wheel chair, and we girls, feeling sorry for him, decided to talk to him for a minute. We were just young girls, less than teenage, but he seemed to welcome our company and after we asked, he told us what had put him in the wheelchair. Harry was a company man at the Ford Motor Company. He worked at the assembly plant down in Fordview Park. However, on this particular summer, he was not working. He couldn't. He had both of his legs broken and would be stuck in that wheel chair for the summer and maybe longer. Harry had made the mistake of crossing the United Auto Workers picket line when the Ford Motor Company was on strike. Industrial unions, especially during the Great Depression, were trying desperately to get a foothold into industry. The deprivation and hardships brought on by the Depression had given impetus to Unions seeking the rights to represent and bargain for American workers. At the same time, industrial leaders saw the unions as a threat to management's control of industry and resisted union forces by any means they could.. An especially bitter fight was going on between the United Auto Workers Union and the Ford Company and neither side was above using strong arm, bullying tactics to achieve their purpose.

When Harry crossed the UAW picket line, the Union organizers had a crowd of men standing by, ready to prevent any such overt action. Harry and some other men had ignored the Union warning, and proceeded through the picket line and on toward the plant to work. The Union gang, armed with baseball bats and clubs, descended upon them with force and beat Harry to a pulp, breaking his legs and putting him in the hospital for weeks. That's why he had free time on his hands to talk with Thelma, Jean and me.

During our idle moments that summer, we made it a point to drop in on Harry now and then when he was out on his porch, not just because we felt sorry for him, but also because Harry was an intelligent and articulate conversationalist. We enjoyed our goodwill visits with him, and he seemed to look forward to seeing us.

The Rosen family lived right next door to us at 500 Fuller. Gus Rosen had at one time worked for Mama's mother, Dazerine, when she ran a boarding house. Gus was from Sweden and at some point between 1918 and 1922; he returned to Sweden and came back to the United States with his bride, Edla.

Edla was from Finland and she often remarked on how superior Finland was to Sweden, and what superior artisans the Finnish were. She had few kind words for the Swedes but she and Gus got along famously. The Rosens had three girls about the same age as Jean and I.

Our houses were only a driveway apart and we children often played games across the yards, tossing balls to one another or other games. Gus Rosen and Daddy had been friends for years. They often argued politics long and loud and sometimes a little too vigorously. Gus, being from Sweden, often voiced support for a Socialist type government such as Sweden's government. Daddy, on the other hand considered Gus's Socialistic points of view to be subversive, and he had a difficult time tolerating them even in an objective argument. At one point, he told Gus that if he liked a Socialist government so much he should go back to Sweden and the two of them did not speak for a long time after that.

Gus was an exceptionally fine craftsman, and at one time, he built a chicken house about 8ft. by 8ft. out of sod and mud. We though the little house would surely fall apart in the first rain but it was still standing at least 40 years, perhaps longer, after it was built. About 1937 or so, Gus built his own travel trailer complete with living quarters and moved his family to Florida hoping to find work. The travel trailer was not the boxy, unwieldy conveyance, you might expect from a home built trailer. To the contrary, it was sleek and modern looking with curved ceilings and aerodynamic construction. We corresponded with the Rosen girls from their Florida home for many years and the family apparently thrived in that state.

The Fordview Drug Store was an important feature to our old neighborhood. It was on the corner of Independence Ave. and Bennington, a block up the hill from Mrs. Weigstein's store, and right across the street from the combined Fire and Police Station. Our parents bought all our pharmacy needs at the Fordview. I don't remember the first Fordview owner's name but I can still see his face. He prepared a special iodine mixture for Daddy that didn't burn as tincture of iodine does. He also made a special mix of glycerin eardrops that soothed many an earache for us.

Phil Levine was the Fordview Drug Store owner I remember best. Phil was a tall man with dark hair and a huge mustache. When you came in to Phil's drug store, he met you with a friendly smile welcoming his customers as if they were members of the family. The Fordview is where all the adult neighbors bought their medical supplies, and it was where all the children got their ice cream cones. At first, it was just one dip of ice cream to the cone, later we were able to buy a double dip, and later still, if we were feeling brave, we would try a triple dip. Many a dip of ice cream fell to the hot sidewalk in front of the Fordview and , and many a tear was shed for the loss of that ice cream on the way home from the drug store, because we knew better than to ask for another cone.

As we got older, we youngsters would go to the drug store and spend some time sitting at the soda fountain bar to drink cokes and rootbeer floats and fraternize with other young people.

Every so often, in the summer months about dusk, we would hear the rinky tink music of the organ grinder and we knew the hot tamale man was coming in to our neighborhood. That's all we ever called him, the hot tamale man, but he was often the highlight of a summer evening.

He played the barrel organ and intermittently, sang out, "Hot tamales; red and hot. Put 'em on your tongue go flippity flop. Get your hot tamales here".

When the tamale man showed up, he was quickly surrounded by smiling children, because not only did he sell some of the most delicious tamales around, to our greater delight was the pet monkey that rode on his shoulder. The little monkey was on a long chain. He wore a perky round red hat on his head and a little tan vest. When the tamale man made a sale, the monkey would swing down from the man's shoulder; go to the customer with a tin cup in his hand and collect the money. Then back to his perch on the man's shoulder he went, doffed his hat, chattering and making funny faces.

As elementary school students, the neighbor children passed the drug store everyday on our way to Henry Clay School. Two huge sections of plate glass met at that point to make a corner. Some one discovered that if you stood directly center of the outside corner where the two pieces of plate glass came together and put your nose on the corner, then raised one arm and one leg on the same side it made a comical reflection in the window. We spent hours taking turns on that glass corner and laughing at our reflections.

My cousin, Ira, was ten or so when he joined the local Boy Scout Drum and Bugle Corp. He met regularly with the scout troop at the local police station. Ira played the bugle. We girls were so impressed to see Little Ira (we called him little Ira to differentiate between him and Uncle Ira) show up at school once a week in his scout uniform. Every now and then the police would cordon off a portion of Independence Ave., and the Drum and Bugle Corp. would parade smartly down the street, led by the Scout Master and Drum major, playing their drums and bugles. There was always a good crowd of onlookers and of course, we girl cousins were there too, waving and cheering for Little Ira.

Our neighborhood was not without its undesirable residents. The most notable being a young, red haired woman we called, "Sheffield Annie". Annie was the curiosity of the neighborhood and we children were afraid of her. We were not sure exactly what drug addict was, but the adults told us, Annie was one. She was more often called a hophead or a dope fiend. She walked in a hoppy gait around the neighborhood, scouting all the trash cans looking for anything of value, muttering and complaining all the while. If someone got close to her, she might take a swing at them. Oddly enough, everyone ignored her as much as possible. No one that I knew did much to get rid of her, or put her away. She was around the neighborhood for years. We children were told to stay away from her and leave her alone and we did.

There were other neighbors around Fuller Ave. and Robert's St. with more or less colorful lives. Some were good natured, easygoing people and some were not, but they all came together in a blend of interesting characters to make a rarely dull neighborhood.

Except for the movies, or picture shows as we called them, there was little cultural entertainment available to us. However, at least once or twice a year the Medicine Show or the Carnivals would arrive and set up their operations at the usual location on a large tract of land, on Independence Ave., near Winter Road, about four blocks from our house. Large crowds turned out for the entertainments.

The medicine shows featured a variety of entertainment. Sometimes it was a play, or more often a vaudeville type show with dancers and singers and comedians. At regular intervals, the performance would stop and the performers would leave their stage to run out in the audience and sell such miracle medical tonics and elixirs as Puritone and other magical cures. There were a lot of out of work actors during that time looking for any gig they could get. While times were bad for the actors, it was a plus for our little blue-collar neighborhood to see some great professional type theater in those Medicine shows. The carnivals featured the latest in thrill rides and side shows at prices we could afford to enjoy. Some of medicine shows performers, such as Red Skelton. Pick and Pat, and others went on to national fame.

Her Name was Lillian but They Called Her Bill.

My mother's given name was Iva Lillian, but everyone called her Bill. It was rare, in those days, for a woman to be called by a masculine sounding name like Bill or even Billie. When Mama was introduced as Bill, new acquaintances were often reticent to call her by that nickname. I could understand their reluctance to call her Bill because, as an adult, the name did not suit Mama. She had acquired it as a child, about ten. Her brother, Ira, dubbed her Billy because she was a quite the tomboy at that age. A few years later, Daddy's brother, John, latched on to the name and started calling her "Wild Bill from Bunker Hill." Mama was neither wild nor masculine. She was five-foot- four and weighed about 125 most of her life. She had auburn hair that as a younger woman, she wore in long braids until the 1920s, flapper age. Then she had it "bobbed" in a fashionable short style. Mama's most outstanding feature was perhaps her expressive, pale blue eyes. Guarded though she might try to be, her eyes reflected her every emotion. Mama thought of herself as plain. To me she looked like what she was, my mother, but even as a child, I heard men remark that she was a "good looking woman."

Uncle John called her Wild Bill because he had known her as a child and he liked to tease her, so he would call her that for fun. By the time she was fully grown, the name was so ingrained there was no changing it. As her new friends became better acquainted with Mama, they soon became comfortable with the name and actually grew to like it because it somehow made them feel closer friends with her.

Mama's sister, Eva, and her family however, did not call Mama, Bill. When they were children, their mother, Dazerine, always insisted that the family should call Lillian by her full given name, not a nickname and not a shortened version of her name such as Lil or Lillie. Aunt Eva always honored Dazerine's wish and she made it clear to her children that they should do the do so as well.

Bears and Dreams and Other Things?

It was June 1935. We were on our way to our dream vacation in Colorado. There were six of us in the car, Daddy, Mama,their best friends, Mildred and Lee Cramer, a my sister, Jean, almost 11, and me, almost 9. We were seated two adults and a kid in the front and the same arrangement in the back seat of the Plymouth sedan. Since Jean and I were both small, the car didn't seem too crowded. Daddy was at the steering wheel and we had just passed the state line marker on Highway 50 going out of Missouri and into Kansas. That's when I remembered my toy bear, Fuzzy. Memory flooded back. I had made my bed hurriedly that morning and carelessly tossed him on the pillow, not looking back or even saying goodbye. Be quiet, I told myself. Don't say anything. Don't whine! They will think you are a baby! However, the next words out of my mouth came in a whine, "I forgot my bear." I said. No one said anything. Mama and Mildred looked at each other in a knowing way. After a few minutes, Mama sighed. "It will be okay. Just look at the pretty scenery." she said. Mama rarely got angry with my sister, Jean or me since my little sister, Audrey died. I sometimes wished she would.

Remorse clouded my joy and I sank gloomily down in the car seat. I wished we could go back but I didn't dare say so. This was our first vacation trip ever. For weeks the lights in our kitchen had burned late into the night as Mama, Daddy, Mildred and Lee sat around our old kitchen table with road maps spread out over the tabletop, planning the best routes to the vacation spots they most wanted to see. For months they had pinched pennies, and Mama could pinch a penny harder than anyone I knew, saving little bits of cash here and there, until they had the $300 needed for the trip. This was to be a camping trip. They bought camp cots and a camp stove and tin dishes, everything we would need to camp out along the way. Only a small amount of money was slated for tourist cabins when necessary. Mama and Mildred had splurged to get new permanent waves and some new clothes.

They had a great time shopping around to find just the right traveling outfits. They both wore brown Jodhpur pants and knee-high, lace-up boots. Perched at a jaunty angle on their heads, they wore little round, beige tams. It was all so exciting. None of us had ever before been out of the state of Missouri except to visit family in northwest Arkansas.

Lillian "Bill" and Mildred in Colorado, 1935

Until this year, the economy had been so gloomy; my folks never thought they would be able to afford such a vacation. These were the Great Depression Years but the 1932 election of Franklin D. Roosevelt as U. S. President, had turned things around, Daddy liked to say. The country, still shedding its mantle of poverty, was responding to the "rosy promise" of Roosevelt's plan for a "new deal." Daddy and Mama responded to the promise by buying a brand new car. The first new one they had ever owned. It was a Plymouth sedan. It cost $800.00 and financed for two years at 6%. Mama marveled at the terrible expense. Daddy and Lee took two weeks of unpaid vacation to make the trip. Only a few weeks earlier, Daddy had come home from work with a broad smile on his face and handed Mama his two-week paycheck. She looked at the check, then wide-eyed back at Daddy. In an awed voice she whispered, "A hundred dollars." Then quickly turned to us children and said, "Now, you kids don't go telling anyone about this."

We left our house at 504 Fuller about noon on that bright June day. The green Plymouth sedan cruised smoothly out on to Highway 24, then on to Highway 50. Daddy said the Plymouth "purred like a kitten"

As I fretted over forgetting my toy bear, I knew, even then, that I was too old to have this fixation over a toy bear and that this was not the time to mention it. However, there it was. I knew I was being ridiculous but I couldn't seem to help myself. What to do? I couldn't expect someone else to understand that saying good-bye to a toy bear was truly important. They had not spent long summer hours with my friend, Fuzzy, watching billowy white clouds float across a hauntingly blue sky. They never pondered the greatness of the earth or snuggled deep into the bed covers on a wintry night and confided secret hopes and fears into his little cloth ear. However, most important of all, that little bear had been my safety net since my four and a half year old sister Audrey died, almost two years before. That fuzzy, little toy helped fend off the dreaded nightmares that plagued me after her death. It was my fault that the bear was home alone. However, I could do nothing about it now.

How Fuzzy warded off my nightmares is a curiosity even to me but the furry little bear with his perpetual smile was an instant and abiding, comfort to me. At bedtime, I would turn my back to Jean's sturdy back and cuddle Fuzzy in my arms. With Fuzzy's help, I schooled myself to think only pleasant thoughts and the plan apparently worked because the intensity of the dreams faded and gradually went away altogether.

Audrey's death had come as a shock to the whole family. It was so unexpected. Before school let out for the summer in June, the Kansas City Health Dept. administered the diphtheria vaccine to all the elementary school children. It was part of a free, citywide, mass inoculation program designed to eliminate the disease. Because Audrey would enter kindergarten the coming school year, she was eligible for the inoculation. She so looked forward to being in kindergarten the next year. All the last school term she had watched Jean and me leave for school each day. When we came home, she was out in the yard eagerly awaiting our return home, wanting to hear what happened at school, and talking about how she too, would pack her little lunch and go to school with us next school term.

Doctor Martin first diagnosed Audrey's sudden illness as scarlet fever. Shortly after that, a man from the health department came to our house with a big white cardboard sign lettered "Quarantine" in bold red letters and below that in smaller red letters it read, Scarlet Fever. After that, only Mildred and Lee, who had no children of their own, came to our house. I looked at the sign with embarrassment. To me, it meant we were somehow socially unacceptable. No one could come see us because we had germs and we must be avoided.

Audrey was sick barely a week. One day she was playful and begging to be out of bed and the next day she was feverish only wanting Mama to hold her and rock her, and sing to her. She asked Mama to sing, " I've a Dear Little Dolly, her eyes are bright blue", only she wanted Mama to say baby instead of dolly. And, she wanted to hear "Carolina Sunshine Girl". Toward the last, she only wanted to hear, Bye O Mama's baby and she would say, "Sing sweet, sweet baby, Mama."

Earlier in the week, after she was diagnosed with scarlet fever, but not terribly sick, Jean and I were outside playing in the yard. We heard a yell from overhead and looked up to see Audrey on the roof of the house. She had sneaked out of her bed and crawled out of the upstairs window and on to the roof. She was calling to us to play with her. The window opened directly onto the roof and offered easy access to the roof outside. Jean and I had pulled this little trick ourselves in the past so we were not surprised to see her up there, running nimbly across the shingled roof in one of her new white cotton nightgowns. It was a warm, sunny, day and we, not realizing the gravity of the situation, gleefully joined in the game .We were all three laughing, yelling to one another, and having a merry time when Mama discovered Audrey and whisked her quickly back inside and into her bed. What a happy child she was! How could this dear little sister be gone, I wondered. It was all too distressing, all too confusing. These thoughts, of course, were never spoken aloud, to speak them aloud would only cause pain or anger.

On his last visit, Dr. Martin came to our house for Audrey's daily examination. Doctors, in those days, regularly made house calls. When people were sick enough to be in bed they were not expected to get up and go to the doctor's office. That day, Dr. Martin, went through his usual routine, he examined Audrey's throat, listened to her vital signs and then, sat straight up, and back in dismay. He didn't say a word for several minutes. Finally, very solemnly, and with great reserve, he rose from his chair and said to Mama that he couldn't understand it, and he blamed himself for not seeing it sooner, but Audrey's illness was not scarlet fever after all, it was the dreaded diphtheria and it was advanced. He said Mama should get Audra to the hospital immediately. Mama and Daddy wasted no time following Dr. Martin's instructions.

How could this happen, they wondered. Audrey had gotten two of the three required immunizations for diphtheria. The last one was only recently. The shot should be protecting her from the deadly disease.

Audrey was soon in the isolation ward of General Hospital with doctors and nurses hovering over her. Mama and Daddy both stayed with her at the hospital until visiting hours were over at 9 p.m. They were then told they must leave. Only hospital personnel were allowed to stay after visiting hours. There were no exceptions, not even for small children. Those were the rules. With great reluctance, Mama and Daddy left Audrey in the hospital's care but not without tears of frustration.

The next morning they were out of bed at the crack of dawn, dressed and on their way to the hospital. They walked in to the hospital hoping to see Audrey much improved. They were unprepared for what happened next. A brisk, unsmiling nurse met them in the hall. Audrey was not in her room, she said. "Where was she?" they asked? The nurse directed them down the hall to another room. Audrey was there on a table with a sheet over her face. The nurse walked in, jerked the sheet back from Audrey's body, and said, "There she is" Mama took one look at the poor little swollen body, and fell in a dead faint to the floor. Daddy was so angry he could hardly speak and the nurse, realizing what she had done, was immediately contrite and apologetic. For some reason, unknown to anyone else, she had assumed Audra was a neglected child. Her actions had been her idea of retribution.

When Mama and Daddy came home alone, they both had an odd look about them. Jean and I wanted to know, "Where's Sister?" The question hung awkwardly in the air for some time. Mama finally said, "Little sister won't be coming home. She is in heaven with Jesus. She still loves us, but God wanted her to be with Jesus. She is his little girl now."

I don't know that Jean or I cried, but neither of us quite understood what had happened. Death was a word with no reality to us. We had never before experienced death of any kind. We didn't know quite what it meant. Audrey was in heaven, they said. We imagined her in her little white nightgown, sitting with other children at Jesus' knee, looking up into his face and he smiling down at her. We accepted Mama's word that Audrey was with Jesus as reasonable, but we would miss her. Why did she have to go?

Audrey was the baby of the family, a bright mischievous little sprite of a girl. She loved to sing and she had memorized several songs, such as "Carolina Sunshine Girl", "The Stars Are Gonna Twinkle and Shine", and many more. She never seemed to meet a stranger, and spent much of her time out in the front yard talking to neighbors passing by. The mail carrier was one of her favorites and he always stopped a few minutes to play word games with her as he walked his daily route. The iceman came by every other day in his truck, hauling 50lb. chunks of ice held in ice tongs to install in our icebox. He usually had a small piece of ice for Audrey. The bread man was another favorite. Our house was the place he chose to stop and have a cup of coffee and share a sweet bread roll with Mama and Audrey. Mama was a regular customer for his bread and pastries. There was the Jewel Tea man and others who came door to door to sell their wares. They took time to visit with Audrey. When they heard of her death, these grown men came close to tears.

Muril.6, and Audrey,4, in homemade coats

Audrey had a favorite game she liked to play to the exclusion of all others. She pretended to be a growling bear and she would chase anyone, who would play her game, all over the house. She sometimes was so carried away with the game that she would frighten a little visiting neighbor boy to tears. "Mrs. Knight, Mrs. Knight!" he cried, "Make Audie stop, she's scaring me."

This little game may have been what triggered my nightmares. Jean and I didn't go to the funeral because Mama wanted to protect us from the pain of seeing Audrey no longer alive. All we knew was that Audrey was gone and would not be back because she was in to heaven with Jesus. She was so sweet and good, Mama said, that Jesus wanted her with him. We accepted this explanation without question, but still there was something unreal and unsettling about it. One day she had been an integral part of our daily lives and the next she was just gone.

For a long time, Mama was almost bedridden with grief. My sister and I were on our best behavior most of the time so as not to upset anyone further. We tried to be quiet and helpful but we were also bewildered. We were told not to be sad because Audrey was happy in heaven with Jesus and yet everyone around us was deep in grief. One day Jean was helping to set the dinner table. She absent-mindedly set a plate for Audrey. When everyone got to the table and saw the mistake, Mildred spoke sharply to Jean and scolded her for forgetting. "It's alright," Mama quickly said. "She just forgot for a minute that Audrey was gone. It's alright Jean." But Jean didn't hear Mama's words, she had run from the room, and I stared miserably at Mama as tears came unbidden to her eyes.

Later, when my cousin Ruthie and I were playing out of doors, I heard someone say, "Just look at the kids playing. They don't even care that Audrey is dead." It was the wrong thing to say. Actually, Ruthie, who was Audrey's age, and I were imagining Audrey up in the clouds, close to heaven. As children, we had lively imaginations and we thought that if we looked closely enough we could see her dodging in and out of the clouds. We had actually convinced ourselves that we did see her there, and we were playing hide and go seek with her. The overheard remark ended the game. We were instantly contrite and quit playing.

The nightmares started suddenly a few weeks after Audrey's funeral and it was always the same dream. Audrey and I were out in the front yard. We were playing hide and go seek with our cousins. It was our favorite game. Our driveway had a 3-foot high retaining wall separating it from the front yard, and that's where Audra and I chose to hide. The wall was close to the street. In the dream, as we sat crouched down beside the wall, we suddenly heard the sounds of a marching band and the footfall of many feet hitting the pavement. We peeped out from around the wall, and there to our amazement was a band of large friendly, bears, marching upright and six or eight abreast. They came around our street corner at Fuller Ave. and Roberts Street. At first, they were happy and smiling bears, rocking back and forth, and bowing in a merry fashion. Where they came from, we could not imagine.

Suddenly, Audrey jumped up from behind the wall and ran straight out in to the street to greet them. I grabbed frantically at her dress to stop her and drag her back but I missed and she kept running toward them. Then in an abrupt about face, the bears stopped smiling and they turned ferocious. Fear swept over me. They were snarling and mean. They slobbered. I could see saliva drip from their long white teeth. I tried with all my might to scream, to move and run after Audrey, to grab her out of their reach. But no sounds come out of my mouth. I was terrified, I couldn't move and the bears kept marching forward, closer and closer to her, more menacing with each step. There was Audrey, to my alarm, standing out there smiling and waving at them as if nothing was wrong. The bears growled and I saw their long claws, but still I couldn't move. Usually, at that point someone or something would wake me and while I thought I had not been able to make a sound, I was told I actually hollered quite loudly. One time, when I was taking an afternoon nap, Mildred was outside in the yard. She heard me hollering from the open upstairs bedroom window.

Once awake, I would be weak with relief to know the nightmare was just another dream, but the sadness lingered. The dreams happened only infrequently, probably once or twice a month but I eventually reached a point when I dreaded going to sleep.

The first time I saw Fuzzy was in Sears Roebuck Department Store with my mother. It was December. Audrey had been dead for six months. Christmas decorations had transformed the department store into a fairyland. Midst all this splendor, spotlighted in a large toy display was a beautiful, golden, toy bear. He seemed to look directly at me with open arms. I stood awe struck and stared at him. "Do you like that bear?" Mama asked me. Oh, yes, I surely did, and that very night I asked Santa to bring him to me for Christmas.

When I crept down the stairs on Christmas morning, it was still very dark. Tiny halos of light winked among the branches of the evergreen tree, and there in the glow of the lights was "my bear". I swept him up into my arms and hugged him to me, swearing my loyalty to him forever.

Now we were on our way to Colorado. He was at home, all alone, and I had not said good-bye.

The car's speedometer showed fifty miles an hour, then sixty, out we went over an almost deserted 2-lane concrete ribbon of highway. The sun bounced balls of light from the sedan's new green enameled fenders and struck diamonds off the chrome hood ornament. All four of the car door windows were opened (no air conditioning in those days). Mama and we girls sang a roundelay of "Go tell Aunt Rodie, go tell Aunt Rodie, go tell Aunt Rodie her old gray goose is dead." Mildred hummed loudly along blissfully unaware of her off-key monotone. "It died a flyin', it died a flyin', it died a flyin' over yonder shed."

In the front seat, Daddy, at the wheel, unaware of the rest of us, sang a waltz version of "Springtime in the Rockies." Lee rode along quietly, absorbed in the scenery.

The Kansas prairies started about 50 miles into Kansas, and they were a remarkable sight. Barren dust fields stretched to the horizon on all sides as far as the eye could see. Midway through the dust bowl that was Kansas in the 1930s, Mama pointed to a bleached gray shack out in the middle of the prairie. The shack stood sharply outlined against a brilliant blue sky. There, standing in the open doorway, was the gaunt figure of a lone woman looking toward our car. Mama raised her arm in a friendly wave. "How do people live out here?" Mildred wondered of the barren stretch of brown earth. Even in Kansas City, Missouri, people were keenly aware of the Great Plains dust bowl and the disastrous effects that over cultivation and mismanagement of prairie farming practices had taken on the Great Plains from beyond Kansas to Texas.

On one occasion during the several years that dust storms plagued the multi-state area, Mildred and I were in downtown Kansas City on what local residents called Petticoat Lane. It was called that for the obvious reason that the wind down that street regularly blew strong enough to blow women's skirts up high enough to see their petticoats.

We had barely left the City transit bus at the corner when a dust storm descended down on us. The wind blew hard and the air turned a dense dirty brown. I was frightened but Mildred, always at her best in a crisis, took charge, reassuring me that all would be well. She maneuvered us toward shelter in a corner alcove at the front of a large office building. We huddled there quite a long while, along with a group of other people seeking shelter. I am not sure how long it lasted but I know my mouth was full of dust, I could barely breathe, and the gritty dirt and grime unrelentingly pelted my tender skin. That happened during the time that President Franklin D. Roosevelt initiated his ambitious soil conservation plan.

"Give Roosevelt a few more years, and you'll see these Kansas prairies bloom," Daddy, a staunch Democrat, predicted.

That night in Kansas, we slept to the lullaby of a cricket concert under the open prairie sky.

"See the falling star?" Mama called as we bedded down. "Make a wish girls."

"There must be a trillion, jillion stars up there," Jean said. "At least," Daddy agreed. And, indeed, it was true. The flat prairie was covered in a crowded bowl of stars, each one brighter than the other. The wind blew cool after the hot day on the road and we all slept soundly in our outdoor campsite along the highway.

Early the next morning, we were back on the road, moving across the plains of Kansas and toward the majestic wonders of Colorado's Pikes Peak and the Garden of The Gods. We toured several little ghost, mining towns and we saw the Cave of the Winds.

Homer Knight in Colorado 1935

On a winding mountain road in Colorado, I got my first glimpse of real working cowboys. Thin, tanned men sat easy in their saddles, whooping and prodding a herd of cattle down the narrow, twisting mountain road, just as we were coming up the road. One cowboy smiled and winked directly at me. I was thrilled beyond words. The road was just wide enough for one car. On one side, the mountain formed a solid rock wall and on the other side, the road dropped away to frightening depths, down sheer mountain walls. At intervals along the road, pockets large enough to park one car in, were carved into the mountainside. We waited out the cattle drive in one of those pockets. The men wore denim shirts and leather pants and waved at us with a wide swing of their broad-brim hats.

Jean, 11, Muril, 9, in Colorado

Alas, before we knew it, vacation time was ending and we were on our way home.

"Look, there's that same woman we saw coming up, still standing in the door," Mama said as we passed again through Kansas going home. Once again, Mama raised her arm and waved. This time the woman waved back.

"Are we almost home," I fretted. "No kiddo, we are not," Mama answered. "And you are not to keep asking that question every ten minutes," she warned. "Kids." Lee complained. "Never know what will please them." "Shut up Lee." said Mildred.

When we finally pulled up in front of our house, I scampered quickly out of the car. "For heaven's sake watch where you're going," said Lee as I nearly ran him over. "Don't go too far," Mama scolded. "I'm going to fix lunch."

"Well," I thought. "I'm not hungry." I bolted through the house and upstairs to my room. I charged into the room to get Fuzzy, but stopped dead still. Fuzzy was there all right, just as I had left him, but his beady eyes stared accusingly at me. He looked so angry. I was sure he hated me. The silence of the room was overwhelming. I whirled around, stumbled downstairs, and out on the porch. Oh dear, oh dear, I thought. What should I do? I slumped down, shrouded in gloom, and sat leaning against a porch post. I'm not sure how long I sat there but I heard the screen door slam behind me and there was Jean standing over me. "I'm sprised you ain't said hello to your old bear," she said and tossed Fuzzy unceremoniously into my lap. I stiffened, and it was a moment before I could lower my eyes to look at him, but when I did, I was happily surprised.

"Ah Joy!" The magic was back! Fuzzy was smiling. He had forgiven me. Now, I was hungry. I grabbed him up and went in to the kitchen where Mama and Mildred already had a picnic lunch set out. It was good to be home. It took a while longer before I outgrew my obsession with the toy bear, but the trip was a turning point and the nightmares never reoccurred. I still have Fuzzy, even after all these years, safely stored on a closet shelf. His once luxurious, yellow fur coat is now threadbare and faded, and the palms of his paws are twice mended, but he is never-the-less a treasured, keepsake toy, a symbol of changing times, and a gentle reminder that a child's world is a time of tender years that can sometimes seem incredibly complicated.

Surgery on the Kitchen table

In the fall of 1933, my mother, Lillian Knight underwent emergency major surgery on the kitchen table of our family home in Kansas City, Missouri, 504 Fuller Ave. to be exact. She was twenty-nine years old, and had borne three children by that time. Her youngest child, Audrey, had died of diphtheria only a few months earlier at General Hospital.

The table where the surgery took place was not a sleek modern piece of furniture. It was a well-used antique, and it had one particular flaw that caused some worry about its use for so delicate a task as surgery. It was a drop-leaf table and therein was the cause for worry. The center surface of the tabletop was probably 24 or so inches wide, and it had two wide leaves on either side that hinged under the table. The table served a couple or easily converted to serve six or eight people by raising or lowering the leaves on either side. When the leaves were raised, they automatically locked in place. They were lowered very simply by pressing upward on the center of the hinge to drop the leaf down. A problem occurred only if the person seated at the table near the hinge inadvertently raised his or her knee under the table hinge. When that happened, the table leaf automatically dropped down. If the table was loaded at the same time, it dumped its entire contents into the persons lap or out onto the floor. That aspect of the table was discussed and it was decided that since no one would be sitting at the table during surgery, the table should be safe enough to use.

No one seemed to know the exact origin of that old table except that it had been in the family for generations. It was made of fine quality, solid, black walnut but had acquired three or four coats of white paint over the years. The stories attached to the drop leaves are too numerous to mention. However, one story about the table that my mother enjoyed, did not involve the table leaves.

The story she got a kick out of, concerned the day my father's mother, Lillie, dropped by our house unexpectedly with her new husband, a Mr. Flanders. Grandmother Knight, to be frank, was not one of our family's favorite people because of things she had done in her children's young lives. Her grandchildren had seen her so seldom as they grew up that they actually did not know her until much later in their lives when she was sick and needed help.

During the latter days of their marriage, my paternal grandfather, Jason Moreland Knight and Grandmother Knight did not get along well. They were, in reality, separated, even though they still shared a house together. During that time, Grandmother Knight got involved with what Mama called a "two-bit gangster", who shall be unnamed. The details of this story are sketchy to me because they happened before I was born. However, I heard the story a number of times growing up, usually in a behind the hand, gossipy sort of way when no one realized the children were listening. The story was usually discussed in whispers within the family, and never in detail. As children, eavesdropping on adult conversation, we knew better than to ask questions. As I recall the story, it occurred some time in the late 1910s. One evening, my Grandfather Knight came home early from work and fell asleep on his bed. He was sleeping soundly when Grandmother's boyfriend came into the house. For some reason, he shot Grandfather Knight while he slept, wounding him seriously enough to put him in the hospital, where they thought he would die. When the police came by the house to investigate the shooting, Grandmother Knight and her boyfriend told them that John, her oldest son, still in his teens, had accidentally shot his father. Grandmother, as the only witness, swore to the story. Their explanation to the family later was that they thought if Grandfather Knight died, Uncle John would stand a better chance in court than her gangster boyfriend would. The police, after an investigation, did not believe for one minute that the shooting was an accident. Uncle John pleaded his innocence to the charge but they arrested him, and he went to jail charged with attempted murder.

Fortunately for Uncle John, and against all odds, Grandfather Knight survived. He quickly absolved Uncle John of the crime but Uncle John never forgave his mother's betrayal, nor did the rest of the family. Uncle John's bitter feelings toward his mother never healed and in later years influenced his lack of trust in people in general.

Grandfather and Grandmother Knight were, of course, divorced and she remarried several times over the years. He never did.

Even with that history, the family was polite to Grandmother Knight and tolerated her on her rare visits to our house.

On the particular afternoon my mother remembered so well, Grandmother's companion on her visit to our house was her third husband, Mr. Flanders. The door had not closed behind Mr. Flanders before we learned that he was by his own words a "born again" Evangelical Christian. Immediately after that announcement, he started preaching. He was not only there to spread the gospel, he announced, he was there to change us all from our wicked ways, and save us from "everlasting hell". We only thought we were Christians, he scolded, and he was there to wipe away our sins and keep us from Satan's grasp.

He started out preaching quietly enough, but I couldn't help wondering just what wicked ways he had in mind that we needed so badly to mend. Although my parents were not dedicated church members, we children attended Sunday school regularly, and you would have to look a long way to find anyone who practiced Christian principles better than they did.

It wasn't long before Mr. Flanders tone sharpened and his voice rose to a few decibels below a train whistle. He began to perspire and his face took on a reddish glow. It was clear to all that Mr. Flanders was becoming overly excited. Mama and Daddy tried to steer the conversation into a less serious vein but Mr. Flanders was not to be deterred. He had something to say and he intended to say it.

After the 1929 stock market crash, many families faced desperate financial crisis. The desperation seemed to bring about a fervor of religious evangelism, and a rash of "would-be preachers" popped up regularly at our door. Some were selling Bibles and preaching the gospel despite the fact that most of them were not well-versed in the Bible. Even so, they swore that by some spontaneous miracle, they were divinely qualified to preach. Maybe some were, but I doubt that Mr. Flanders was one of them.

Mr. Flander's newly found zeal came about after a night of heavy drinking and carousing. He had not had time for a long, serious study of the Bible, he admitted, but felt compelled to preach anywhere and anytime he could.

It being their nature, Mama and Daddy tried to be patient and respect Mr. Flanders tender feelings but the more he talked, the louder he got. It didn't take long before Mama and Daddy realized that Mr. Flanders didn't know what he was talking about, and their patience began to wear thin.

At some point during his preachy monologue, we had migrated to the old drop-leaf table and sat down. We sat patiently around the table, willing ourselves to be polite just a little longer, as Mr. Flanders loudly expounded his views on redemption.

It was getting close to mealtime, and I, personally was a little preoccupied with visions of fried chicken and apple pie.

Unnoticed on the table, up to that time, lay our large black, thick-volume, home-remedy, doctor book. Mama liked to keep it there as a handy reference.

Our evangelical visitor was in high gear now, quoting chapter and verse on how Satan stood at our door that very minute ready to snare us into a life of sin when someone at the table questioned one of Mr. Flanders Biblical statements. I don't remember what it was, but he stopped dramatically, mid-sentence, red -faced and indignant. Then, in a self-righteous maneuver, he reached over and planted his hand, firmly down on the old black doctor book. "I tell you it's the gospel truth, and I can prove it right here in this book." He thumped the old doctor book a couple of times for emphasis, obviously mistaking it for a Bible. It did look like a Bible.

Mama quickly rose up in her chair to advise him of his error. She did not like to see anyone embarrassed especially on such a sensitive subject as religion.

"No sir," she began, "You see that's a…" but Mr. Flanders assumed she was challenging his word. He would tolerate no such interference, and he cut her off rudely in mid-sentence, brushing aside further attempts to correct his error. "No," he shouted, "its right here," and down came his hand again on the book.

Daddy, who had been quiet up to this point, interrupted Mr. Flanders to say, "Excuse me sir, I don't think you're going to prove it with that book," and he emphasized, " that book". Even Daddy was uncomfortable with what was obviously coming. "No, no!." Mr. Flander's shouted. "I tell you. I will show you, right here in this book. With a grand flourish he threw open the pages of the old book. The cover fell back and the pages rippled down to rest mid-center of the open book. Mama gasped, and for a moment, no one said a word, the silence was deafening. Because there for all to see, on the centerfold of that old book, was the garishly colored, well-defined picture of a man's internal digestive system. Daddy could hold it no longer, he roared with laughter. We kids snickered, but were afraid to laugh. Satan would surely grab us and do something terrible, and if he didn't, Mama surely would. Mama fluctuated between apologies and smothered titters of laughter. And Mr. Flanders… well, Mr. Flanders did not handle it well. He slammed the book shut, clamped his jaw in humiliation and stormed out of the house with grandmother right behind him. We never saw or heard from him again, and, it was several years before we saw Grandmother again.

On the day of the surgery, Dr. Olaf Coleman, a promising young surgeon, performed the hysterectomy on my mother. He was, at the time, newly in practice. . Dr. Mackey, a rough- talking old retired Army field surgeon, who had tended the war-torn bodies of soldiers on the battlefields in World War I., assisted him. It wasn't planned that way, but, my mother's best friend, Mildred Cramer, probably 19, with no prior nursing experience, was the surgical nurse.

This story now seems incredible, even to me, and I was there when it happened. People who did not experience the Great Depression era, and who did not live the experience of poverty-stricken times, may find it difficult to understand the hard decisions described here. The doctor's decision to perform home surgery must be considered in the context of the times. There were few if any public financial medical programs to assist people in need. That was an accepted part of everyday life. People today may find it difficult to understand the depth of poverty that existed during those days and how money or the lack of it influenced what a person could or could not do. There were charity hospitals, but as a rule they were poorly funded and poorly managed. Most people of that time viewed them only as a last resort, a place to go to die. The ill frequently preferred to take their chances at home rather than die in a charity hospital alone as they surely believed they would. As for Mama, she chose to take her chances with home care.

The family had spent the morning cleaning and disinfecting the entire kitchen. "We scrubbed the kitchen down in Lysol and got all the white sheets we could find to cover the table and hung the sheets around the table to close it off from the rest of the room," Mildred said. "We had an old-fashioned, coal heated cook stove," she said and waved her hands to indicate a direction where the stove was, "and a granite dishpan. Dr. Coleman put his surgical tools in the granite pan and we boiled them," Mildred said.

Prior to the surgery, no one had even considered using Mildred as the surgical nurse, especially Mildred herself. Dr. Coleman's wife, Dolores, was scheduled for that duty. However, when Dr. Coleman's scalpel drew blood from the first incision across Mama's abdomen, Dolores passed out cold. I was seven when all this happened and I could remember only bits and pieces of the events. However, in an interview with Mildred in her later years before she passed away at the age of 86, she verified the entire story, as she remembered it, to my sister, Jean and me.

"It was just Dr. Coleman, Dr. Mackey and the nurse, but she passed out cold and fell flat in the floor. Dr. Coleman told me, Mildred you have to take over, so I just took over," she said.

"There was your Mama laying wide open and Dolores out cold. Dr. Coleman would say, 'hand me this and hand me that' and I thought, 'Ohhh, I can't do this' and then I said 'yes, I can, yes, I can,' and I did," said Mildred. She gave God credit for enabling her to carry out the doctor's instructions.

When asked why she thought the doctor would take such a risk as performing surgery on someone in his or her home, Mildred answered simply. "Well, it was that or let her die. We had to do it."

Mildred said the decision on surgery came after Lillian had a miscarriage without doctor's care.

"She was just tore up. There was so much infection; she was actually bleeding to death from it. Her health just kept getting worse. One day we went shopping at Montgomery Wards and while we were walking home, she left a trail of blood. Dr. Coleman had to go in there and take all that stuff out."

The surgery was successful, but seven days later, after all the precautions of scrubbing and sterilizing the room, Mama developed a staph infection. The results of the staph proved more harrowing than the surgery.

"She got that old staph infection and it rotted out all the stitches," Mildred said and went on to describe what happened a few days after the surgery.

"I was staying with Bill the whole time but I made a quick trip to Mrs. Weigstein's grocery store on the corner," Mildred said.

"When I got back from Mrs. Weigsteins," Mildred said. "Bill was in the bed and blood was coming through the mattress and onto the floor.

"I was so scared I didn't know what to do. I put your Mama's feet up higher than her head and sent you kids for your Uncle Ira. Then here came Ira, and he said 'she is going to General Hospital.' And, I said,' No, she ain't going to that old place.' Every one was scared of that durned old General Hospital. They just let you die out there. So we propped Bill up and I called the doctor. Dr. Olaf Coleman was out of town but his father, also a doctor answered the phone. He said, 'Get every thing white you can find and cram it in her until I can get someone there'. Ira said, 'We're not gonna do it' but I said, 'Yes, we are gonna do it,' and Bill, well, she was just scared to death."

All the while Mildred worked over Mama, she and Uncle Ira argued heatedly about whether Mama was going to General Hospital. Mildred said she didn't believe Mama could survive the ambulance ride and she had no confidence in the hospital.

"Ira was so scared and he was crying and that was scaring Bill. I didn't know what to do. I told you kids to go over to the Rosen's, (our neighbor's next door) and stay there, and then, I told Ira to keep his mouth shut. And, I sent him to get Homer from work," Mildred said. Uncle Ira must have sensed the rightness of Mildred's decision or realized that it was useless to argue with her because, whatever his reason, he did what she said. He went out in the front yard where a crowd of neighbors had gathered. How they knew what was happening is anyone's guess, but they were there. I watched the crowd from Mrs. Rosen's porch swing not really comprehending the seriousness of what was happening. During all this time Dr. Coleman still had not come. His office was trying frantically to get word to him but he was attending an out of town patient, and there was no phone service there. Even after he got the message, because of the long drive, it took him a while to get back to town.

Meanwhile, Daddy had rushed home after receiving word at work that his wife was near death. No one we knew had home phones then. Any phone messages we made were at a pay phone at the corner drug store, a block away.

When Daddy walked in and saw Mama, he was stunned at her condition. He could see that she was dying and knew he must act quickly. He decided that if Dr. Coleman couldn't be there, he had to get another doctor. He raced to the drug store and phoned another doctor who was just three blocks away. After hearing the circumstances of the case, that doctor refused to come. At that point, Daddy was not going to take no for an answer, he said. In a white-hot rage he told the doctor that he, the doctor, would come, or he, Homer, would come up there and "blow his head off." When asked later if he actually would have done it, Daddy said he was prepared to do just that. The doctor agreed to come.

At the house, Mildred had followed all the instructions to control the hemorrhaging, she packed Mama with the white cloth and propped her feet higher than her head. Mama was very weak by that time and convinced that she was dying. She told Mildred. 'I want you to raise my kids.' Those plaintive words struck fear in Mildred and she felt a moment of panic, but she knew she couldn't give in. "I knew I had to get some fight in to her or she was going to die on me. I was never so scared in my life but I couldn't let her know that. I said 'Now listen here Bill; I've had enough of this. There ain't nothing goin to happen to you. We've gotta go here and we've gotta go there. I ain't gonna raise your kids. I've got other things to do. Just forget it. I don't want no babies to take care of. Now quit being a baby. You're gonna raise them kids yourself'," she said. "And then, Bill got mad and that's what I wanted, to make her so mad, she would fight to live. We got her feet up high and then Dr. Coleman and the doctor that Homer had called were both there at the same time. When the other doctor saw Dr. Coleman had arrived, he left. I think he was happy to get out of there."

"Dr. Coleman told us we had done a good job and then he took over. He gave Bill a shot of something that ran her fever up real high. He said it was the only way to fight a staph infection. He stayed right there with her all night, watching the fever and keeping her cooled with wet towels. Penicillin and other antibiotic medicines had not yet been discovered. Dr. Coleman said the fever would burn out the infection or she would die," Mildred said.

The fever apparently did the work because Mama made a full recovery. She lived to be 78-years old. Dr. Coleman went on to become one of Kansas City's prominent surgeons. Many years later, Mama happened to see Mrs. Coleman at the doctor's office .When Mrs. Coleman brought up the subject of Mama's surgery; Dr. Coleman was reluctant to acknowledge that it had ever happened.

The McIntyre cousins

The McIntyre cousins were an amazingly sturdy lot. They were far tougher than my sister, Jean or I. They had fewer colds, fevers, upset stomachs, etc. Hard knocks that left me bleeding, bruised and crying, seemed to roll off their backs like water. I have often wondered if being part of a large family had anything to do with it.

There were only five McIntyre siblings, Ira, Thelma, Charlene, Billy and Margie, when, one Saturday morning about 1937 or so, Uncle Ira and Margurette had scheduled all of the kids to have their tonsils out in the doctor's office. Today's doctors only remove tonsils in dire necessity and then only in hospitals. But back in the 1930s, most doctors professed to believe that tonsils were just something left over from an otherwise efficient evolutionary process. They may have been helpful in ancient times, but they no longer served any useful function. A round of sore throats or tonsillitis might cause the doctor to recommend getting the annoying things out. Having tonsils removed in the doctor's office was a common practice in those days. However, I think it was probably somewhat unusual even then, to have five sets of tonsils removed in one morning office visit. Mama fussed at Uncle Ira about it because when Jean and I had our tonsils out earlier, on separate occasions, we were ill and in bed for a few days. Mama didn't think it was wise to have all five of the children's tonsils removed in one visit. She pointed out how much trouble I had when my tonsils were removed. I was puny for months after the surgery. The doctor said that when he administered the anesthetic, I went under just enough to lose control and then I began fighting. I remember starting to count backward to ten when the ether was being administered, but midway through the count a shrill ringing in my ears and a horrible drifting feeling terrified me and I thought, "I don't want to do this," then I was out. However, the doctor said I never really went all the way out. He said I fought him to the point that the knife slipped and he nicked the inside of my throat just a bit. He finally had to quit and leave a fraction of the tonsil in. The result was, when I got hot, my throat and nose bled. Uncle Ira listened to all the warnings and advice but he had his mind set. Nothing was going to happen. He was convinced, and the tonsillectomies went on as scheduled.

That Saturday morning, the family was up early and in the doctor's office by eight o'clock and back home by noon. Mama need not have worried because, just as Uncle Ira said, the McIntyre kids came back home jolly as could be and went right out to play. I was amazed and perplexed. It hardly seemed fair to me that I should have so much trouble and they skipped right through it. Only Charlene had a few complications.

When Mama saw the children out playing so soon after the surgery, she was once again annoyed at Uncle Ira for letting the kids go out to play so soon after their surgery, and she promptly told him so. Mama and Uncle Ira had a way of speaking their minds to one another with no long lasting ill effects. Uncle Ira told Mama that the kids were fine and if they got tired, they would come in and rest.

Probably reacting to what I had heard Mama say, and being a nosy 12 year old, maybe a tad envious that they had fared so much better than I did, I decided it was my duty to keep an eye out for the younger kids. I knew the older ones would not listen to me anyway.

We were all playing ball on our corner of Roberts and Fuller when I noticed Margie, four years my junior, sitting on the back of a car looking rather wan. I decided to tell her "for her own good" of course that she shouldn't be there playing in the street after just having her tonsils removed. "You should be home resting," I told her in my most maternal fashion.

Well to my chagrin, she looked me straight in the eye and sassy as you please, said I should mind my own business, that she was fine and she did not intend to go home until she was ready. Well, she was just fine, and so were the other young McIntyre siblings. They all recovered with no ill effects. In addition, I learned a lesson as well. From that experience, I learned that well meant intentions do not always warrant getting in to others people's affairs. That's how the McIntyre/ Knight children played off one another to learn life's lessons growing up during the Great Depression.

Uncle Clell

After his mother died, Uncle Clell lived with one of his older married siblings and then with another. He lived first with his sister, Eva and her husband, John, then with Lillian and husband, Homer, and then his brother, Ira and wife Margurette. Until he married, he bounced from one house to the other as the mood struck him. As a result, his nieces and nephews all formed a special bond to him and each family thought they had a special claim to him. We were all a bit possessive of Uncle Clell. I'm not sure he ever realized that.

When Jean was nine and I was seven, Uncle Clell lived with our mother, Lillian. He taught us how to make crepe paper and melted wax flowers. When the flowers were finished, he would heat one of those large old round 78 records and shape it into a vase for the paper flowers. It made a surprisingly pretty bouquet. When Jean was ten, he taught her to peel potatoes without leaving the eyes in. When she was twelve, he taught her how to cut crafts out of wood using a jigsaw, (a table jigsaw). She made all kinds of things with his help; bookends, corner shelves, matchbox holders and other pretty things. After Clell married Pearl Barrett, Jean and I would go to their house and play a card game called spoons, or dominoes. He would pop corn or make fudge. He always had time for us and actually seemed to enjoy our visits. "Sometimes, we would laugh till our jaws hurt," Jean said.

Thelma McIntyre remembered some years back, that Uncle Clell was, in her words, "a good cook and made the best pies I ever tasted." When she was nine, she said, he taught her how to bake a lemon meringue pie. Thelma said her pie turned out beautifully. The meringue of whipped egg whites and sugar stood in high peaks. She was so pleased with her pie that she danced around the kitchen throwing the dishtowel in the air. Then, to her dismay, the dishtowel came down and landed right on top of that beautiful meringue. She looked at that dishtowel and, "Unhappy would not come close to what I felt," she said. "But, Uncle Clell came to the rescue. He carefully lifted the rag from the pie and smoothed the meringue. Thelma said she swore she would never tell the rest of the family and she never did, "until now." Thelma thought her Uncle Clell was the greatest uncle ever.

Jean recalled that Uncle Clell started smoking when he was still in his teens. "Back in the 1930s,' she said, "it was the style for a man to roll his own cigarettes. They carried a little white drawstring sack of tobacco with cigarette papers stuck in a brown paper band around the sack. The drawstring was thin yellow twine that drew the bag closed. On the end of the string was a round tag that named the tobacco company, usually Bull Durham. "Uncle Clell always had that little yellow string hanging out of his front shirt pocket and he never stopped rolling his own cigarettes even after the modern pre-rolled cigarettes became popular," she said. The last time she saw Clell at the age of 79 before his death in 1990, there was that little sack and tag hanging out of his shirt pocket, she said. "He sat down, leaned back in his chair and rolled his own cigarette. Then, he started talking about the good old days. I just wanted to give him a hug and I did," she said.

Uncle Clell could play almost any musical instrument he picked up. I especially remember the banjo, harmonica and mandolin. He could pick a jig on the banjo like a pro. Some of those harmonicas he had, we called them all French harps, were fancy. As I recall, at least one of them, had as many as four rows of holes on one side and just as many on the other side. There was also some sort of a slide feature that let him warble the sound. To our delight, Uncle Clell would blow that harp first on one side and then flip it over to play the other side never missing a note. In addition to the more conventional instruments, he could also play the musical saw and washboard. He loved old-time music and he was always willing to show us kids how to play whatever instrument he happened to have at the time.

Billy McIntyre was born in 1932. He was Uncle Ira's fifth child and his second son. Billy's given name was William Clell, but we always called him only Billy. He was named for Uncle Clell and his Uncle Homer whose first name was William. Thelma was seven when Billy was born. Up to that time, all of Uncle Ira and Margurette's kids were born at home as were most of the children of that time. When her two younger sisters were born, Thelma was too young to pay much attention, but at seven, she was much more aware of activities going on around her.

When the due date arrived, Thelma had no idea what was going on, but she knew things were not normal. The doctor came and Uncle Clell took all four of Uncle Ira's older children downstairs. When the baby started being born, Thelma could hear Margurette crying and she didn't understand what was happening. She thought that the doctor was hurting her mama and she tried to run back upstairs. Uncle Clell picked her up screaming and crying, and held her. He explained to her what was happening. He then made some hot cocoa for all the kids. Uncle Ira and Margurette would go on to have four more for a total of nine children and it wasn't long before Thelma was like a second mother to her younger siblings.

In those days women had to stay in bed for about ten days after childbirth because doctors didn't take stitches, there was no penicillin or antibiotics and recovery was generally slower for new mothers. After the baby was born, Uncle Ira had to get back to work. While Margurette recovered, Uncle Clell took on the household chores of cooking the meals, keeping the house clean, and helping to take care of Margurette and the baby, changing diapers and sending the older children to school. When she wasn't in school, Thelma, even at the age of seven, was there with Uncle Clell, helping to do whatever needed to be done.

When Billy was five, and started attending Henry Clay School, his kindergarten teacher asked him for his name. He told her it was Billy William Uncle Clell McIntyre. Slightly confused by the odd name, the teacher spent some time trying to get Billy's name straight, but without success. She finally sent Billy to Miss Flaven, the principal's office, to verify his name. Miss Flaven had no better luck getting his name straight than the kindergarten teacher did, and she called for one of the older siblings to come to the office. She didn't mention why they were to come to the office, and as a result of that, it was whispered all over school that Thelma or her older brother, Ira, must be in trouble because they were called to Miss Flaven's office.

To be called to Miss Flaven's office struck terror in the heart of even the toughest kids in Clay School. She was a feared, no-nonsense administrator, well known for her harsh disciplinary methods, such as the leather strap for whipping some of the older boys who misbehaved. The word around school was that she also kept a large wooden paddle with holes cut in the center for the more severe disciplinary problems. Another rumor held that she wore a ring on her finger that had at one time cut a boy's face when she slapped him with her backhand. Miss Flaven even intimidated some of the parents who knew her when they were in school. She was a tiny woman, no more than five-foot tall. We never knew her age at that time, but even when my parents attended Clay School, they thought of her as elderly.

In her younger years, she had been head master of a military school and when she arrived at Clay School, she brought her tough no-nonsense administrative methods from the military school with her.

Henry Clay School was a two story red brick building with a full-length basement. The building and playgrounds took up an entire city block.

When we attended school, there was a rule that boys played on one side of the playground and the girls played on the other side. One of Miss Flaven's cardinal rules was that no boys should ever come onto the girls' side of the playground for any reason. The same rule applied to the girls. To break that rule was a major infraction and meant a visit to Miss Flaven's office. Another strict rule was that no students were allowed in the building until the bell rang. When the bell rang, we formed a line and came into the building single file. There was no talking in line and we went directly to our classrooms. Those children who had class rooms on the second floor filed up two flights of concrete steps without holding onto the banister. The banisters as well as the hardwood floors were always meticulously polished and heaven help the child who messed them up. When the weather was freezing, Miss Flaven relented and opened up the cafeteria room. Students were allowed to sit in the cafeteria until classes started but we had to be quiet.

When the school day ended, we lined up in an orderly fashion just outside the classroom door and waited for the recorded marching music to sound over the loud speakers. With the first notes, we stepped smartly in place for a short time in a left foot/right foot cadence. Then, with a signal from the teacher, we stepped out, four abreast, and marched down the hall to the first flight of stairs, hesitated there just long enough for the first-floor students to clear the downstairs hall, then on down the stairs we marched and out of the building in an orderly fashion to the rhythm of marching music. All the while, Miss Flaven stood militantly erect, outside her office door observing each class as it marched past her. Small though she was, she loomed large as an authority figure in her ankle length skirts and sleeves to her wrists. Her arms were primly down at her sides as she watched our orderly and well-disciplined exit.

Yes, Miss Flaven was a formidable figure, and to be called to her office was no small thing. Therefore, when the word went out that Ira and Thelma were summoned to Miss Flaven's office, and the other family children didn't know why, there was no end to our curiosity. When school let out, there we were, family and school friends, gathered around Thelma and Ira clamoring to find out exactly what had happened. After we heard the story about Billy's name, it became another family favorite repeated down the years. Billy never quite lived it down.

Daddy builds a Swimming Pool

Back in the 1930s, my Dad, Homer Knight, was a seemingly boundless source of strength and energy. He was young, still in his twenties, and he was healthy. Mama said he didn't know what it meant to be tired. She, on the other hand, often found it difficult to match his energy. Daddy didn't mind working hard if it brought pleasure to himself or someone he loved.

Daddy was about 5 ft. 10 and weighed in the area of 160pounds. He had black hair and dark blue eyes. He was of a muscular build, and had worked hard all his life.

Mama and Daddy knew each other as children. They were married in 1922 and were together 60 years later when he died in1982 and she in 1983. We, their children, could not have had better, more dedicated parents. Our family, and that extended to the grandchildren, and great grandchildren, had no doubt in our minds that that was true.

A resourceful man, who grew up poor, Daddy, enjoyed nothing more than creating something from little to nothing. One summer during the Great Depression when he had more time than money, he built his own swimming pool in our back yard. The swimming pool idea occurred to Daddy after he came home tired several days in a row from hot, exhausting work and dreamed of jumping in a pool of cool water.

Daddy enjoyed swimming with a passion, and a torridly hot summer, and no car, were enough to keep him preoccupied with dreams of a swimming pool. The summer I spoke of, as stated, was particularly hot with temperatures soaring into triple digits for weeks.

Daddy always worked steady to meet our necessities but luxuries such as a swimming pool during the Great Depression were out of the question. Daddy often worked three or four 10 to 12 hour-days in a row but then he would be off for four, and there was no guarantee that he might not lose his job entirely.

However, Daddy didn't complain. No, he was not one to sit around and bemoan hard times. He was a man of action. As the summer wore on and the days grew hotter, the idea of a swimming pool became more and more attractive. Then one day, he made his decision. He had thought long and hard about it. Bags of cement and water were cheap and something he could afford. He would provide his own labor. He began immediately to finalize the plan in his mind. He had never built a swimming pool or even seen one built, but he had a plan and he had no doubts that he could accomplish it. He was going to build a swimming pool in our back yard.

Mama just shook her head. Our old garage had a dirt floor and occupied the space where he planned to build the pool. It was then we learned that it was to be a covered swimming pool. "Why not," Daddy declared. We didn't have a car so why did we need a garage. On the other hand, swimming in a covered pool would bring refreshing relief from the oppressive heat for swimmers and provide a nice shade at the same time.

Daddy was not reckless but he was known, on occasion to rush into things, sometimes prematurely, without thinking them through.

Without further ado, the next thing we knew, Daddy was out digging a hole in the dirt floor of our old garage. He hauled out his shovel and wheelbarrow from the basement of our house, and the swimming pool project began. The dirt flew and the hole got wider and deeper by the day. In a matter of weeks, Daddy had dug a rectangular hole about eight feet wide by 12 feet long, four feet deep at one end and about six feet deep on the other. Some of our close neighbors who had time on their hands, helped with the digging. Gus Rosen, Lee Cramer, Uncle Clell, and my cousin Johnny, who was a teenager, helped on occasion.

Once the hole was dug, Daddy mixed the cement by hand in a mud box and hauled it by bucket loads into the hole, no concrete mixers or fancy machines for this job. He had occasional help with this process also and finally the pool was completed. The finished pool wasn't perfect, but as I recall, it wasn't bad. When the concrete dried, and Daddy filled the pool with water, the sun shone through the open door of the former garage and the water sparkled clean and cool. With an excited howl and a huge splash, Daddy jumped into the pool. The next thing we knew eight or ten people were in the pool, splashing and having a big time. The neighbors dropped by often that summer and anyone who wanted could take a dip in our pool. There was no drain in the pool, but every day or so Daddy dumped a gallon of laundry bleach in the water to purify it. Being covered, the pool got little debris in it and the water stayed clean and clear. It may not have been completely sterile but it was a wonderful relief from the dreadful heat. We all had a grand old time in that pool all summer and late into the fall. No one got sick or suffered ill effects from it and we anticipated other summer seasons playing in that pool, but that was not to be.

The winter came in cold and blustery that year with months of ice and snow, and freezing weather. The pool froze solid. When spring brought warm weather and the pool slowly thawed, we could see that it had cracked and would no longer hold water.

"Not a big deal," Daddy said, because by then the economy was picking up and he had a car. We could drive to a lake.

Since he now had a car, he needed a garage so, he backfilled the pool with the excavated dirt from the pool and parked his car in the garage. Oh, but that does not the end the history on the old garage. No, that garage had a long history.

When the pool was backfilled and the garage restored, Mama used part of it to store some old furniture she was no longer used, but wanted to keep. Included in the storage were two old, solid walnut, platform rockers that had belonged to her dearly departed mother, Dazerine Petty McIntyre, long since passed away.

One weekend, Daddy inspected the garage and declared it a "damned mess." Daddy was one of those men who found it difficult to express himself without using a few swear words. Without further delay, he decided to "clean out the damned garage." He worked most of the day hauling out stored canning jars, old magazines, boxes of old junk, and old furniture, from the garage. Out it all came, and out came Grandmother Dazerine's old wooden platform rockers.

Mama had saved those old rockers for years, moving them first to one storage area and then another. Someday, she promised herself, she would reupholster them and put them back in the house to use.

While Daddy was in a big way of cleaning out the garage, Mama was in the house otherwise occupied and unaware of his activities.

He stacked all the old stuff in a high pile, including the old rockers, stuffed in some dry paper, splashed on some gasoline and lit the fire. The fire caught quickly and the trash burned hot and fast. It had burned down almost to ashes when Mama showed up.

She had finally noticed the activity, and had come out to admire his work. Oh, it was true, the garage was immaculate and Mama, always quick to praise a job well done began to admire Daddy's hard work. My goodness, it did look neat, but words of praise froze in her throat when she took a closer look at the burned down ashes. For there, at the fire's edge, was the telltale, charred remains of Grandma Dazerine's old rockers. A look of disbelief crossed Mama's face to be replaced by a flush of anger. Mama's smile froze in mid-sentence. She stared at the charred remains for what seemed an eternity while Daddy fidgeted. " Is that Mama's platform rockers?" she asked, knowing full well that it was. She turned unbelievingly toward Daddy and what followed was not pretty. "What have you done to Mama's chairs?" she demanded. Daddy stepped back. He knew he was in for it. He hung his head and seemed to grow smaller by the minute. Mama followed up with a tongue-lashing and tears, the like of which I had never before seen.

More embarrassed than angry, Daddy blustered back, he didn't think she wanted any of that old stuff especially those old rockers. He tried to say they were not much good anyway, but Mama would hear none of it. "They only needed reupholstering," she declared and kept declaring many times again, loud and long over the years after the calamitous event occurred. That story had a way of resurfacing at the oddest of moments, with Mama just as angry and Daddy just as defensive as the day it happened. I'm not sure she ever forgave him for that, but they finally seemed to agree not to mention it again.

About twenty years later, quite innocently in casual conversation, Mama's brother, Ira, asked, "Sis, whatever happened to Mama's (meaning Dazerine) old platform rockers?" He recalled the beauty of the wood, mentioned how his mother enjoyed rocking in the old chairs. He reminisced how old they were and remarked on the considerable worth of the fine antiques at that time. Mama said not a word, but drew herself up tall and tight, folded her arms across her chest in that special way she had of doing, and looked Daddy, straight in the eye. The old wound was back, raw as ever. Daddy didn't say a word but he turned brick red, took a breath and mumbled something under his breath. Then, quicker than you could cuss a cat, he changed the subject.

Visiting Uncle Okla

My parents got along famously well most of the time. They had similar backgrounds and values and agreed on most financial and other family decisions. On almost everything, they were a good solid team. There were however, a few things that they could never seem to agree on, and anything to do with Uncle Okla was one of them.

Along those same lines, there were times when ordinary events seem to come together to produce experiences that might not have happened otherwise. For example, one summer afternoon about 1936 several factors came in to play to produce the following story that was added to our family collection and brought up to rehash and joke about at family gatherings during the depression and prohibition years.

During the 1920s thru the 40s, or thereabout, the Pendergast Machine, a corrupt political power operated freely in Kansas City, Jackson County and throughout Missouri, and had for decades. The Machine's awesome power extended, in some cases, to Washington D.C.

Under the Pendergast rule, Federal Prohibition laws in force in Kansas City at that time, designed to forbid the sale of alcoholic beverages and gambling nationwide, were no problem to the more sophisticated party folks in Kansas City. In fact, Prohibition only ran the sale of alcohol underground and became a financial goldmine for bootleggers and political greed. The appropriate password by those in the know could open doors at speakeasies, gambling joints and other forbidden party spots in Kansas City, and alcohol was readily available with the appropriate wink of an eye. Red-light districts promoting prostitution were not uncommon. They operated wide open in certain areas of downtown Kansas City. They were, however, limited to those designated areas, and respectable people avoided those areas like the plague.

The only air conditioning available to the average home or many businesses at that time was an open window or an electric fan, and the only telephones available to most people were at the corner drug store or some other public building. Children in those days stayed younger and more innocent longer, and there's little doubt in my mind that my sister Jean and I were more naive than most.

All of these factors came together one warm and pleasant afternoon when Daddy heard that his brother, Okla, was back in town. Uncle Okla traveled out of state a lot and Daddy hadn't seen him for a good while. Daddy wanted to go find Uncle Okla's new apartment and visit him.

It would be an impromptu, unannounced, visit because Uncle Okla didn't have a phone and neither did we.

Daddy asked Mama how she would like to go visiting. She told him it was okay with her if he wanted to visit Uncle Okla, but she did not intend to do so. That was not what Daddy wanted to hear. He wanted the whole family to go, he said. Mama and Uncle Okla had grown up knowing each other and had never gotten along well. A long-term animosity left from their childhood skirmishes was still well entrenched between the two of them. Okla had been a brash and outspoken young man, and Mama was not one to tolerate rude behavior. Uncle Okla also had a reputation within the family, for being an adventurer and a rogue with the women. He knew the location to speakeasies around town and had close acquaintances with lots of questionable women. Those qualities made him popular in some social circles, but they did not endear him to my mother who tended to be a somewhat judgmental along those lines.

Daddy kept insisting that he wanted the family to go along, and at last, Mama began to reconsider her refusal. After all, she reasoned, Okla was Daddy's brother. He hadn't been around for a long time. Perhaps she was too critical; perhaps he had mellowed, and changed. He was, after all, her children's uncle and we had not seen him in years. Perhaps, she was being selfish by refusing to go visit her husband's brother, she thought. Finally, she decided she would forget Okla's past transgressions, it was a nice day for a drive, and we children would enjoy a little outing. Yes, she decided, we would all go. Uncle Ira's daughter, Thelma McIntyre, was visiting us that day and she was invited to go along. It was to be a fun occasion.

Uncle Okla was Daddy's bachelor brother. He had married once and had a daughter but his wife left him and took his only child with her so Uncle Okla had been single for some time. As he traveled, he often managed apartments in exchange for his rent and now that he was back in town, he was managing an apartment in downtown Kansas City. Daddy had the address. Although he didn't know exactly where it was, he was sure he could find the place.

We children looked forward to the outing. In spite of the fact that Mama didn't approve of Uncle Okla, we girls thought he was a fun person and enjoyed his visits.

Uncle Okla was slightly older than Daddy. He had the same dark hair and blue eyes that Daddy had but the resemblance ended there. He was a short, dapper man and a little on the thin side. He always showed up at our house with a big toothy smile and came in swaggering about and spouting the latest 1920 phrases such as, "Oh you kid, Twenty Three skidoo, So's your old man" and other popular, idioms. He carried quarters in his pocket which he generously handed out to us children upon arrival, and which we accepted joyously. However, the minute, Mama found out that he had given us money she promptly made us give it back to him, but we appreciated the gesture anyway.

Jean and I were eager to go driving. It didn't really matter where. Going riding in a car was not something we did on a regular basis and we were excited to go. It would be even more fun with Thelma going along. Thelma and I were both ten and Jean was twelve. We were easy to entertain and the thought of going for a ride in the rumble seat of Daddy's little coupe was a joyous treat indeed. For the uninitiated, a rumble seat is a compact little passenger seat located at the rear of a coupe. A compartment, much like the trunk of a car, houses the seat. The lid opens up and back to reveal the backrest, and the cushioned seat. The rumble seat accommodated two adults or, as in our case, three children. Jean, Thelma and I loaded ourselves into the rumble seat. It was a tight fit, but we didn't mind. Mama and Daddy sat in the front and the little car was full. It was a fine day and we girls were ready to go. It would be an adventure.

We sang joyously as we rode along down the City streets. The wind grabbed our hair, blowing it in every direction, in our eyes, our mouth. It was wonderful. Our songs were caught by the wind, and swept swiftly away behind us. As we neared downtown, Daddy slowed the car and began looking for addresses. Daddy did not have a great sense of direction so it came as no surprise to us, after driving up one street and down another, that we were lost. Somewhere along the way, Daddy managed to turn on a one-way street, going the wrong way.

"Now, you've done it," Mama said. She was hot and tired by this time, and what's more, she said, she did not like the looks of this neighborhood.

Young though we were, we girls were inclined to agree with Mama, that this neighborhood did look different. As we drove slowly down the street, we could see men, dressed in flashy looking suits, lounging on the street corners. They laughed loudly and one man was weaving about as though he might fall. There was trash in the street and in a large building across the street from us, all the windows were wide open, and scantily clad women sat two or three in the open windows. They held hand fans and slowly fanned their rouged faces and scarlet lips.

Daddy acted as though he didn't see them.

Not one to hide her displeasure for long, Mama advised Daddy. "Homer Knight, I think this is a red light district. We should turn around and go right back home," she declared. She should have known Okla would live in a place like this, she added.

Daddy was frustrated at not finding Uncle Okla's address, but he was not ready to quit looking. He decided to park the car and ask someone for directions. Perhaps a more observant man might have been more aware of his surroundings, but Daddy had one thing on his mind, and that was to locate his brother's apartment.

He had barely cut the car engine, when the women in the windows began to call gaily down to him. They leaned seductively far out of the upstairs windows, their scanty outfits showing much more cleavage than we girls were accustomed to seeing. They waved and smiled. "Yoo hoo, sweety." they called. "Come on up. We're waiting for you." There were more friendly invitations.

"Hey Mama," we girls said in surprise, as if Mama hadn't noticed, "Those ladies are hollering at Daddy. Do we know them?" "No," she replied curtly, "We do not." We girls smiled and waved back to the women. The women paid scant attention to us but kept laughing and waving at Daddy obviously having fun at his discomfort.

He ignored them and even seemed angry. He turned back to the car and jerked the door open to get back in. Mama, a normally friendly person, was stiff with indignation. She glared in the direction of the women in the windows her nose in the air and her jaw clenched. I was embarrassed for the friendly ladies but they seemed unaware of my parents' rudeness, ignoring my mother's glares and Daddy's cold shoulder treatment.

"Homer Knight," Mama said, "You had better get me out of here. Right now! This is the last time I ever visit your brother at his place," and she sounded like she meant it.

Meanwhile, a police officer was walking slowly toward our car. As he approached, we heard the slap of the nightstick against his leg. "You're going the wrong way on a one-way street buddy," he said roughly to Daddy.

Of course, Daddy already knew that, but he replied politely. "Yes sir." He explained to the officer that he was looking for his brother's place, and had gotten lost. He was trying at that very moment to get back to where he belonged, he said. However, the officer wasn't satisfied. "This is no place for the wife and kids," he persisted. Daddy was agreeing, but we girls were not pleased with the officer's attitude. This was our father he was speaking to after all.

Jean and I accepted without question that our parents were the final authority, that they were all wise and always in control. Who did this police officer think he was to lecture our father? We decided it was our place to defend our father and we spoke up. We told the officer that he should stop bothering our Daddy and go do whatever he was supposed to do and leave us alone. To our surprise, Daddy quickly turned to us and told us firmly to "Hush up." Then he turned back to the officer and apologized for us. We hardly knew what to think, but lucky day for us, the officer was smiling. "Okay Buddy," he said. He told Daddy that he wouldn't give him a ticket this time but he should get on out of there. He even asked Daddy what address he was looking for and then gave him directions to the location. As we left, the officer was shaking his head and smiling. When I got older, I realized that the friendly women were actually prostitutes and we, most assuredly, had ventured in to a red-light district. The women in the window had probably had a field day teasing and embarrassing a family man caught in that area with his wife and kids.

With the new directions, we finally got to Uncle Okla's apartment. He was glad to see us but a little nervous and distracted. He was apparently busy with party guests. The women in his apartment wore pretty, low cut dresses and high heels and they laughed a lot. The men were all in suits with cocktail glasses in their hands. There was loud music, the clinking of glasses and an occasional outburst of male laughter. We only stayed a short while and left.

As we left, Mama's normally good humor returned for the rest of the day. Before going home, Daddy drove us out on 24 Highway to one of those new ice cream places called the Dairy Queen and bought us all one of the biggest ice cream cones I had ever seen. It was delicious.

To read these stories you might think my parent's marriage was one of conflict. You would be wrong. The good times far outweighed the bad. Over the years, stories like the above made rich fodder for family humor. However, stories about the old rockers were not mentioned in Mama's presence and as I recall not in Daddy's presence either. There was give and take, fun times and sorrow, in their marriage, all the things that make marriage a rich partnership. Perhaps, the reason marriages such as theirs grew rich in memories and lasted is because they both, and I emphasize both, cared more for the family unit than about themselves. I doubt that divorce ever occurred to them.

Uncle Ira's Kids

Thelma was the second child of Uncle Ira and Marguerite's nine children and the first daughter. She was two years younger than her brother Ira, who was the oldest child. Thelma was only five months older than I was, but she had, by far, more work and more responsibilities than I ever did. At home, I helped with the dishes and dusting or sweeping and other little odd jobs but nothing of great consequence, beyond feeding the cat or dog, I had few responsibilities at that age. By the time she was twelve, Thelma had five younger brothers and sisters, two more came later. By then, she was an old hand at baby sitting, cleaning, changing diapers, and bottle-feeding babies with ease, and of course, cooking. She did a lot of that.

At twelve, she could fry potatoes better than anyone I've ever known. My sister, Jean and I often watched and admired Thelma's ability to cook. If we could help we would, but usually we just waited for her to get finished with her chores so we could all three go to play. Thelma peeled those big white potatoes, and sliced them thin and round, into one of the biggest frying pans I have ever seen. It was a thin steel skillet with deep sides. First, she popped a big chunk of white lard into the skillet. As the lard melted, she loaded the skillet, heaping full with the sliced potatoes, and stirred them with a spatula without dropping a single slice over the side. Jean and I marveled that she could do that. After a time, with frequent stirring, the potatoes came out steamy tender and crisply brown on the bottom. She served them with hamburger steaks and white gravy. Uncle Ira was especially fond of sliced canned peaches and they were often a part of the meal. That must have been a favorite meal because that's all I remember seeing Thelma cook. The whole McIntyre family would gather around a long kitchen table for their supper meal, and in short order, the bowls of food were empty. I vaguely recall that Thelma could also bake a good pie.

After supper, Thelma was free to join Jean and me for long bicycles rides or other games around the Fuller and Roberts Street neighborhoods.

We older cousins attended a Lutheran Church for Sunday school back in the 30s. On one particular Sunday, Thelma and I were both ten years old and spoiling for mischief. As part of the routine Sunday school practice at our church, all the classes came together for singing at the end of Bible study. On this particular Sunday, Thelma and I had already made plans. As the music started, I looked at Thelma and her eyes sparkled in agreement. We waited for the song we knew was coming. The preacher had chosen that Sunday to visit the youth group and lead the singing. Finally, the song we were waiting for came up. It was "Bringing in the sheaves. bringing in the sheaves. We shall come rejoicing bringing in the sheaves". The music started, voices rose in sweet harmony and Thelma and I sitting close together in crime, belted out our own special revised version of the lovely old hymn. When the chorus came round, we sang, "Shucking In the corn. Shucking in the corn. We shall come rejoicing shucking in the corn." We sang it with gusto and we sang it loud. As each chorus came around, we did it again and again. The song ended. We waited. We looked at each other. Nothing happened. No rebukes, no recriminating looks. We had been so bad and we weren't caught. It was marvelous. We caught each other's arm and walked out, but I could not resist looking at the preacher as we passed by him and sure enough, he was looking at us, but oddly enough, he didn't look angry. Indeed, quite the opposite, he too had a merry look in his eyes.

The Big Muddy

The Missouri River, around the Kansas City area, is a swift, treacherous, muddy river, full of whirlpools, sand bars, and an ever-changing course. How Aunt Eva and her family wound up living on an island in the middle of that big muddy river during the late 1930's is a question to me. However, that was Aunt Eva's way. She was one of the sweetest women in the world, a caring, undemanding, moral and dependable woman, but she was also unpredictable.

During my growing up years, Aunt Eva lived alternately in northwest Arkansas and Kansas City, Missouri. She would be in Arkansas for a year or so, and then the next thing we knew she would be riding in with her kids to our house at 504 Fuller with a truckload of furniture and other belongings and move back to Kansas City. Jean and I looked forward to those visits in Kansas City because Aunt Eva's girls were close to the same age as we were, and we knew when they showed up that we were in for some good times.

One day, Jean and I (we were quite small) got the idea that Aunt Eva was coming to Kansas City. We were so convinced of the idea that we went to the corner of Fuller and Roberts Street to watch for her. After a long wait, to our delight, we saw this big, stake bed, three quarter ton truck come rolling down the street and there she was, Aunt Eva and her children waving and calling to us out the open truck windows. I have often wondered if perhaps there might have been some subtle hints from our parents to nudge us in that direction, but at the time, it seemed quite magical.

Aunt Eva was a marvelous cook. As I recall, she was partial to fried chicken, mashed potatoes, green beans, corn on the cob, and blackberry cobbler. It makes my mouth water to think of Aunt Eva's cooking.

She was my mother's sister and 13 years Mama's senior, but Mama worried about Aunt Eva. Daddy, on the other hand, got a kick out of her unpredictable lifestyle. He had a song he liked to sing to her. It was "She'll be comin round the mountain when she comes." I can remember him singing other parts of the verse, "She'll be wearin red pajamas when she comes," and "We'll all go out and meet her when she comes." Then he would grab her up (she was tiny) and swing her around and Aunt Eva would laugh that special laugh that she had. Her laugh was hearty and infectious and somehow wound up sounding like a hen cackling. When she laughed, everyone laughed.

One of my earliest memories is standing outside on the front porch at 504 Fuller with Mama and several other people. Aunt Eva and Uncle John had lived there up to that time. I had to be less than five. Mama was begging Aunt Eva not to leave Uncle John and go to Arkansas. Aunt Eva was leaving, just she and the children, that very day with her good friends, Sam and Bea Reeves, who were also moving to Arkansas. Aunt Eva and Uncle John were separating after six children and 14 or so years of marriage. At that time, Uncle John and Aunt Eva owned the house there at 504 Fuller and we lived next door at 506 in a much smaller house. Uncle John was behind on his house payments and was about to lose the 504 house but Daddy agreed to take over the payments and the house became our house.

Mama didn't blame Aunt Eva for leaving Uncle John. She had good reasons to leave him. Uncle John had gotten involved with another woman, and had married the other woman while he was still married to Aunt Eva. Aunt Eva adored Uncle John and the betrayal was almost more than she could endure. Perhaps, that is what motivated her to take the drastic step of moving out of state to Arkansas. Whatever Aunt Eva's motive was, she would not be swayed from it, and Mama's pleadings were ignored.

When some years later, Aunt Eva moved to the Island, I was twelve or so. It must have been about 1938 or 40. Aunt Eva's oldest daughter, Ina, was married, her only son, Johnny, lived away from home, (Eula had died when she was ten) and Shirley, the next oldest must have been about 15. Shirley matured young, and at 15, seemed almost an adult. The rest of us, Jean, Betty, Ruthie and I, were still immature and tomboyish. We loved to run barefoot in the sun and play, and that is what we did on the Island.

The Island was located off a remote and lonely stretch of road not far from Sugar Creek, Missouri on the outskirts of Kansas City. There were no neighbors for miles, no electricity, no phone, or running water, but Aunt Eva managed to make her Missouri Island house a comfortable home on that 24 acre somewhat primitive location. There were two other homes on the island. Sam and Bea Reeves had a home there and an old bachelor, who lived alone in a tiny cabin, lived on the property. At one time, there was an old horse named Sadie there, but unfortunately the poor creature got into a patch of wild marijuana and after ingesting a considerable amount of it, she died.

The island was named Rabbit Island but we always called it simply, "The Island." I believe it was named Rabbit Island because of the abundance of wild rabbits native to it. Island tenants often trapped and caged the rabbits. They fed them out and when the time was right, butchered and cooked them for a fine meat dish. There was also plenty of fish to catch for a meal.

Aunt Eva had a vegetable garden on the island. She also raised popcorn. Betty and Ruthie had a small popcorn stand on a road directly across the river and in season, they sold popcorn to passersby. They shelled the popcorn by hand, rubbing one ear of corn against the other to loosen the kernels. Shelling popcorn in this manner resulted in continuously sore hands throughout the popcorn season. However, it also brought in some cash money.

One morning, Ruthie and I were walking on that remote road when we spied a brand new package of Dentyne Gum on the pavement. Dentyne Gum was a new product at that time. Neither of us had ever tasted it and we were curious. We debated, at some length, whether to chew it or not, because we had heard some scary stories about drug dealers who put drugs into candy in order to get children hooked on narcotics at an early age. We studied the package carefully. We could see that the gum was tightly packaged so we thought it should be safe to chew. We peeled the wrappers back, popped a stick of the pink gum into our mouth, and began to chew. We tasted the spicy flavor of this new product. It was indeed very different from any other gum flavor we had chewed. It had an odd taste but we kept on chewing. Then one of us brought up the news story we had heard about drug dealers lacing candy and gum with narcotics. Our imaginations kicked in and within minutes Ruthie said she felt a little odd and I decided that maybe I felt a little odd too. We had convinced ourselves that we had been duped into chewing narcotic laced gum. We grabbed the gum out of our mouths and threw it on the ground, and sat down by the roadside waiting for the full effects of the drugs to begin. As we waited, something else distracted us and within minutes, we had forgotten all about the gum and we were off on another imaginary adventure.

The main Missouri river channel was on one side of the island and a sluice, which was larger than many rivers I have seen since, was on the other side. The island probably came about as the result of a large scale, federal flood control project in the 1930s to control flooding along the Missouri/ Mississippi River basin. The only way to reach the island from the mainland was by boat across the sluice.

The sluice was by far the more tranquil side of the river, but even there, the water moved with such force that the boat handler had to start rowing about a city block up from their destination point to reach their chosen landing. Even with strong, steady rowing the river current carried the boat far down stream. We girls usually rowed in pairs crossing the swift water, sitting double on the center seat of the old wooden rowboat. One person handled an oar on each side. We soon developed good teamwork and maneuvered the boat quite well. We wore no life jackets (few people did in those days) but we were always cautious and we became strong, proficient, oarsmen. Sometimes we would discuss the pros and cons of what we would do if the boat should capsize. On one occasion, Aunt Eva's youngest daughter, Ruthie, about ten at that time, discovered just how treacherous the Missouri River waters could be. She took the rowboat out in to the sluice alone thinking she could handle it. To her chagrin, Ruthie lost control of the boat and found herself moving ominously down the sluice to the main body of water. A fully grown, strong, man would have been foolhardy to try to negotiate a rowboat in the main channel of that rowdy river at that point, and the little rowboat was moving ever closer to the main channel with Ruthie screaming her lungs out. Finally, some patrons of a local beer tavern near the water's edge saw Ruthie's plight. A group of the men came swiftly to her rescue and Ruthie, overwhelmed with gratitude, fell into their arms in relief.

For the most part, we girls were dependable and well behaved and our parents trusted us. We were allowed to run barefoot and unsupervised, like natives, on the island. We swam in the less treacherous section of the river and laughed as the water sloshed muddy streaks down our faces. We took nature hikes or just wiled away the hours watching tug boats push strings of barges up and down the river and waved at the crews. We all gained many happy memories of our island adventures.

Only once did we almost get in to serious trouble. Later, my cousin, Ruthie, graciously blamed herself for the incident but actually, we were all in it together, me for non-intervention and Jean and Betty for active participation. It all came about because Ruthie got the habit of mixing dry cocoa and sugar to eat from a cup. She often shared this delicacy with me. Not satisfied to eat it with a spoon, she developed her own individual style of imbibing the sweet chocolaty concoction through her teeth. She said this method of sipping, enhanced the flavor, and made it more fun.

Then, she took on the task of teaching me her special sipping technique. I quickly became a chocolate sipping fan. The technique is simple: First, you put a teaspoon of the mixture between your lower front teeth and lip and allow your saliva to moisten the dry mixture. When it is properly moist, you slowly suck it through your teeth and into your mouth, much like dipping snuff. I had to agree that chocolate sipping in this manner added a certain verve and panache to the act and we made quite a game of it.

Ruthie, a charming girl when she chose to be, had another habit that irritated the rest of us. She catered to the grown ups, going out of her way to compliment and be sweet to them. Ruthie was the youngest of Aunt Eva's children, and she may have developed this habit out of self-preservation to compensate for the fact that the older children sometimes, thoughtlessly, left her out of their activities. In our family, the simple fact that she was the youngest child would naturally gain her more attention from our parents than the older, children got. However, Ruthie went even further to endear herself to the older generation, complimenting them and laughing at their jokes. They thought she was the sweetest child ever, but it annoyed us. As a result, we sometimes picked on her for that very reason.

Just how the disagreement between the four of us erupted on that particular day, I am not sure. I think it was because Ruthie refused to share her cocoa mixture with Betty and Jean, or they thought she had swiped their chocolate mixture, I'm not sure how it started, but during the discussion, something was said about Ruthie "shining up" to the grown ups and the argument escalated from there. The end result was that Ruthie, who was probably about ten, still a small, undeveloped girl, flat as a board, got stripped of her clothes and tied, stark naked, to a small tree on the island and left in clear sight of the tug boat crews. To be stripped naked of her clothes was the height of indignity for Ruthie. She may have been young but she was a modest girl and to be put in that state of undress for all to see was humiliating to the last degree.

Although I did none of the stripping or tying, I also did absolutely nothing to stop it. Then the three of us, Betty, Jean and I, partners in crime, walked glibly away and left Ruthie there, tied up and begging to be freed. We had not left her long before Adrian Reeves, Bea and Sam's older son, caught up with us and told us, in no uncertain terms, to get back there and untie her or he was going to tell on us. Well, we certainly did not want that, and we lost little time in hurrying back to Ruthie, getting her untied and helping her to get dressed. After she settled down a bit from her embarrassing ordeal, Ruthie, in her usual charitable manner, quickly forgave us. Looking back, I can see no excuse for our bad behavior. It was totally out of character and a dreadful way to behave, but that story became another family favorite with Ruthie, who grew up to become a vice president for the prestigious Bank of America in California, laughing as hard as any of us as we told, and retold the story many times over through the years.

After their divorce, Uncle John and Aunt Eva both remarried to other people, but none of the family believed they ever cared as much for anyone else as they did for each other. Therefore, while it may have seemed ironic to those outside the family, the immediate family was not surprised when Uncle John and Aunt Eva, in their late 50s, after years of acrimony and hardship for Aunt Eva, and after their children were grown, remarried. They lived out the rest of their lives to the ages of 78 and 79 happily married in Arkansas.

The Cliff Drive Incident

During my young life, growing up in Kansas City, there was a decidedly strained relationship between Italians and Caucasians. Many Americans, at that time, believed that if you were Italian you were very likely part of the notorious "black hand" gang later called the Mafia.

The Kansas City Italians, most of whom were well off financially, were a proud people in general. They obviously didn't care what the Caucasians thought. They wanted nothing to do with Caucasians anyway. Many of the older generation did not speak English. They established their own neighborhoods and businesses, and went about their lives, doing very little to correct their gangland image.

The Mafia was known to have a stronghold in Kansas City, and it was rumored to have a heavy population in areas of a scenic road named Cliff Drive. Cliff Drive was only a short distance from our house.

When Mama recovered from her surgery and the ill-fated after effects of the staph infection, she suffered a "nervous breakdown." She was afraid to leave the house and experienced symptoms of depression. No one even thought of a psychiatrist but Mildred took matters in hand. She planned situations that forced Mama back in to social events. Daddy bought a yellow Chevrolet convertible with a rumble seat. Even though it wasn't new, Mama was thrilled with it. When Mama had a bad day, Mildred would practically drag her out of the house for a drive. Eventually, going shopping and joy riding once more became fun for Mama.

Lillian "Bill" and her yellow roadster

One afternoon, she and Mildred took a scenic ride along Cliff Drive, in a wealthy immigrant Italian neighborhood. It was a beautiful drive, with hills and outcroppings of limestone, beautiful lawns and fine homes.

Mildred and Mama were not driving carelessly or fast, but as they maneuvered through the winding streets, a small dog ran out in front of the car. Mildred veered the car and tried to miss the little dog but could not avoid hitting it. She slammed on the brakes to stop the car and both she and Mama got out to see what they could do for the animal. Suddenly, the entire neighborhood of Italian women came rushing out of their houses. They were shrieking in angry Italian words and shaking their fists at Mama and Mildred. Images of the rumored Italian Mafia or "Black Hand" organization raced through Mama and Mildred's thoughts.

Only that week another news story of a drive-by shooting involving Italian gangsters was headlined on the front page of the Kansas City Star Newspaper. Mildred and Mama were so frightened that they immediately jumped back in the car and sped away from the screaming women. When they were safely within two blocks of home, the humor of the situation hit them and they laughed so hard they had to stop the car. Laughable though it was, they avoided that neighborhood from that day on.

Grandmother Knight Comes to live with us

I was about 13 when Grandmother Knight suffered a massive stroke and came to live with our family. She must have been predisposed to strokes because she had several before she died. The strokes disabled her physically but did not impair her mental abilities. No one in my family was particularly happy about her move to our home, but none of her other children would take her into their homes.

My sister, Jean and I didn't know Grandmother. We had seen her so seldom over the years, that she was a stranger to us, and we didn't look forward to a stranger living with us. Grandmother's children, Uncle Okla, Aunt Vera, Daddy and Uncle Noel had all met at a tourist cabin to discuss who would take her in. Uncle John refused to attend the meeting and made no apologies about it. He still harbored bitter memories of serving time in jail after Grandmother Knight falsely accused him of shooting his father.

Homer Knight and his mother Lillie Culver, 1939

"You know who will have to take her, don't you?" Mama asked Daddy before we arrived at the tourist cabin.

"You don't know that," Daddy answered.

At the time of her stroke, Grandmother was married to a Mr. Culver, a lawyer who was serving time in prison for some kind of fraudulent activity in which he had been involved. He couldn't help her. There were no special nursing home programs or other public health programs for the sick and elderly. Therefore, Grandmother's care was solely the responsibility of her family, or in our case, my Dad.

One of the first things that Grandmother did, after she moved in, was to censor all the mail that came into the house. She would come hobbling in on her crutch to the living room early in the morning and wait patiently for the mail delivery. She then sorted through it and removed all letters addressed to my Dad. She hand delivered them to him when he arrived home. Most of his mail was advertisements, bills and similar items that

Daddy did not want to look at. Mama just ignored Grandmother's mail sorting activities and eventually Daddy got annoyed with it and told Grandmother to "just give that stuff to Bill," he didn't want to be bothered with it. Mama handled all of that stuff, he said.

Grandmother practiced a number of other little annoyances such as thinking she needed to chaperone all of my and my sister, Jean's young visitors when they dropped by to see us, but the height of my chagrin, the thing I had the most difficulty overlooking, was her homemade sauerkraut. Anyone who has been around homemade sauerkraut will know immediately what I'm talking about but the uninitiated person who has never smelled this process could not be expected to know the height of embarrassment this process caused me.

To make sauerkraut, cabbage is cut finely. It is then, salted heavily and stored in a very large crock jar, with a lid to cover it. In Grandmother's case, she kept the jar under her bed. All was well as long as the lid was on the jar but when it was removed, a most unpleasant odor wafted out of the jar and filled the entire house with a most unpleasant and foul odor. At first, it wasn't so bad and we didn't notice it much. Then one day, my mother and I were sitting in the kitchen when this dreadful odor filled the room. "Oh my, what in the world is that," Mama asked. She fanned the air with her hand, looked accusingly at our old Collie dog and immediately threw him out of the house. When the smell continued to crop up at odd moments and it began to be a problem, we finally tracked down the cause. It was Grandmother's sauerkraut. When the sauerkraut fermentation process was underway, Grandmother would lift the lid on it daily or more often.

My big problem with the kraut making was that Grandmother seemed to choose the very moments when my friends came by to pull the old crock jar out from under her bed and remove the lid. I thought she purposefully left the lid off overly long. When that happened, and the penetratingly foul odor filled the room, the strangest look would come across my friends' faces. They would stop talking in mid sentence and look cautiously around. At this point, I would hurriedly explain that my grandmother made sauerkraut and she had obviously removed the lid to the crock jar. That, I explained, is what they smelled. After a while, they all knew what was going on and when the offensive smell invaded the house, we would, in spite of ourselves, burst helplessly into gales of laughter.

Childish behavior perhaps, and not an especially acceptable behavior, but what else could we do?

After a couple of years, Grandmother was finally able to live on her own, and Daddy found a reasonably priced rent house for her that he could afford to pay. Grandmother had also, by that time, started receiving a small pension check of some sort. The rent house was large enough so that she eventually was able to rent a couple of rooms to a young couple to help cover the rent. Since her health had improved that allowed Grandmother to be somewhat independent, and I, for one, was certainly happy for her.

Learning Life's Hard Lessons

In 1945, when I was nineteen, I thought I was pretty much in control of my life. Not that I was overly confident, things had not always gone my way. However, I had a good job, a fair social life, and generally speaking, I had been through enough to consider myself a competent person. So I thought, as I said, at this point in my life I was pretty much in control. It took only one chaotic, brutal evening to change my mind.

That evening started out bad, and I should have listened to my more intuitive self that screamed at me to go home. I didn't really want to go out that evening but my cousin Betty's husband was home from World War 2 and she wanted to go out for an evening of fun. The war had ended in August but it was November before her husband, Dub, got home.

I had a couple of reasons for not wanting to join Betty and Dub on their night out. One reason being that I knew Dub never liked me. I wasn't sure why but I knew it was true and I accepted it. Another reason I resisted was that I was between boyfriends and I didn't have a date. I never mentioned my first reason for not going, and Betty dismissed my not having a date as a good reason. She said, it would be the three of us and we would have a good time. Her enthusiasm was hard to resist, so I agreed to join her and Dub for the evening out.

When I arrived at Betty's place, she had heard me come in the downstairs door, and she and Dub met me coming down the stairs. Betty came down first. She was all smiles and ready for a good time, but behind her Dub's face was like a rain cloud, a glum mask of simmering anger. He was still in uniform. As part of the Army Reserve, he was required to wear it. One look at Dub's face and I wished I could turn around and leave. I knew something was not right but it was a little late for me to back out gracefully.

Betty grabbed my arm. It was easy to be swept-up in her happy mood, and off we went for an evening of fun, we thought. On our way downtown, we swung by some friend's house to see if they wanted to join us for the evening but they didn't. They later said it was because they could see that Dub was in a foul mood.

I had expected that we would go to a nightclub or some place with music and dancing, or a floorshow, but Dub was doing the choosing and he took us straight to a downtown bar. It was a no frills, beer joint, with a long L-shaped bar lined with men drinking beer. Betty and I looked at each other, not sure what to think, but we decided to be good sports and humor Dub in his choice of entertainment, at least for a while.

We had not been there long before Betty and I began to be bored. We played the jukebox and chatted, but we were sending each other signals that we were ready to leave the place when a uniformed soldier seemed to materialize out of nowhere. He came over and sat down close to Betty. I don't know if Dub knew the soldier but he didn't seem to. The soldier moved even closer to Betty and began an animated conversation.

I was concerned that Dub, who was normally a jealous husband, would get angry and start a ruckus with this other soldier, but he didn't. In fact, he was unusually cordial to him. In short order, Betty's conversation with the soldier turned from animated and friendly to argumentative and loud. I am not sure to this day, what it was about, but it escalated quickly and I was concerned by the intensity of it. It was unusual for Betty to start an argument with a complete stranger. I couldn't quite follow the gist of the conversation but it was heated. I could see the soldier was goading Betty into a verbal fight, and to my consternation, Dub was doing absolutely nothing about it, in fact, appeared oblivious to what was happening. I decided it was time to put a stop to this ridiculous situation, and I got between the soldier and Betty and began nudging her toward the door. We were outside the door but the soldier had followed us out still arguing loudly. It was clear to me that things were getting out of control and I was looking for a City bus stop so that Betty and I could get aboard and get out of there.

As I searched the area for a bus stop, Dub came out of nowhere and grabbed my arm. He pulled me away from Betty, and was ushering me down the dark street away from the tavern. I could not understand this chain of events. Here was this man whom I knew did not like me, practically dragging me down the street, away from a gathering crowd and leaving his wife in front of a beer joint arguing loudly with a complete stranger. Dub was muttering something to me about getting us out of there but I wasn't hearing too clearly what he said because I was too confused about what was going on to hear anything. I finally jerked loose from him and headed back to Betty but Dub got there ahead of me. Before I knew it, to my utter amazement, I saw him grab Betty, draw back a doubled up fist and slug her in the face. I had never heard the sound of a fist hitting someone in the face before and it was a sickening thud. At that point, I was no longer thinking, I was just moving, trying to do something, anything to stop this awful fighting. I managed to get a hold on Betty and drag her away but she was addled from the beating and angry beyond control. Once free of Dubs grasp, she ran back into the tavern and was behind the bar rummaging around, searching for something. "What are you doing," I screamed at her. "I'm looking for a gun," she said. "They always keep one behind the bar," her voice was deadly serious. I froze for a minute and I was never more convinced that if Betty found that gun, Dub would be a dead man.

I may not have known what she was looking for, but the bartended certainly did. He was there, before I could make a move, pushing Betty out and away from behind the bar. "Oh no. you don't," he warned her and told us to get out.

We had no choice then but to go back out the door, and Dub was there, waiting. We no sooner cleared the door, and he was on Betty again, slugging her senseless. My attempts to free Betty or do anything to stop his assault were pitifully inadequate. Somewhere during this assault, the soldier had disappeared. I'm not sure if that was before or after the police car pulled up. But, to my relief, there the squad car was and two police officers rolled out of the car. At last, I thought our dilemma was over. My relief was short lived because this one cop was barely out of the car door when I heard him say, "That's okay soldier I know just how it is." Absolutely, dumbfounded, I watched him as he took Betty by the arm and shoved her into the squad car. What is going on here, I thought? Everyone was ignoring me and little by little, my brain began to function.

If there was one thing my mother stressed to us girls, repeatedly, when we were teenagers, it was that whatever happened when we were out together, we should always stick together. There was safety in numbers, she said. I was remembering that statement, and again, without stopping to think, I walked around to the other side of the police car, and got in the back seat with Betty. I worried that the door would be locked but it wasn't. No one told me to get out. Later, in court, the arresting officer said I chased the car three blocks and jerked the car door open to get in. Although that never happened, the statement triggered a bit of levity at the court hearing, and the image of myself racing down three dark City blocks in high heels chasing a police car; added a bit of comic relief to the Monday morning court hearing.

In the police car, Betty and I were driven downtown to the City jail. We were fingerprinted, photographed and booked into jail. At one point, the arresting officer called us both a "couple of dames". My frustration at this entire, senseless mess boiled up, and anger at his unfair statement took over. I threw my purse in the floor and asked him how he dared to call us dames. I may have called him a big jerk, and a few other words but I didn't use any profanity. He also mentioned that little exhibition in court.

Betty and I were the first women in the large round jail cell that night but about midnight, the local ladies of the evening and other women of dubious character began to filter in to the cell. This was something new to Betty and I and we watched them with curiosity. Then abruptly Betty and I were singled out, removed from the main jail cell. We were removed to a private cell with white sheets and clean bunks. We later learned why.

While Betty and I were being hauled off to jail, Dub had gone to Aunt Eva's house and told Betty's family his own concocted version of what had happened. He told them that Betty had gotten drunk and was completely was out of control. He had to subdue her, he said. For some reason they believed him. Ruthie came by the jail for a brief moment and seeing Betty in her addled, half-conscious state from the beating, she assumed that Betty was drunk. From there, she went to my folk's house and repeated Dub's story. Mama and Daddy listened and then promptly said they didn't believe one word of it. Mama called a lawyer immediately, and the lawyer, who knew our family, said that while he couldn't do anything until the next morning, he could see to it that we were treated well, thus explaining our removal from the main jail cell to private quarters.

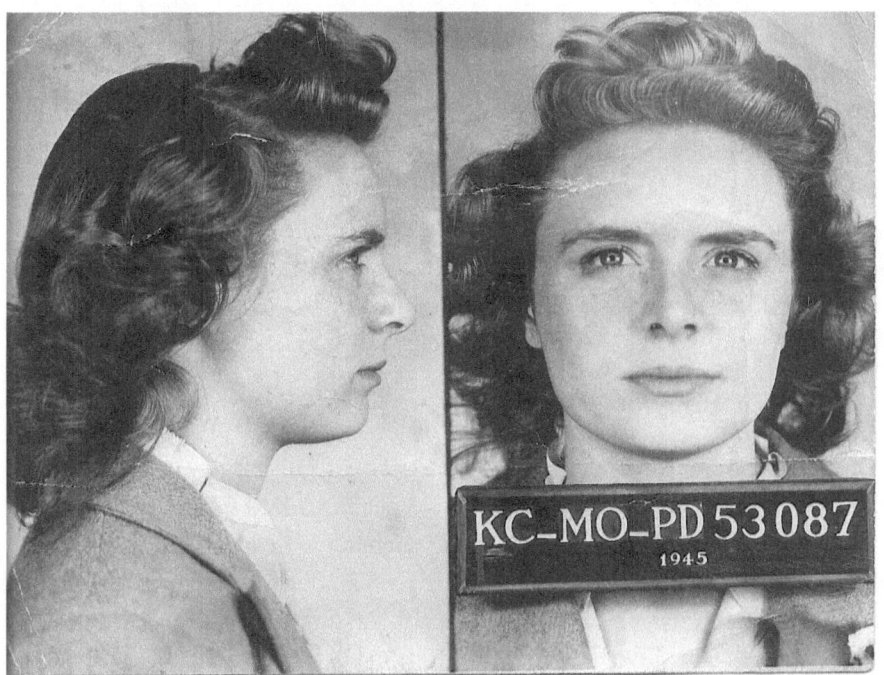

Muril Knight 1945

The next morning, Sunday, Betty and I were released. Aunt Eva and Dub were there early to take us home. Mama had called Aunt Eva to tell her we were released and because Aunt Eva lived closer, she and Dub were at the jail before Mama and Daddy got there. When we arrived at Aunt Eva's house, she began to question and lecture Betty, with Dub standing there. That was a mistake because I was immediately angry. I contradicted everything Dub had said. I turned to glare at him and staring him right in the face, I described the entire evening in detail. I dared him to contradict me. He didn't. Almost immediately, Mama and Daddy came into Aunt Eva's living room and took me home.

As a result of the Monday morning court hearing, Betty and I were cleared of all charges. The arresting officer was reprimanded and demoted to a less desirable position. About six months later, I got a call from the police department. It was one of the male file clerks asking me some foolish questions and then asking me if I wanted my mug shots from the police files. I said yes and he sent them to me, but not before trying to arrange to meet me somewhere. That didn't happen but I did get the mug shots, in the mail.

About five years later, I was married with children, when Betty called me and thanked me for standing by her that evening. She said she was not sure she would have done the same for me. I appreciated her gratitude but confessed that I had often thought I acted stupidly in staying there that evening. It would have been wiser to leave and get help, I said. I confessed further that everything had happened so quickly that night that I was not in control, acting only on reflex and impulse. Very little thought went into anything I did and though I appreciated her gratitude, I didn't really deserve it. After our little talk, we were both able to laugh about that disastrous evening and another misadventure was added to our collection of family stories.

Missouri to Texas

September 1946 Kansas City, Missouri.The day was perfect fall weather in Kansas City, Missouri, a warm day filled with sunshine and bright autumn colors. Recent frost had turned tree leaves to myriad shades of yellow, burnt orange and burgundy and they rustled noisily in the wind. I spent the afternoon riding double on a motorcycle around northeast Kansas City. That night about 10 p.m., I was aboard the Twin Star Rocket, a sleek ultra modern, fast train headed for Houston, Texas, an unplanned, spur of the moment trip, the type of thing I was more and more prone to do in those days following World War II.

Muril Knight 1946

To say I was restless and lacking direction would have been an understatement. The war started when I was 15. For four years, my social and work life was structured around war related activities. While most Americans in the 1940s were expecting European hostilities with Germany to boil over into the United States, no one was prepared when Japan bombed American facilities at Pearl Harbor Dec.7, 1941. When President Franklin D. Roosevelt called for an all-out declaration of war on two fronts, both Germany and Japan, that same year, this country was thrown head first, largely unprepared, into World War II, a full-fledged confrontation that we thought would end all wars.

Now it was over, and let there be no doubt, I was glad to see the fighting and dying ended, but nonetheless, my lifestyle was derailed. My job as an overhead crane operator at Alcoa was fazed out, my circle of girlfriends, which included several married girls, had eroded. Their husbands were home now, or coming home. They had formerly been free to spend time going to nightclubs, partying at each other's homes and so forth, but with the war over, my girlfriend's focus turned solely to husbands who were either home or on their way home. In my wartime patriotism, I had developed the habit of dating military men almost exclusively. Now, those young men were headed to their respective homes in other states. I found myself temporarily footloose, out of the circle, needing to make adjustments to begin a new life. However, it was difficult to find that new direction.

And there were memories! My dear friend, Denzil O. "Denny" Barber, the first boy to propose to me, a beautiful, idealistic, dark-haired, brown-eyed Marine died on a filthy battlefield on the island of Iwo Jima in the Japanese war zone. He was 18 and I was 15 when he left for boot camp. He asked me to wait for him until the war was over. I never saw him again. We were, of course, too young to be so serious and to be honest, I wasn't, but nevertheless, I wrote to him regularly, always careful to send bright, cheerful letters. I couldn't believe it when he died after four years of dirty ground fighting, battle after battle in the Japanese sector, just a few months short of the war's end. Raymond Mitchell, a tall, athletic neighbor boy came home a paraplegic in a wheel chair. Our old friend Robert Salley, my sister's first boyfriend, had been a prisoner of war in the German sector. When the war was over, there was very little wild celebrating in our neighborhood. We were grateful to see the war over, but there was also overshadowing sadness, too many gold stars signifying a son lost to the war hung in the neighboring windows. Later on, we would throw off the melancholy and celebrate but it took a while.

On April 13, 1945, my cousin Ruthie Knight wrote in her journal that she later shared with me. She wrote; "The President died yesterday evening at 3:30. It came as a tremendous shock to me and a despairingly dark foreboding for the future. Truman (Vice President Harry S.) was sworn into office at 7:30 last night. I was at work when the news came. Tomorrow we get off from work at 3:00 o'clock as a tribute to a great man, Franklin D. Roosevelt.

I wonder if this will effect Edward's (her boyfriend) coming home sooner or later.

Johnny (her brother) came home from New Guinea Sat.23rd and Cleo (her sister's husband) came in Wed 20th from Panama. That was in March. I was happy to see them both.

Johnny finally obtained a divorce from Emily Daniels Wed.11th. He expects to marry Rose Mary Powers tomorrow.

Denzil Barber was wounded and died in the hospital at Iwo Jima. The telegram came Sat.7th. I did not go to Muriel's house until Sun. about 12:00. Edward is now in Germany. He has crossed the Rhine and will be in combat anytime. First, he went to France, then Belgium, then Germany.

Billy Hicks is engaged to be married to Charlene (cousin) McIntyre. Charlene got home from the hospital Tues. 10th. after being operated on for appendicitis.

Today is Sandra's (her niece) birthday."

In that same journal, a month later, she wrote in the first paragraph, "May 7, Monday 1945. Hooray the war is over in Europe and I don't have to work tomorrow. I also got a letter from Edward. What more could a girl ask for in one day."

It had been fun riding the motorcycle all over town that autumn afternoon; I think it was a Saturday. Horace King, we called him only King, a family friend, had come by the house at 504 Fuller to show us his new "Harley Hog", a big, first-class, Harley-Davidson Motorcycle that was his pride and joy. He asked me to go for a ride and without a second thought, I hopped on the back of the motorcycle behind him. King was younger than I was by a couple of years and, at 19, I thought him too young to be considered a boyfriend. King had a birth defect. Looking at one side of his face you might have thought him handsome. However, the other side of his face was twisted and distorted and he was very sensitive about it. I could tell he was pleased to have me riding with him, not because I was so special but because some girls were repelled when they saw King's face and made no effort to hide it. His feelings would be terribly hurt. We rode around to several of his friend's places that day pretending I was his girlfriend. He was showing off his motorcycle and me to his friends. I went along with his charade to please him. It was not a problem for me. King was just a nice kid to me. I had no serious romantic attachments and I liked him. He was a good friend. A few months later, I was glad I had done it because he attempted suicide by shooting himself in the stomach. I had no idea he was that unhappy. He lived but the wound caused some sort of abnormal reaction that started him growing again and he grew to almost giant proportions.

If someone had told me I was going to Texas that same September afternoon, I would have thought them crazy. It came about because Mildred, my mother's long-time, best friend had been visiting us from Texas for a couple of weeks. Now she was going home. Mildred and her husband Willis (Red) Stone, close family friends, had moved to Texas in 1940 from Independence when World War 2 was brewing in Europe. Most Americans could see the war with Germany coming and, companies like Sheffield Steel, where Red and my Dad worked, were expanding facilities into other states like Texas, building new modern plants to accommodate the war when and if it came. Plant managers had asked my dad to go and head up the construction of a new foundry near Houston but he chose not to go because of family ties. Red and Mildred, on the other hand, had no strong ties to Kansas City, and welcomed the opportunity to help organize the fledgling mill and advance Red's career.

I can't remember what prompted me to join Mildred on her return trip to Texas but there I was, aboard the Twin Star Rocket, a sleek, super-fast train, that originated in the twin cities of Minneapolis/St. Paul, Minnesota. It stopped briefly in Kansas City, Missouri and ran overnight to Houston, Texas. The Rocket was a beautiful train with a fresh, new look, nicely upholstered seats and fine dining cars. The waiters dressed in black uniforms, starched white shirts and ties.

Military men, returning home from the war, crowded the coach cars that night with many standing three deep in the aisles. We assumed they were soldiers returning from the war fronts. They appeared bone weary, exhausted. I'm sure they had probably been traveling for days. Even so, a couple of the men who were seated got up and, though we protested, gave us their seats. I wonder if such chivalry still exists in this modern day. The train left Kansas City that night about 10:30 or 11 p.m. It was my first train ride and I was excited as I stepped aboard. We got off the train about 1 p.m. the next afternoon in Houston, Texas, and I unknowingly, stepped in to that new direction I had been looking for. I never guessed then that I would meet the man I would marry, a year later, on that very day.

Sept.1946 Channelview, Texas

World War II was over and Troy H. Hart, aka Curly, was back in his hometown of Channelview, Texas after military service in the United States Navy from Jan.4, 1945 to July 22,1946. He was an Electrician's Mate 3rd class aboard the U.S.S. Keersarge, a newly commissioned aircraft carrier.Troy was proud and a little excited to be part of the originating crew for the giant carrier. Launching fighter planes from the middle of the ocean was a relatively new innovation to warfare during World War II. It had not been done on a large scale before. The Keersarge was 888 feet long and housed almost 4000 men. The flight deck was 870 feet long and the ship had nine decks.

Troy H. Hart
U.S. Navy 1945

Even before being drafted into the Navy, Troy had tried at age 17 to volunteer for military service, but because of his young age, he was required to have written permission from his parents to enlist. With one older son already in the U.S. Coast Guard, Troy's parents were reluctant to put another son in harm's way, so they refused to sign. However, at 18, he was drafted, and given the choice of his branch of service. It was not surprising that Troy chose the Navy. Although he was born in North Central Texas in a small town named Holiday, the family moved when he was small and he grew up on the Gulf Coast waterfront in Aransas Pass, a coastal fishing community. The second son of a poor family, he got his Social Security Card when he was 11 and went to work in a shrimp house, heading shrimp. He worked and played as a child around the waterfront. His older brother, Coy, eight years his senior, was in the U.S. Coast Guard, and was for a time the lighthouse keeper at Port Aransas. Troy was familiar with both large and small ships and other seafaring craft. His father, who in his early years was a farmer and carpenter, became a commercial fisherman and then went to work on dredge boats. He worked to help clear and deepen the ship channels for ocean going traffic. Those were the "Great Depression" years and a man did what he could to provide for his family. In 1939, as the Depression years eased and, new and better employment opportunities arose, the family moved to Channelview, a raw, new community that evolved with the discovery of oil in the surrounding areas and the growing importance of the shipping industry out of Houston. Troy and his family lived at 311 Bayou Drive when he was drafted into military service in WWII. After moving to Channelview, he had worked in war-related industry. His first job was at the Houston Shipyards as an outside machinist aboard ships He worked there for a year and moved to work at Brown Shipyards as an electrician. Brown Shipyards sent him to school for in-depth study of the electrical trade, a skill that would serve him well for many years.

After his discharge from the U.S. Navy, and a long wearying trip home, Troy's homecoming was something he said he would always remember. He got off the Greyhound Bus at Old River Terrace Park in Channelview. As the bus door swung open, his old neighborhood buddies came running around to the bus door in a strip-down, Chevy, nearly running him over to greet him. They were whooping, and cheering, "Welcome home". Before he knew what was happening they grabbed him in big bear hugs and a round of friendly back pounding. Someone handed him a bottle of bourbon and tossed his sea bag in to the back of the strip–down. "Get in", they hollered. Troy bolted over the side of the car, into the seat, and was headed down Bayou Drive toward home. It was great to be home, and the Lord knew he was ready to be home. He wanted to see his family to get reacquainted with friends and civilian life. Even before his tour of duty in the Navy, he had put in long evening hours during the war at the Houston Shipyard from 5p.m. to 4 a.m., seven days a week. Those hours left little time for socializing and he couldn't even play hooky from work, as some young men did, because he rode to work with his father. Now, all that was behind him, he was carefree and looking forward to a more relaxed lifestyle. The next few months were spent sleeping late, running around with friends, and having a good rowdy time. He dated a few girls, but none of them seriously. He wanted nothing serious just yet, no one to tell him what to do or when to do it. He was not ready to settle down. He just wanted to be footloose for a while. He was not even seriously looking for a job. Then one evening at Rosie's Bar and Grill, a local, favorite nightspot, Jack Goodson, the owner of a service station was complaining about needing good help to manage his gas station. He asked Troy to take the job. Troy had tentative plans to go back to school and get a degree in electrical engineering, but he knew he wasn't quite ready for the long hard grind that a degree would require. So, after some thought and with nothing better to do at the moment, and possibly needing some extra change in his pockets, he agreed to accept the job as manager of the station but only on a temporary basis.

When the Twin Star Rocket pulled into Union Station at Houston with Mildred and Me aboard, Red was there to meet us. As we drove through Houston it seemed to me that time had been set back a month or so. Everything was green. I had never been this far south and it surprised me to see the grass and trees still green, not the autumn hue I had left in Kansas City; and it was hot. Houston was also a cleaner looking city than Kansas City. Kansas City was a coal-fired city; meaning coal was a chief source for heat and energy. Most homes were heated by coal, trains were fueled by coal and industries like Sheffield Steel and other large industrial companies, not too far from our home, were powered by coal. Smoke stacks and chimneys belched black smoke 24 hours a day and small particles of soot settled on buildings, homes and, laundry hanging outside on the clothes line, making them all a bit grimy (they called it tattletale gray) and hard to keep clean. No one liked the dirty air but it didn't occur to us until years later that we could actively protest against the companies causing the pollution. It was accepted as a necessary side effect to keeping people working. Those were the Great Depression years. People of that time were more involved with keeping their jobs and earning a living than protesting about pollution controls. Kansas City was in 1946 also a much older and larger city than Houston. And, Houston was not the giant megalopolis it is today and its industries must have been fueled by a source different from what was used in Kansas City, because, whatever the reason, in 1946 the city looked markedly cleaner than Kansas City. I also noticed there were fewer sidewalks in the residential areas of Houston. I was accustomed to seeing sidewalks along every street, even along major highways that went through town. For some reason the lack of sidewalks caught my attention and surprised me. Arriving in Channelview was a new experience for me. One of the first things I saw was a drunken cowboy riding a Paint pony down the middle of the main road. Even though I had spent some time in the country around Independence, Mo., I had never seen a cowboy, complete with boots and wide-brim hat, riding a horse in town. It was almost like an early frontier town. All the buildings looked brand new…like a movie set… with one row of stucco shops on the corner of Market Street and Sheldon Road and further down the road, on the opposite side, a string of beer joints and icehouses. The buildings were painted white and the glare of the bright sun on the white shell roads and white buildings was almost blinding. On down the road a short distance, there was a service station. We stopped there for gasoline before driving to Mildred and Red's home on Old River.

The owner and one attendant were at the station along with a couple of young men who were apparently just hanging around. Mildred seemed well acquainted with everyone. She introduced me to the station owner and to the young men and, finally to the one person who seemed to be actually working there. Everyone called him Curly but Mildred introduced him as Troy Hart. I quickly noticed that he was good-looking and had a nice smile but he appeared to be rather shy. He was quick enough to acknowledge our introduction and we exchanged a few polite words but then he went right back to work and if he noticed me further, I couldn't tell. "Oh well", I thought, "Better luck next time."

Troy said later he certainly had noticed me and that he liked what he saw but he was girl shy and not sure enough of himself to try and get better acquainted. He said he was impressed by my self-confidence and liked my open friendly manner, but he never expected it to go anywhere. I guess if a couple of things hadn't happened to change the course of events, it wouldn't have.

A couple of the young men I met a few days later asked me out and I went to a movie with one of them but the other boy was a braggart and had an obviously high opinion of himself. He also asked me out but I thought I knew his type and wasn't particularly interested in going out with him; still, I didn't want to offend any of Mildred's friends so I told him I already had a date. He wasn't satisfied with that, and wanted to know with whom. Without thinking, I blurted out "Troy Hart" and was pleased to think I had settled that. However, Mildred had overheard the conversation and she was not at all pleased with my answer. "You shouldn't have lied to him," she cautioned me. "This is a small place, and Sunny will probably run right over and say something to Troy. Word gets around fast here. You had better call Troy, tell him about it and hope he backs you up."

"Boy," I thought, "this really is small town stuff" but I decided to follow Mildred's advice so I called Troy at the service station and confessed what I considered my little white fib. He listened. There was a pause and I said, "Okay?"

"Sure," he answered, " When shall I pick you up."

Then it was my turn to hesitate. "What do you mean?" I asked.

"Well, if we're going out I need to know when to pick you up." he answered. "How bout tomorrow afternoon? We could go horseback riding."

Horseback riding! That sounded like fun. It had been quite awhile since I was on a horse but I was confident I would enjoy riding again, so I agreed to go. The next day was a sunny afternoon. Troy arrived to pick me up in his old strip down Model "A" truck. I stared at it in amazement. It was truly a jalopy and it must be 20 years old, I thought. The fenders were painted a dull powder blue and there was no hood over the engine.

Troy and his strip down Model A truck

The truck had originally been a four-door sedan; Troy explained as we drove to Jack Goodson's service station where the horses were tied. However, sometime back, he wrecked it in a collision. The collision occurred one night when he and his buddy, Milton "Speedy" Brasher, were returning home from a "big party" in Houston.

They had turned off the main highway on to the road home. Speedy was driving and the night was dark. He failed to see that the road was under construction and crashed into the ripped-up roadbed. The right wheel struck a slab of concrete rubble throwing the car up and over. Troy, who was asleep in the back seat, hit his head on the plywood top of the old sedan. He was knocked semi-conscious. He was out of the car and walking around but not aware of what was going on. Speedy was not seriously injured. Another motorist happened along, loaded the young men into his car and took them to the home of a doctor in Baytown. Troy said he came to himself and was aware of his surroundings as they were ringing the doctor's doorbell. The doctor apparently wasn't at home. If he was, he didn't answer the bell. Now, fully conscious, Troy decided he was not seriously hurt and convinced the others to take him home. The next day he and Speedy went back to the site of the wreck. The sedan was a crushed mess but they managed to hook on to it and tow it home. In the process of repairing the old sedan, he decided to convert it into a truck. The back section of the chassis was removed with a cutting torch, moved forward, and welded into place to form the back of the cab. Behind the cab, sheet metal was secured to the car frame, over the back wheels to form the bed of the truck. The engine, he remarked proudly, was in perfect condition. I could easily see that he was proud of the thing. Well, I could appreciate the effort involved in the transformation of the old car to a truck. I too had grown up in hard times during the Great Depression years and understood well the effort involved in making something out of little or nothing. It was certainly not the first jalopy I had ridden in. However, that would be another whole story that I may tell later. Thus far, Troy's and my first date was off to a good start. We seemed to have a great deal in common, but the day was not over and it was not to be without a couple of memorable glitches. Our horseback ride while largely successful hit a snag at one point. Troy was not well acquainted with the two horses he had borrowed for our little excursion. They belonged to his boss, Jack. He knew the mare I was to ride was gentle; so gentle in fact, that it took considerable urging to get her to move. However, the gelding Troy rode was jittery and shied at every turn. A piece of paper blowing across the street would start him humping up in the middle and prancing about like an Irish jig dancer, a sharp noise could start the gelding snorting and break into a wild run. At one point in our ride, these tendencies threatened to cut short any chance that Troy and I might have of being better acquainted. We rode into some heavy brush. I was in the lead on the mare with Troy, on the gelding, close behind me. We came across some low branches that blocked my way and I reached out to move a limb aside. I knew the minute I caught the branch that I had made a big mistake because, to my dismay, it was so tough and springy that I couldn't turn it loose without causing a swift backlash that would probably hit Troy or spook the high-strung gelding into who knew what antics. As I held tight to the branch, I envisioned the calamity that loosing my grip might precipitate. A mental series of unwanted events flashed through my mind. I envisioned the gelding charging off into the woods and in the process dragging Troy to the ground or, the horse rearing up and dumping him hard to the ground, possibly stomping him in the process. Well, what to do, what to do? I couldn't decide. Time seemed to stand still as I worried about my next move. To make matters worse, the mare I was riding, which had not wanted to move earlier, now kept inching forward ever so slightly, making it harder for me to hang on to the limb. The gelding, seeing the mare move ahead, wanted to follow, staying close behind. I felt the branch tighten and begin to slip from my grasp Meanwhile, as my dilemma grew, Troy watched the branch with awe, trying to anticipate the worst. Dreading the consequences but desperate for an end to the dilemma, Troy finally grew impatient. "Just let it go," he yelled. "Let's get it over with!" All of a sudden, the branch flew out of my hand and made its backward swing. With a grand flourish, it lifted and flew swiftly back, shuddered momentarily, and settled into place; and we waited. The gelding pawed the ground in agitation but to our immense relief, nothing happened. The offending branch came short of hitting either the horse or Troy. The gelding shied a bit and then actually settled down. We could hardly believe our good luck. "Whoooee," Troy cried out in relief. "I'm sorry," I said. Slowly, we moved ahead, each absorbed in our own thoughts. Was Troy angry, I wondered? The answer seemed to be no but I wasn't sure. Looking back on it, I thought his "Just let it go," outburst had been rather brusque. Of course, he was nervous, I could understand that, but I hadn't meant for it to happen, and that crazy horse, whose fault was that? Plus, I didn't think it was at all necessary for Troy to say, soon after the crisis had passed, that he wished I had just "not held on to the limb so long." What was he thinking now? I couldn't tell. However, he seemed quite nonchalant, as if nothing had happened. Why didn't he say something? Well, if he wasn't going to say something, I wasn't either. We continued our ride, but the fun had gone out of it for me and we shortly decided to go back to the service station, tie up the horses and go in search of other entertainment. Troy said later that of course he wasn't angry, not at all, perhaps a bit edgy, he said, that was all. He said once he saw me on the mare he knew I had ridden horses before, and I had, but very little. My experience was limited to one horse. My family had moved out from Kansas City, Missouri to a farm in Independence when I was about 14. My sister, Jean, and I each had a horse of our own. My horse was a brown Hamiltonian with a long, black mane and tail, a well behaved but spirited mare. She had a white star in the center of her forehead so we called her "Star". She was an ordinary looking animal until you got a halter and bridle on her. Then, she would arch her neck and prance in a measured gait that set her apart from the other horses. Her back was soft and I often rode her bare back and without a bridle. All she needed for direction was a squeeze of the knees in her side and lacing my hand in her mane to pull it in the direction I wanted her to go. She was a gentle, reliable mare and I was sorry to lose her when we moved back to the city four years later.

Back at Jack's service station, we had a long visit with Jack. Troy told him about the gelding's bad behavior and Jack roared with laughter, at the same time kidding Troy about his horsemanship. Jack had a few stories of his own to tell about the wayward gelding and it was evening before we got away from the station. The horse, Jack said, had been okay until he experienced an injury to his neck that required serious medical attention, including long-term injections in his neck and other painful medical treatments. After its neck finally healed, the horse remained high-strung and the least thing startled him. The visit with Jack had been fun and as we left, Troy was clearly in a good mood. He asked if I would like to see some of the entertainment available in Channelview. No need to change clothes, he said. Our riding clothes would be just fine where we were going. The local nightspots, he said, were mostly family oriented places where neighbors gathered to enjoy a meal, drink a beer or soft drink, listen to amateur musicians perform, or dance to the jukebox. No one dressed up to go there, he said. The casual country atmosphere was intriguing. We stopped in one place that Troy's dad had built that very summer. The place was called The Southern Inn; a nice middle-aged couple from Oklahoma owned it. It was a simple white frame building with wide pine wood floors and lots of open windows and doors. Someone had sprinkled cornmeal on the floor for a smoother dancing surface and a few couples were dancing. Everyone was on a first name basis. We had dinner and danced a little. Several people came by our table to say hello to Troy and meet his new girl friend. Thus far, the evening had been pleasant and I was enjoying myself until at one point, Troy excused himself and left the table for a few minutes. He had barely left when a girl I hadn't met came over and plopped herself down in a chair beside me. She didn't introduce herself but with few preliminaries, said, "See that girl over there," she pointed to a corner table. I looked over to see a rather forlorn looking blonde dabbing at her eyes with a napkin and looking sorrowfully back at me. Puzzled by her odd behavior I said 'Yes'. "Well," the girl continued, "That girl is my friend and she is crazy about Troy. They have been dating and she is terribly upset to see him here with you. I think you should leave him alone."

I sat there, dumbfounded, and looked at her, at a total loss for words. I had little time to react before Troy was back. The girl hurriedly excused herself and returned to her table. I told Troy what she had said.

"What the heck is that all about?" I asked. For some reason I, felt insulted. I couldn't decide whether to get angry or laugh?

"Is she your steady girlfriend or something?" I asked." No," he answered abruptly, obviously irritated. "I went out with her a few times, and that's all there is to it." That was the end of the explanation. He brushed aside any further comment

I was still curious but decided not to question it further. I probably should feel sorry for the girl, I told myself. But I didn't. Was I being callous? Maybe, I'm not sure. The whole scene had been a bit melodramatic for me to take seriously. To the contrary, I was somewhat turned off by the tragic little episode. I didn't know that girl, I rationalized. In fact, I didn't really know Troy that well, and I would soon be going back home anyway. With little effort, I decided it was not my problem and put the girl out of my thoughts. I enjoyed the rest of the evening and there were more dates with Troy. We were together every evening I was there. I didn't understand my attraction to him. He was good looking and comfortable to be with but he was different from the boys I was used to dating. His reserved manner took some getting used to, and he was not big on conversation but he had an easygoing, relaxed manner, we seemed to enjoy many of the same things, and he was attentive with a quick sense of humor and, more importantly, he surely seemed to like me. That was good enough for me. I went back home after two weeks knowing I would like to know him better. I imagined he felt the same about me. We agreed to write each other and hoped there would be another time for us to get better acquainted.

I can't remember what prompted my next visit to Channelview, but it was the middle of April, 1947. Troy and I had exchanged many letters. I had changed jobs and was now a keypunch operator for TransWorld Airlines, (TWA). Keypunch was a relatively new business technology that had come about some time in the '40s. I was company trained by manufacturers of the machines, International Business Machines(IBM). I had also managed to maintain a busy social life. I dated several boys and had a somewhat steady boyfriend, but that restless streak that had prompted my earlier visit to Texas still nagged at me.

Whatever the reason, I found myself once more exiting the Twin Star Rocket at the Houston train terminal. This time it was Troy and Mildred who met me at the station. My friendship with Troy fell back on track as if I had never left. Troy had made changes in his life. He no longer worked at Jack's service station, he had gone into the business of electrical contracting with a friend. He did mostly house wiring. We saw each other every day. Troy introduced me to all his friends, had me over to his parents home for dinner to meet his family and before I left to return home he had asked me to marry him. What he actually said was that his family liked me, his friends all liked me and when was I going to marry him? I don't remember the details but Troy said I answered him by saying that was not a "Yes" or "No" question, but from that point, it was understood that we were engaged. We made tentative plans to get married sometime in September and I returned home. About that same time, my mother had serious surgery and was having difficulty recuperating. My dad decided a trip to Texas and a visit with her old friend, Mildred would be just the thing to revive her spirits and assist her recovery. I suggested she call Troy when she got there and get him to show her around and she did. They became immediate friends and Troy and his buddies took Mama under their wing to insure that she had a good time. It must have succeeded beyond their expectations because she came back home several weeks later well and happy. On the spur of the moment decision, Troy made a big switch in his planned trip to Kansas City in September and joined Mama on her return

trip home in July. Our wedding plans were rescheduled from September to August.

A Baptist minister, Kenneth Lambert, who later joined a part of the famous Billy Graham Evangelist Troup, married us August 10, 1947. It was a simple ceremony at a small church, The Bethel Baptist, on Independence Ave. and Bennington Street.

Wedding, Muril and Troy Hart, 1947

In reflection, it would be easy to ask, what chance did our marriage have to last? The odds were not with us. We hadn't known each other very long. We were from different states. Neither he nor I had a good job at that time although he soon went to work for Sheffield Steel Corp. Neither of us had much money, but married we were and married we have stayed for 62 years with three adult children, five grand children and five great grandchildren at this time in 2009.

This Book
Part iii
The Ancestors

This Book Part 3: The Ancestors*

Maternal Family

The Fishers*
The Pettys*
The McIntyres*
The Tompkins*
The Sisneys *
The Mefford/Masters*

Paternal Family

The Boones*
The Coffees*
The Knights*

The * and bold lettering is used to show direct family lines.

The following family histories are a collection of stories about the McIntyre and Knight families. The information gathered from various sources is an attempt to show the winding paths and circumstances that started in early America and eventually brought the Knight and McIntyre families together about 1914 in Kansas City, Missouri. Credits for help in gathering information for this book are listed in a separate section of this book.

The descendents of Dazerine Petty and Elija Jackson McIntyre like to call their family line the "Daisy Chain". Daisy stands for the descendents of Dazerine Petty McIntyre or "Daisy" as she was known. The word chain represents the strong family links that connects Dazerine's descendents. Shirley Knight Collins of Prairie Grove, Arkansas came up with the name Daisy Chain for a family newsletter written and circulated by Muril Knight Hart, to family members for a number of years.

The Daisy Chain and Knight family ancestors were pioneers of early America. Both sides of the family were among those who spearheaded moves into new uncharted territories and staked claims in unsettled land. They cut trees and built their log homes in untamed forests, and wrested a living from wild country that no white man had before touched. Some were victims of Indian raids. Written records of the families, some dating back to the early 1700s, before this country was settled, support those statements, and mark the families' progress across the unsettled frontiers of early America.

In researching Daisy Chain/Knight ancestry lines, surnames such as Petty, Fisher, Mefford, Coffee, Sisney, Boone and others of our fore-family seem to cross and re-cross in the same time period and the same places. It's interesting to speculate on whether these ancestors may have known each other during those early frontier days of Virginia, Kentucky, Pennsylvania, Ohio, Illinois, North Carolina and Missouri. However, that is something we have no way of knowing.

One thing is clear; those early ancestors in the formative years of America had to be a sturdy lot just to survive the effort of their sojourns into the new frontiers. Horses, or covered wagons pulled by oxen were the choice of travel by land, and quite often hand-built, keelboats, flatboats, and rafts were the choices for down river journeys. The men were hunters, trappers, blacksmith, saddlers, carpenters and farmers, all work that required strength and stamina. The church seems to have figured heavily in their progress across the country with sanctuaries and meeting places established soon after their arrival into new territories. A number of preachers also show up in the Daisy Chain family records

A testimony to the toughness of the women ancestors is the fact that they bore eight to twelve children over their adult lives, averaging one child every two years or so after their marriages, while also managing their wilderness homes and moving from one location to another. The great majority of these women managed to deliver their babies by natural childbirth and lived to be old women but there are some, who apparently were not so fortunate, and judging from the time their babies arrived, and when the mothers died, it is reasonable to assume that childbirth played a part in the early demise of some mothers. Records show that several family members had a sound knowledge of, and practiced herbal medicine in the various generations. Apparently, the knowledge needed to practice herbal medicine was passed down from older generations to the younger generations as the family grew.

There are many fascinating stories associated with siblings of the Daisy Chain and Knight family. Jean Knight Fisher wrote a more comprehensive and expanded genealogy that includes research into extended family genealogy. However, the focus of this book is the direct family lines. Still, there are a few exceptions to that goal when the background of a particular person or something they did played an important role in shaping the lives of direct descendents and where, for one reason or another, it might warrant mentioning.

The Fishers,

An exception to the goal of showing histories of direct-line family ancestors only is the story of Solomon Fisher and the town of Frankford, Missouri, a town owned by Solomon Fisher. A number of Daisy Chain family units came together in Frankford, and members of the direct Daisy Chain line figured heavily in the settling and building of the town, lending significance to the story of the town and its owner. While he was not a direct ancestor, Solomon was a close relative of Dazerine Petty McIntyre's extended family.

Solomon came to Missouri sometime in the early 1800s. He was the first settler in that part of the country. With his family, Solomon and several other families left Kentucky and came down the Ohio River into the Mississippi River. They turned into the Salt River and moved on to the mouth of Peno Creek. Traveling along the banks of Peno Creek, they discovered a large cave with spring water flowing out of it. There, in that cave, Solomon made his home for several years and began laying groundwork for a new town.

In 1818, he laid out the plans, donated and deeded land for the streets, the Public Square and public buildings to build the town. He gave land for a church and a park. Solomon's son, Adam directed much of the work until his premature death in 1825. Solomon then took over. His nephew,*Absolom Petty (the son of his brother, Ebenezer Petty) moved to Frankford and took on a major role in setting up the town.

When Solomon died, a large boulder was taken from his land and placed in the Frankford Park by the Daughters Of The American Revolution. It was inscribed as a monument to Solomon's dedication, and contributions in building Frankford. The stone is still there and Frankford is a thriving small town with a city population of a little over 400 but it also serves a larger agricultural area outside the city limits.

As often happened, in those days of large families and close-knit small towns, a sister and brother of the Fisher family married a sister and brother from the Petty family. In Solomon's case, his sister, Mary Elizabeth, married Ebenezer Petty, previously mentioned, who was Dazerine's great grandfather. Ebenezer's sister, Mary Ann Petty, married Solomon Fisher.

Solomon and Mary Elizabeth were the grandchildren of Sebastian Fisher, a German immigrant and a direct ancestor of the Daisy Chain. He and his family came to America in 1709.

The Fisher Family,

Like many early American immigrants, *Sebastian Fisher came to this country to escape religious persecution and political abuse in his fatherland. Sebastian, his wife Susanna, and their two young sons, were part of a mass exodus from the Palatine region of Germany in the early 1700s. The Palatines were Protestants living in an area dominated by the Catholic Church. Kraig Ruckel, in a genealogical paper (date unknown) wrote the story of the Palatine Emigrants. He begins his paper with, "The winter of 1708-1709 was very long and cold in the Rhineland. It was a bleak period. People huddled around their fires and considered quitting their home and farms forever."

It is noteworthy that ancestors of at least two different families of Dazerine Petty McIntyre's line came to America from the Palatine area of Germany in the 1700s for similar reasons. However, they arrived in America several decades apart. The Sebastian Fisher family arrived in America about 1709 and the *George Mefford family arrived in America 42 years later in 1752. The two families probably didn't know each other in Germany since they seem to have come from different levels of society. The Fishers were a well-educated family with large holdings of land and families of prominent political influence. The Meffords were apparently of the middle working class families. If the two families were acquainted, they went separate ways for several years after landing in America, but much later, in the 1800s both families came together and made their homes in Frankford, Missouri, the town owned by Solomon Fisher.

The Mefford name shows up in the Revolutionary War as well as the Petty, Sisney, Tompkins, Coffee and Boone names. These same names also show up in the Civil War. Daisy Chain ancestors are recorded in the two wars, with soldiers on both sides of the conflicts sometimes within the same family units. Stories from older generations state that family members fought in the War of 1812, the Blackhawk War and several Indian wars, but those records are yet to be proven.

Palatine families did not leave their homelands in Germany willingly. Family histories there dated back hundreds of years. The Fisher family was at one time well placed socially and secure, but thirty-two years of war had taken a heavy toll on their well-being. Since 1702, their country had endured war and the future offered small hope of improvement. It was a period when the Palatines were heavily taxed and endured cruel religious persecution. One out of every three Germans, during those years of unrest, perished.

The first mass emigration of Palatines was about April 1708. The land was still frozen, and most of the Palatine's vines had been killed by the bitter weather when they boarded their small boats and set out down the Rhine River for Rotterdam. Many of the émigrés had only the basic goods they could carry and their faith in God. Queen Anne of England had invited these people to go to England. She promised them that they should be sent later to America to settle in new homes.

Sebastian, a native of Germany, with his wife Susanna and their two small children, embarked for England at Rotterdam, Holland, on June 28, 1708. From Rotterdam, they went to England and from there to America. In early June 1709, Sebastian and Susanna reached New York, but only one of their children had survived the harrowing journey. The hardships and misery from Rotterdam to New York plagued all the emigrants and their troubles did not end upon reaching the English colonies in America.

Sebastian Fisher's circumstance was somewhat different from most of these immigrants. He came from a family prominent in political affairs. Sebastian had somehow become involved in poaching laws. However, there was more to it than infringement of poaching laws. He was heir to a large estate on what is now Hanover. Sebastian had disagreed with those in power and incurred their displeasure. As a result, he was obliged to leave Germany, losing his title and estate. It also necessitated his leaving with only what he could carry with him.

Sebastian was well educated, probably at a German University. He was a man of learning and reportedly a man of courage and tenacity of purpose. When the emigrants landed in England, before their final trek to America, they soon learned that provisions for them were inadequate and their circumstance did not improve when they finally reached America. The Palatines were met with mixed responses in England. Many of the English welcomed them but the poor people of England felt that English food was being taken from them to feed the Germans. British newspapers printed differing reviews on the Palatines, with some praising them and others highly critical of the Palatines.

Upon arrival in America, shelter, rations of food and clothing had to be provided for the immigrants until they could be established and provide for themselves. Sebastian Fisher and some of the other refugees had money but supplies could not be bought with money in those days. Work was provided for many of the immigrants but trouble between the English colonists and the German immigrants erupted early upon the Palatines arrival. Homes to house the German immigrants were built along the Hudson River on the Livingston Manor, and in 1711, Sebastian lived in Annsburg, one of the small villages. Later he was at Berne, New York. The immigrants eventually tired of what they believed to be discriminations against them, and Sebastian and other men engaged in trying to get justice for their compatriots.

Sometime before 1717, Sebastian and some others bought land in the Schoharie Valley and moved to Gerlachsdorf, previously known as Neu Cassell.

Cassell in 1717 was the seat of one branch of Sebastian's family line. Researchers into the Fisher family (Deutches Gescglecter Buch) state that other members of Sebastian's family had immigrated to America at an earlier date; it was apparently the only Fisher family of which this fact is recorded. They bore the same Christian names, such as Sebastian and Adam, as did the early American branch. They were reported by researchers to have been "men of higher learning, holding responsible positions." It was also noted that a wealthy descendent of Sebastian Fisher in the early part of the 1900s sent a lawyer to Germany to look into the supposed fortune due the American branch. The trip bore no results except to verify some of the early family traditions.

After the German's had paid their money in good faith for the purchase of land in Schoharie Valley in New York State they learned they could not get title to their land because the English who sold them the land had no title from the Indians. They were extremely angry and disappointed at this state of affairs.

In the spring of 1723, Sebastian and 14 other families decided to move to Pennsylvania hoping to find better treatment there than they had in New York. After crossing the Schoharie Valley to the Susquehanna River, they built boats and rafts, and the families proceeded down the Susquehanna 150 miles down river to the mouth of Swatara Creek, they crossed over the watershed to Tulpehocken Valley, which is about 17 miles northwest of the present city of Reading, Pennsylvania,. and settled there. They prospered in this new location and others joined them, from New York and Germany. At first, there was trouble securing title to their land, and a petition is recorded in the Pennsylvania archives regarding the matter. Sebastian signed this petition in Latin, Sebastine Piscator.

Although he was taxed in 1725, it is doubtful if Sebastian ever received title to his land in Pennsylvania. Dr. Charles A. Fisher, Selinsgrove, Pa., genealogist for the Fisher and many other Pennsylvania families, states that he has searched thoroughly and has found no record of title. Even so, Sebastian Fisher helped found two of the oldest Lutheran churches in Pennsylvania. One was Reeds, or Reids Lutheran church situated about two miles east of the present town of Stouchsburg, and the Tulpehocken Lutheran Church, now Christ Church a few miles southwest of Stouchburg. Reeds Church was founded in 1727 (and in 1730, they built a log schoolhouse near the church and hired a schoolmaster). When the Reeds, who were one of the fifteen families who came from New York, began to lean toward the Moravian Doctrine, Sebastian Fisher headed a list of a 150 members who withdrew from Reeds church in 1743 and founded the Tulpehocken Church. Sebastian's name was signed to many petitions for roads, sometimes he signed, as "Sebastine Piscator", his name has not been found in the Pennsylvania records since 1743. Dr. Charles A. Fisher, who has researched the Fisher family lines in depth, thinks that he may have migrated with one of his sons or perhaps returned to New York State. Some think he may have gone to Virginia. No record of Susanna Fisher has been found but she bore one child after they moved to Tulpehocken, P.A.

Children of Sebastian and Susanna Fisher:
1. Ludwig (Lewis or Lawrence), b. probably 1706; d. July 1773; m. Barbara Blankenbaker Ludwig was the one surviving child (of German birth) of Sebastian and Susana Fisher when the family arrived in

America in 1709. Little is known about him except that he lived and married and may have had descendants living in Missouri

2. George Ulrich, b. 1712; died 1770 m.
3. Peter, b. Oct. 4, 1714, m. Dorothea Ball
4. John Jacob, b. 1720; d. 1803; m. Mary Elizabeth Frederick
5. Ann Elizabeth, b. 1722; d. 1777; married John Anspach
6. ***John Adam**, b.1724; d. March 1783.

*John Adam Fisher was Dazerine McIntyre's direct ancestor. Birth records from the Old Christ Church near Stouchsburg, Pa. establish that he was born in Pennsylvania. More often than not in family histories, John Adam is referred to as Adam so we presume it was the name by which he was known. He married Christina Burkstoler. They moved to West Virginia probably sometime after 1761 because the birth of their fourth child, John, is recorded in the Pennsylvania church.

Indian raids were occurring in Tulpehocken Pennsylvania at the same time that Adam and Christina moved to Virginia. Many settlers believed the whole country would be destroyed. However, that did not happen. West Virginia settlers were also subjected to Indian raids. Eyewitnesses gave vivid descriptions of the terrors they experienced. It is firmly believed by some researchers that Catherine Fisher, the youngest daughter of Adam and Christina Fisher was a casualty of those raids. However, researchers were unable to prove that fact because members of the Fisher family refused to discuss it.

Adam and Christina settled on land that was part of the Lord Fairfax Manor. It was part of the land surveyed by the young George Washington in Hampshire County, Virginia. The county land was later divided and the Fisher's land was then part of Hardy County. Some time later, the state was divided and Hardy County became part of West Virginia. There were other members of Adam's family living in Madison, County, West Virginia.

By the time the Revolutionary War began, Adam was too old and frail to serve in the armed forces but he provided flour and other supplies to the Army. Records in Romney, Hampshire County, Virginia show in the form of a receipt signed by Abel Randel that Adam furnished six hundred and sixty nine pounds of flour. There are records of other donations. Three of Adam's sons served in the Army.

One family researcher noted in his/her research after reading Adam Fisher's will that Adam's movable property was a history of the lives of "these hardy pioneer families". The list showed no luxuries but there was an abundance of the necessities. The researcher mentions that, "Even in this wilderness they had their books and slates because the education of their children was never neglected."

Joseph Petty was Adam Fisher's neighbor and good friend in those early frontier days and it was during that time that three of Adams and Christina Fisher's children married children of Joseph Petty's family.

Children of Adam and Christina Fisher
1. Adam Fisher, b---; died 1816. m. Jemima Mace.
2. *** Mary Elizabeth, born Aug.29, 1757; died---Married Ebenezer Petty.**
3. (John) Jacob r, born Oct. 29, 1758; died 1839; m. Susan Burns.
4. John, b. Sept.29, 1761; died; m. 1st. Mary Baylor; 2nd._____ Levens.
5. George r, born March 1, 1765; died Jan. 15, 1824; m. Sarah Petty.
6. Catherine, Born 1771; died 1780s
7. Solomon, b.Feb.6, 1773, d. May 28, 1841, m. Mary Ann Petty.

The Petty Family:

Family researchers have traced Dazerine Petty McIntyre's ancestors back to the mid 1600s to a John Petty, found in England. He sailed to America before 1662. Although John Petty is quite likely of the Dazerine Petty line, that connection has not been proven. John Petty settled in Windsor, Connecticut and later moved to Massachusetts. He and his wife, Mary Ann Canning, are recorded to have had seven children: James, Hannah, John, Mary, Joseph, Ann, and Ebenezer. All of the children have been traced except for Ebenezer. However, a Mister Petty and his wife, Elizabeth, are a proven family connection in the Petty line. They were found in Hampshire County. That part of Virginia eventually became part of West Virginia. Because of an abundance of similar names found in their research, some family genealogists believe that Ebenezer may be Dazerine's family connection to England but that remains to be proven.

Mister Petty's first name is not known, and Elizabeth's last name is not known. They lived in Hampshire Co. Virginia. Before moving to Virginia, Elizabeth lived in Philadelphia County, Pennsylvania, and owned land there for some time after that. Records show five children born to Mister Petty and Elizabeth. Mister Petty died while the children were young, and Elizabeth married again to Gysbert Bogard.

Elizabeth, on April 10, 1784, had her son, Joseph, who was also her attorney; sell 100 acres of land in Pennsylvania. On that same day, she transferred her Hampshire County property out of her name and into Joseph's name. The next year in 1785, Elizabeth died She was buried in Hampshire County.

Children of Mister Petty and Elizabeth were:
1. *****Joseph,** born about 1735 or 36.
2. Ebenezer, b. 1737- died 1797. m. Elizabeth C. 1763.
3. Ann, m. Nicholas Mace before 1776.
4. Eunice, b 1772, m. John Harness. d. June 1, 1810.
5. Female (name unknown) m. Jacob Harness. d. before 1785.

*****Joseph Petty.** Joseph married Mary Ann Fisher, a relative of his close friend and neighbor, Adam Fisher. They lived in Hampshire County, Virginia. When Virginia was divided into two states, the Petty and Fisher property fell into the new state, called West Virginia. They, along with a number of other families in the new state, were dissatisfied with the new laws of the land so they all decided to move on to Kentucky. It was in Bourbon County, Kentucky that four of Joseph's children married into the Fisher family. Elizabeth, born March 3, 1765 married John Fisher; Sarah, born June 25, 1771, married Michael Fisher; Mary Ann married Solomon George Fisher in 1799. *Ebenezer, Dazerine's ancestor, married first to Mary Elizabeth Fisher and second to Susanna Sladge.

Joseph's sons served in the Revolutionary War. After the war was over, Ohio allotted land to the war veterans. Joseph and his children, grandchildren and great grandchildren all moved to Ohio.

Joseph and Mary Ann Petty's children:
1. Elizabeth, b. March 3, 1765. D.1842. m. John Fisher
2. Eunice, b. Feb.22, 1767 m. James A. Hall, 2nd Jacob Harness
3. *****Ebenezer, b. Dec. 15, 1769. D. June 1839. m. Mary** Elizabeth Fisher. 2nd Susanna Sladge
4. Sarah, b. June 25, 1771. d.1859. m. Michael Fisher.
5. Mary Ann. b. Feb.13, 1774. m. George Fisher, Nov.24, 1799.

6. Joseph, b. Dec.14, 1776. d. July 26, 1845.m. Eve Mare Nov.24, 1799
7. George, b.Aug.6 1779. D. 1837, m. Jane?
8. Ezekiel, b. Dec.28, 1781. m. Margaret Scott
9. Jemima. b. Sept.5, 1785.d. Aug.8, 1821. m. Solomon McCullock
10. Maxamillan, b. May11, 1788. d.. before 1861. m. William Fyffe Aug.20, 1809

*Ebenezer Petty grew up in Hampshire County, Virginia, which later became West Virginia. He married Mary Elizabeth Fisher, the daughter of Adam Fisher of the same County, sometime before 1790.

When Hampshire County became part of West Virginia, the Fisher and Petty families were unhappy with the changes that involved and moved to Bourbon County, Kentucky.

Ebenezer was a Captain in the Revolutionary War. He served three years from 1793 to 1796 in the Second Battalion, 14th Regiment of Bourbon County, Kentucky. When the war was over, Ohio allotted land to the war veterans and the Petty and Fisher families moved to Franklin County, Ohio and sometime later to Pickaway County, Ohio.

Mary Elizabeth died in Pickaway County sometime after 1800 but before 1811. Ebenezer remarried Susanna Sladge, sometime after 1811. Susanna was born in Franklin County, Ohio. She was a widow with three children. She and Ebenezer had two sons.

Ebenezer died in Pickaway County, Ohio in 1839.

Ebenezer and Mary Elizabeth Petty had three sons. They were:
1. ***Absolom,** born 1790 died 1865 in Kentucky
2. Solomon, born 1792 in Kentucky, m.
3. Mary Ann Franz; he died 1855;
4. Fisher, born 1799 in Ohio, died 1865, m.:
   Sarah Jackson.

Ebenezer and Susanna's children were:
1. Joseph Narval, b.1814 or 1815. m.Nancy Prosser.
2. Napoleon Bonaparte, b. 1815 1st.m. Mary Ann James, Aug.4, 1837;
   2nd. Lucy Ann McCallister, Nov. 28, 1881.
   3rd. Goldie Watson, Feb.24, 1898.

*Absolom, Ebenezer's oldest son, was born in Bourbon County, Kentucky in 1790. He was a young man when the family moved to Champaign County, Ohio. Later they moved to Pickaway County, Ohio. He married Louisa D. Bailey in Pickaway January 7, 1814. Louisa was born in Virginia.

Records show that the couple had six children born to the marriage but researchers are sure there were more.

Absolom & Louisa D. Petty's children
The six children recorded are:
1. Adam, b. in 1816; in Ohio m. Margaret in 1845, she was born in Ohio.
2. William, b. in 1817, in Ohio
3. ***Solomon K.,** b. 1818 in Ohio.)m.1st. ***Sophronia Mefford** 2nd. Elizabeth Sisney
4. Louisa Dazerine, b. in Pike County, Frankford Township, Missouri, 1828, named for her mother, m. William Milburn, Sept. 14, 1853 d.Aug, 1913, Pike County, Missouri.
5. Cinderella Jane, b. in Pike county, Frankford Township , Missouri, 1830.m. Caleb Mefford
6. Katy E, b. in Frankford Township, Pike County, Missouri, 1832

Family researchers believe more children were born to Absolom in the years between Solomon K. and Louisa D. but there are no records on them.

It was in the town of Frankford, Missouri that several of the Daisy Chain family units came together, and at this point in the family history, the Pettys, Fisher and Mefford family histories intertwine to the point that it is difficult to sort out details.

Absolom and Louisa moved there about 1824. Absolom's Uncle Solomon owned the town. Solomon had Absolom clear and fence a block in the southeast part of Frankfort. Absolom built a log house there, where he and his family lived. Absolom died there in 1865. His daughter, Louisa raised her family there in the same house.

The following story from an early edition of the Frankfort Missouri Newspaper gives some insight as to how things were in those earlier times.

(*Louisa Dazerine is Solomon's, sister.*)

The story is as follows and the editor made note of the fact that it was hand written.

————————————————————————————-

Reminiscences of Frankford's Early Days.
by Louisa Dazerine Petty Milburn
Dateline 1913

The Times takes the liberty of publishing the following letter, as it will interest many readers. It is from the Frankford Chronicle:

Dear Editor: I have been thinking for some time I would write and thank you and my many friends for nice cards and a letter I received for my birthday. I heard from old friends and relatives I thought were dead. It was a great pleasure to me to hear from them. One friend requested me to write a little history of Frankfort: as I guess, I am the only one living that knows anything about the beginning of it. I thought you would like a little sketch for your newspaper that they could all read it.

The land where Frankford is built was owned by my old Uncle Solomon Fisher, (an Uncle of my father who was Absolom Petty.) The town was laid out in 1818, nine years before I was born. Uncle Solomon had father clear and fence a whole block in the southeast part of town: he built a log house and lived there until he died in 1865. When Uncle Solomon died father bought four lots for $10. I was born and raised right there, under the shade of an old elm tree, and raised my family there. I lived there until I was 57 years old. My children played under the shade of that dear old tree where I was born: now they tell me it's gone, they have cut it down. It makes me sad to think about it. In 1810 father built a large hewed log house near the first one. The first doctor in Frankford was Doctor Winn: the next Doctor Tate; then Wilburn then came Smith, Tolliver, Craven and Henry. That was all the doctors up to 1878. The first merchant was Jerry Stark: the first blacksmith was Caleb Mefford (Gabe Meffords father): Benson Vermillon was the first cabinet workman: He made all the furniture and coffins, never heard of such a thing as a ready-made coffin: Fisher Petty was the first tanner, and Jack Bullin, the shoemaker, made all the shoes. Solomon Petty was the first saddler: Patrick Glenn was wheelwright: made large wheels for women to spin wool rolls on, and small wheels to roll flax. The women made most all the clothes. Little Tom Cash and a man named Estes built the first carding factory; I don't remember the exact year but I think it was 1837 or 1838. One of my brothers worked in it. Uncle Solomon's father had a mill on land operated by water power. He ground all the wheat and corn for bread for the town and farmers until 1850 or 1851 when Jeff Thompson and two other men built a steam mill in town. Among the first preachers was Timothy Ford, Sandy Jones and Ruby. The first church was a big hewed log house; all denominations preached in it. We only had mail once a week. Uncle Solomon came in once a week to make up and open the mail at my father's house. No one was allowed in the house while it was while it was being opened or made up.

The first newspaper that came to Frankford was the Salt River Journal, printed in Bowling Green; the editor's name was Noyes.

In 1833, we had our first case of Cholera. A man name (Dismake?), who lived at Bowling Green, had been to Palmyra on business and stopped in Frankford, and died in a few hours. His grave is right at the steps at the old brick Presbyterian Church. I guess I am the only one who knows it is there.

Among my cards was a picture of the high school at Frankford. I just thought what a difference in it and the house the first school was taught in. It was a little log house with a dirt floor and fireplace; the seats were logs split and two holes bored in each end and legs put in. My brother, older than I, went to school there. The first school I went to was taught in a little log house on the hill, near the Pitt residence; then I went to school in the old log meeting house. Children in those days didn't have such a good chance for an education as they do now. They studied or read in any book they happened to have; the first one to get there in the morning was the first one to recite; many a race I have had to get there first so I could recite first. I knew the old Blue Back Speller by heart. I remember getting a prize, when I was nine years old for getting the most tickets for standing head most times during the term. It was a belt for the waist made of light green calico; I was prouder of it than children are nowadays of a gold medal. Aunt Polly Stark was the teacher. She was Bina Campbell's aunt. The last school I went to they had them classed.

I owned the first coal oil lamp ever burned in Frankford. We used candles. Gabe Mefford's mother owned the first sewing machine and the first sausage grinder; our sausage was beat out on a big block of wood. Colonel Mase got the first cook stove. All the cooking was done in the fireplace. My husband W. M. Milburn helped charter the first Masonic Lodge; I think it was 1858. There were only five Masons besides himself. Bird Gordon, Billy Penix. Harve Stillwell, Judge Phillips and David Stark. Mr. Milburn went to Hannibal and *got old Mr. Denn and another man, I have forgotten his name. That was the beginning of the Masonic Lodge at Frankford. In my recollection, deer and wild turkey were plentiful; there was very little hog meat eaten. It was no trouble to go out before breakfast and kill a deer or turkey. Wild honey was plentiful too, my father used to get it by the barrel full.*

Now if you think this sketch written by an old lady is worth publishing you may publish it in your paper. I am 85 years old and I am in fine health, and can see to sew and do fancy work. I make a lot of my own clothes by hand, as I like it better than machine work. I help too on housework, as I still like to work. I live with my daughter, Molly Guyton. She is all I have left; my daughter, Rose, has been dead nine years; and my only boy, Willie, died one year ago last February. Mollie and I are all that are left of the family. The good Lord has sustained me through all my troubles, and I realize he is a very present help in time of trouble and thank Him for all his kindness and care. Am just waiting for his summons to go home to be with my dear ones who have gone before.

I will close now by wishing you and my many friends and relatives a Merry Christmas and Happy New Year. Louisa D, Milburn.

December 14, 1913

Generation #6

*Solomon Petty, Absolom's son, and brother to Louisa Dazerine Milburn, grew up in Frankford along with their neighbors, the Meffords. (He was Louisa Dazerine Petty McIntyre's grandfather).

Solomon at the age of 23 married Nathan Mefford's 18-year-old-daughter, Sophronia. In her 1913 letter to the Frankford newspaper, Louisa D. mentions that Solomon was the first saddler in Frankford.

Sophronia's brother Caleb Weden Mefford, was one of that town's earliest preachers. He married Solomon's sister, Cinderella Jane Petty.

Solomon and Sophronia had eight children, the first five were all girls and the last three were boys. Their first son was named for Sophronia's brother Caleb Weden.

Solomon and Sophronia Petty children:

1. Louisa Dazerine, b. 1842. m. Bargay. Louisa died in childbirth. Her surviving twins were Lodon and Lureen.

2. Mary Ann Elizabeth (Polly). b 1843. m. William Long April 17. 1861.
3. Susan C. b. 1845. b. Bigler.
4. Lucinda A. b. 1847. m. John Sinclair June 4, 1886. Lucinda died when their only child, Edward was young.
5. Artamissa Ellen b. 1849. m .John A. Bramlette. Artamissa died when their only child was young.
6. ***Caleb Weden,** b.1854. Married Martha Amanda Sisney Huffman. Caleb was named for Sophronia's brother, Caleb Weden. Caleb died a young man of pneumonia
7. Samuel B., b. 1855. d. between 1870-76
8. Titus J., b. 1862. He never married.

Generation #7

* Caleb Petty grew up to marry Martha Amanda Sisney, a young widow with three children. They lived in Ozark County until 1881 and had two daughters by that time. Later they moved to Barry County to a 160-acre homestead and had two more children, both sons. Caleb died a young man in his 30s. Before he died, he asked Amanda to bury him on his homestead and she did. Legend has it that when the land was divided, a fence cut through his grave.

Martha Amanda Petty
(Caleb's wife)

Caleb & Amanda's children were:

1. Elizabeth Sophronia, b. Sept. 8, 1879 in Ozark County, Missouri (named for her grandmother and Aunt Liz). d 1900.
2. ***Louisa Dazerine,** b. March 7, in 1880, in Ozark. d Jan.17, 1924. *(named for her aunt and great-grandmother)* m. 1st.Charlie Scott, 2nd. Elijah Jackson McIntyre. He died in 1912. Francis Knapp, he died 1914.
3. William Thomas, b. May 10, 1881 in Barry County, Mano, Missouri. m. Cordelia Youngblood. She was half Cherokee Indian. She died June 24, 1958.
4. Isaac "Ike" Robert, b. April 25, 1882, d. Dec.16, 1950, Cassville, Missouri.m.1st. Elsie Sylvania Brock, Dec.25, 1906. 2nd. Vena Bickford, Feb.20, 1931. Ike made his living as a trader in furs and later as a horse trader. He and his Uncle Titus traveled around the country hunting and trading furs. After 1901, Titus went into Oklahoma trapping for fur and was never heard from again. The family believed he was killed by Indians because at that time Oklahoma was Indian territory.

Generation # 8

* Louisa Dazerine's story is told previously in Part 1 of this book. She first married Charlie Scott, 2nd, Elijah Jackson "Jay" McIntyre, 3rd. Francis Knapp.

Dazerine and Charlie Scott's child was:

Eva Mattie Sylvania Scott. b. May 30,1896, in Arkansas, d.April9,1975

Children by Elijah Jackson McIntyre: Ira Jay, b.Oct.10, 1902, d. July, 1983. m.1st. Margurette Leedom, 2nd. Ethel 3rd. Etta..

*Iva Lillian McIntyre, b. June 29, 1905, d.March22,1983 also featured elsewhere in this book, married Homer Knight in 1922.

Clell Vandoren, b. Jan17,1911. d.Oct.1,1990 m.1st. Pearl Barret 2nd. Genevia

The McIntyres:

Jean Knight Fisher traced the McIntyre family back to1650 in Scotland. The name McIntyre is spelled several different ways for various reasons, McIntire, Macteer, McAntire, and other ways. The Daisy Chain McIntyre's stem from Scottish Highlanders. . For example, Scottish ancestors came from Ireland with the spelling Macateer. The Britains spelled it MacA'tar, Mactear. Those immigrants who came to America changed the name to McIntyre and McIntire. Phillip of Jay McIntyre's descendants used the McIntyre spelling. The name McIntyre is of Highland origin and stems from a handicraft or vocation. McIntyre means "works with wood", according to family research.

The McIntyre family was of Gaelic origin and occupied land in Glen Noe. Historic family research indicates that they were a branch of the McDonald Clan of Sleat Skye. The Gaelic people were a tribe of fair–haired, blue-eyed people who migrated from an area called Germany. It was not the small country that we know as Germany today, but an area that covered most of what is now known as Europe. At that time, the Gaelic tribe traveled over the country not calling any place home for centuries until they arrived in an area called Britain at that time. They decided they liked the area and wanted to make it their permanent home. That band of the Gaelic tribe was called Scots, and they renamed the area Scotland. However, others also wanted the area that the Scots claimed. The Scots had to fight one battle after another to retain ownership of the area. As a result of the frequent battles, the Scots trained their sons for war early in life and they were veterans of the Highland clan army of war by the time they were in their early 20s.

*****Philip** was the first of our McIntyre family to land in America. He was a Scottish Highlander of Glen Noe, Scotland. He was deported with his two brothers, Malcom and Robert, and other Highlanders, by Oliver Cromwell, the "Lord Protector" of the British Commonwealth, following the Battle of Dunbar, Sept.3, 1650. Before marching on Scotland, Oliver Cromwell had defeated the English Royalist, beheaded King Charles and left Ireland in "a bloody shambles."

He then moved on to Scotland, the last kingdom loyal to the Stuarts and in time, marched on Dunbar, a town on the east coast of Scotland. Cromwell's seasoned army of 15,000 soon defeated the untrained Clansmen, killed 3000 Scotsmen and took 10,000 prisoners. At least three of the McIntyre clan, Philip, Micum and Robert were among the prisoners. A number of authorities believe they were brothers.

The prisoners were taken first to England but England refused to let them in. They were then sent to Holland but were allowed to stay only a short while because Holland could not support them. Finally, in 1660 they sailed for America.

In all 150 Scottish prisoners were taken aboard the good ship Unity to New England. More prisoners were taken to the colonies in other ships. John Baek of London, who was interested in the Saugus iron mines, financed the passage. They weathered rough, wintry seas and suffered from scurvy. Many of them died from the disease before reaching the colonies. In the colonies, they were sold into slavery, and distributed to towns in Massachusetts, Maine and New Hampshire.

It took Philip, then in his 20s, seven years of indentured service to work out the expenses of his transportation and sustenance. He then settled in the northeastern part of Reading, Mass. near Salem, where he eventually acquired land and on Sept. 6, 1666 married a girl named Mary. Her last name is unknown. They had ten children.

In 1685, the town decided that persons living on the north side of Ipswich River should have two pieces of common ground that belonged to the town. The land was located at the upper end of a Mr. Billingham's farm. Phillip was one of eight persons to receive this grant. Three years later, he contributed ten pounds to build a new meetinghouse. Phillip spent the rest of his life in Reading and was buried there. On April 14, 1719, shortly before he died, he signed over his homestead to his son David.

Generation #2

*Phillip II. was the oldest son of Phillip and Mary. He grew up in Reading and became a farmer by trade. Phillip spent much of his time in Salem where he met his future wife Rebecca Wilkins. She was the daughter of Henry and Rebecca Wilkins.

Phillip and Rebecca lived in Reading only a short time. Their first son, Ebenezer was born there on December 5, 1696 but died on Jan.20, 1697. After their child's death, they moved to Salem close to where Rebecca's parents lived.

Henry and Rebecca Wilkins were members of the Salem Church of Christ. Phillip also joined that church in 1699.

All eight of his and Rebecca's children were baptized in the Salem Church of Christ.

Phillip moved his family once again to Thompson, Connecticut in 1725, and lived the rest of his life there just north of Quinnatiset Hill

Generation #3

*Joseph, born 1708, was the sixth child of Phillip II and Rebecca. He was baptized Sept.2, 1716. Joseph married a girl named Lydia whose surname is unknown. In May 1738, they lived in New Hartford, Connecticut. All six of their children were born and raised there.

Generation #4

*Joseph II was born May 1739. He married a girl named Mary and they had one son, Abraham.

By 1775, the rumblings of the American Revolution signaled that war was imminent and in 1776, The Declaration of Independence was signed. Joseph and his two brothers, Benjamin and Richard rallied to the battle cry. The old bitter sentiments against the British who had caused their forefathers so much grief and caused them to be deported still lingered in minds of the clan descendants. Joseph II and Mary moved to Vermont with Joseph's two brothers, and the three men joined the Green Mountain boys in battle to defend Vermont.

The Green Mountain boys were a paramilitary militia organization established in the decade prior to the American Revolution in the territory that is now Southwest Vermont. The organization was made up of settlers and land speculators who held New Hampshire titles to land between the Connecticut River and Lake Champlain area known as New Hampshire Grants. New York was given control of the area and refused to respect ownership and the town charter of the New Hampshire Grants.

The Green Mountain Boys, several hundred strong, managed to effectively control the area where the grants were issued. They played a significant role in the Revolutionary War.

The Green Mountain Boys leaders were Ethan Allen, his brother Ira Allen, and their cousins Seth Warner and Remember Baker.

The territory of Vermont was claimed by England after the French Indian War and Vermont became a part of the New Hampshire Colony. The colonists of Vermont wanted their independence, so during the

Revolutionary War they fought on the side of the Colonists and called themselves the Green Mountain Boys.

In April 1778, all three McIntyre brothers enlisted in the service of Ebenezer Allen, under the command of Nathan Smith. They fought together until June 12, 1781. At that time, Benjamin and Joseph II transferred to Col. Ira Allen's regiment of the militia in defense of the frontier state of Vermont. Benjamin was put under the command of Capt. Gideon Ormsby, and Joseph II was under command of Abraham Underhill. Richard, as a sergeant, was engaged in taking Tories up on Rupert Mountain for the duration of the Revolutionary War.

Generation #4

*Abraham, Joseph's son, grew up during all this battle and the conflict left him with restlessness. He spent his life moving from place to place. By 1790, he had married Abigail. By 1795, they had two sons both in Vermont. He had moved to Herkimer County where three more children were born. They had one child that year and in 1802, their last child was born in Essex County New York where they had moved. By 1803, they were living in Oneida County, New York.

Abigail died giving birth to their last child. She was buried in Whallamberg Town Cemetery in Essex County, NY. Abraham remarried to Jemima Brackett in 1807. They had a son born 1808 in Essex NY. By this time, Abraham was tired of moving from county to county and spent the rest of his life there.

Generation #5

*Nathan McIntyre, Abraham and Abigail's third child, was living in Cayuga County, in the town of Cato, New York in 1816. He married a German Dutch girl with the surname Van Rauesdaer. Her first name is unknown. They lived in Cato until 1828. Three of their children were born there. Nathan and his family were living in the town of Victory, not far from Cato in 1829. Three more of their children were born there. They had moved again by 1835 to the town of Elbridge in Onadago County, NY. Their youngest child was born there. Nathan's wife died sometime between 1840 and 1850 and he never remarried.

The 1850 census shows Nathan McIntyre, age 54 with his four children:

1. Penelope, 23;
2. Nancy, 21;
3. ***Stephen Van Rauesdaer, 18**;
4. Aloman, 15.

After his children were grown, Nathan moved to Schoeppel and lived first with his daughter, Penelope, but by 1860, Nathan was living with Stephen and Louisa.

Two of Nathan's children married in to the family of Conrad and Maria Harper of Lysander, N.Y., (a neighboring town). **Stephen married Louisa Harper** in Jan.1, 1852, and Penelope married George Harper a year later in 1853. Stephen and Louisa moved to Hannibal in Oswego County, N.Y. and George and Penelope moved to the small town of Schoeppel.

By March 17, 1861, Stephen and Louisa had four sons. The 1860 census records show that Stephen, then age 28, had a wife, Louisa, 24 and three children.

Stephen's father, Nathan lived with them in Oswego, County in the town of Hannibal.

When he was 32, Stephen was listed in the census as a farmer. He volunteered to join the Union in its fight with the Confederacy on Sept.2, 1864. Some researches believe his youngest brother, Aloman, may have enlisted in the Union Army in 1862. Records show an Aloman McIntyre from the same location enlisted in 1862 and there is no trace of him after May 28, 1862.

Some Army papers state that Stephen was 5ft.6 tall but one form shows him to be 5ft. 4. He was a private in Co. A, of the 185th. Regiment of New York States Volunteers. He had black hair, blue eyes and a dark complexion. However, other papers describe his complexion as light in color.

After mustering in at Syracuse, he served as an infantryman until Jan. 28th, 1885 when he died in the Division Field Hospital in Virginia. His commanding officer, Capt. S.O. Howard cited the reason of death as dysentery. Other sources have cited typhoid fever as the cause of death. Writing on the service form is not clear. A filed inventory of his last affects showed Stephen to have no affects. Upon joining the service, he was paid a bounty of $33.33 with $67.67 owed to him by the U.S. government. His papers show that he received no money during his service but did receive United States clothing valued at $41.24.

Stephen volunteered for one year of service. Why did he leave his young family to fight a war? We can only guess. When he volunteered for service, Stephen's oldest son was only nine, his youngest child three. Was his reason for joining the army loyalty to the Union cause? Perhaps it was because his brother, Aloman, if it was he who joined in 1862, that influenced Stephen's decision to join the fight. There was also a family heritage of fighting men in the McIntyre clan shown in early family records and written separately in this book. Perhaps the need for money influenced his decision to enlist. At that time, the Union forces were pressed for a victory and the U.S. Government was carrying on an ambitious recruiting program. The U.S. government in order to enlist volunteers offered a bounty for their service. We will probably never know Stephen's motives for joining the war effort.

In reading Civil War history, it appears probable that Stephen was a casualty of General Grant's Virginia campaign 1864 to 1865, a bitter long fought struggle to retake Virginia and end the war. The war ended in April 1865. Stephen had four months of service and was three months short of the war's end.

Stephen's wife, Louisa, received a widow's pension of ten dollars for her sons until they reached the age of 16. When Stephen joined the Army, Louisa and her sons moved to Lysander. Nathan moved with her. A year after Stephen's death, Louisa had moved to Phoenix and married David Flatt. After her marriage to Flatt, they moved to Victor N.Y. in Ontario County and lived there until after John and Jackson had married. Willard died some time between 1867 and 1875.Louisa died in 1880.

Stephen and Louisa's children were:
all born in New York.
1. John A., b. 1855
2. *Elija Jackson, b.1858
3. James A., b.1859,
4. Willard, b. 1861 in Oswego County, NY

John and Jackson both married and moved with their families, to Oswego.

Something happened during the time before 1900 that prompted Elijah Jackson (Jay) to leave his home, join a railroad crew as an expert in the use of dynamite, and travel to Arkansas where he met and married Dazerine Petty Scott, a young divorced woman with a four-year-old child, a girl named Eva.

The Tompkins Family

Generation #1

#Benjamin and Elizabeth Tompkins didn't live to see the War Between the States (1861 to 1865), but during their lifetime, they saw their own family torn apart by the strife and conflict of principals between Northern and Southern doctrines that preceded the war. Benjamin and Elizabeth were Dazerine Petty McIntyre's fourth great-grandparents. Matilda, one of the couple's older daughters, was Dazerine's grandmother. Matilda is not the focus of the first part of the family history. However, it was her younger sister, Eunice, and her brother, James, who brought about the disastrous events that tore the family apart, and caused Benjamin on his deathbed to declare that he "regretted having trafficked in human souls." There is more about Matilda later in the story.

Benjamin was a Missouri planter. He and his wife, Elizabeth Hampton were both born in North Carolina, he in 1780 and she in 1782. They married in 1799 and moved to Virginia in 1820. They moved again to Kentucky in 1825, to Illinois in 1836 and finally, still pursuing new opportunities, to Schuyler County, Missouri in the 1840s. Benjamin's will written in 1855 in Schuyler County, Missouri says that Benjamin and his wife had 12 children but one family legend says there were 16 children.

According to family legend, Benjamin and Elizabeth in 1800 lived in Carter County, North Carolina where they owned land and an iron forge. During that time, Carter County records show that Benjamin acquired two families of slaves, which do not show up in the 1820 census. Family legend has it that Benjamin freed his slaves in Kentucky, but one elderly, freed slave couple followed them to Missouri, and the old slave woman taught one of Benjamin's daughters, Fannie, how to cook.

Benjamin and Elizabeth were living in Russell County, Virginia in 1820 and had one slave in their household. In 1825, Benjamin and two other men owned 25,000 acres of land there. From there the Tompkins family moved to Kentucky for a few years, bought and sold property there and moved on to Warren County, Illinois. Family records show the Tompkins family arrived there in 1836 and owned land in Ellison and Tompkins Townships. They lived there for ten years until they moved again to Schuyler County, Missouri. It was there that Benjamin and three of his sons put together a 1240-acre plantation in the late 1840s and early 1850s.

Robert J. Flygare, a descendant of the Tompkins family, in 1970, collected the following stories on the Benjamin Tompkins family. The 1240-acre plantation that Benjamin and his sons put together was in and near Schuyler and Scotland Counties. These counties are located in the northeastern part of Missouri on the Fabius River. It was in this area that Kentucky planters tried to establish plantations, worked by slaves, prior to the Civil War. It was generally well known that Benjamin and his sons owned and traded slaves.

The location of Benjamin's plantation in Northwest Missouri made it a target for the Underground Railway organization because of its proximity to Illinois residents working the Underground Railway. The Underground Railway was part of an anti-slavery group, abolitionists who aided runaway slaves to escape their owners, and find a safe haven in free, anti-slavery territory. The organizations were centered in the Quincy, Illinois area. Raids on the Schuyler County area plantations occurred frequently. The Methodists were so active in this movement that they were chased out of Marion County.

Eunice, the younger daughter of Benjamin and Elizabeth Tompkins, married Jared Cox, an avowed abolitionist. Eunice's brothers were angry about the marriage. A man such as Cox would quite naturally have been unpopular with his slave holding, planter in-laws. Eunice's brother, James, further complicated matters when it was learned that he fathered a daughter with a black slave girl. The combination of events triggered a major rift in the family.

Jared Cox was born in Delaware, one of eight children. His family members were all strong Methodists and his grandfather William Biggs had been instrumental in getting Illinois admitted to the Union as a free state.

Jared, an outspoken young man, enraged Eunice's brothers with his antislavery rhetoric to the point that they ran him out of Missouri and would have killed him if Eunice had not stopped them. Two of the brothers pursued the couple for several days before they escaped to Illinois.

Jared and Eunice had five children before she died at the age of 27. The children's names were Elizabeth Amanda, George, Margaretta, Nancy and Eunice Olive. After Eunice died, Jared returned to the Missouri plantation and Benjamin would pay a dear price for trafficking in slaves.

Jared brought two of his and Eunice's daughters, their oldest child, Amanda, and her sister, Olive, to visit their grandfather's plantation in Missouri. Amanda remembered it was a mile from the gate to the house. She said, they were served on a silver tray by a slave boy. When they departed, Benjamin's wife, Elizabeth sent a girl from her household along with her widowed son-in-law, Jared Cox, to help care for his motherless children. The girl's name was Louisa.

Before Jared left, Elizabeth took her granddaughter, Amanda, aside and told her the story of Louisa, in case Jared "took a notion to marry her." Her grandmother told Amanda that Louisa was the daughter of Benjamin's son, James Tompkins, and a slave girl. She said Benjamin took Louisa into his household along with her sisters and a brother, and raised her as a daughter because "he wouldn't have his own flesh and blood raised as a slave." Jared apparently chose to ignore his mother—in-law's advice and that same year of 1855 in Burlington County, Iowa, he married Louisa and they had three children.

Information on James Tompkins is sketchy and confusing. However, records in Lee County, Virginia show that James first married Nancy Mills in 1825. According to the Lee County records, James left Nancy there with the couple's two sons, Benjamin and William, when he moved to Clay County, Illinois in 1830. Records also show he met and married Mahala Brooks who was believed to be the daughter of a freed, black man. James and Mahala had six children, including Louisa who later married Jared Cox. Mahala was dead in 1848 when James died.

With the death of their parents, James and Mahala's children faced an uncertain and possibly dire future. On May 4, 1848, William T. Brooks (Mahala's family) was appointed guardian of the minor heirs of James

Tompkins. The minors were Elizabeth, Eliza (also known as Louisa), Washington, Nancy, Martha and James K.P. For some reason, the children's guardian, William T. Brooks moved on to Missouri with his father, Michajah, in 1849, leaving the six minor children of James Tompkins in Clay County, Ill. Why he left them is not known, but on October 24, 1849, the Clay County Sheriff, Strawther B. Walker, who was also an old Army friend of James Tompkins, was made guardian of the children. (James served as a Sergeant in the Black Hawk War, in 1832, before he was discharged with a disability.)

Six minor children, who were wards of the Sheriff in 1849, would have been farmed out to Clay County families as servants. We can only assume that at this point the sheriff notified Benjamin of the children's plight because Benjamin came to their rescue. He took the five younger children back to Missouri. On May 7, 1849, he was appointed their guardian.

What happened to Elizabeth, the oldest child, is not clear but she was alive in 1855. Benjamin died in 1857 two years after he had written his will, and she was mentioned in Benjamin's will.

Between 1855 and 1860, Louisa, Jared, and their family moved along with several other pioneer families to Minnesota. They bought land in the newly opened area near Red Wing. Some families gave up and went back home, but the Cox family was among those who stayed. Jared and his oldest son, George, served in the Civil War in 1846. After the war, Jared returned to Minnesota and farmed. He spent his last years in Sac County as a laborer, and died in 1894. After Jared's death, Louisa lived with the Wm. Cooper family as a housekeeper. She died in April 1909.

Robert Flygare, the Tompkins family researcher, said Benjamin's hilly land never became a productive plantation. Like many Eastern pioneers, he settled in the woods above a creek where he found water, game, shelter, and lumber for his home, and soil that he could clear and till. He had neither the knowledge nor the plow to break the tough prairie sod. Benjamin held his family together on the land until he died, then they scattered to find more productive land. With the advent of the Civil War, even the slaves deserted the area. Three of Benjamin's daughters married into local families. Their descendants still lived a few miles away but in 1978 when Flygare spoke with them, they had no memory of the hardy pioneer who moved there from North Carolina before 1800 with his family, to search for a new land where he could build a plantation for his clan. Benjamin's land never produced bumper crops. For a while, horses were raised there and exported all over the world, then it was sheep country until competition from Australia and an influx of coyotes made sheep raising unprofitable. Fine cattle were also raised there.

Louisa and her family assimilated into the main stream of society leaving no traces of their slave ancestors in the archives, only the closely held family legend remains. It has quietly been passed down through the generations.

Mr. Flygare mentioned that he visited the Schuyler Co. Missouri plantation in 1978, many years after he heard the stories. He said, "The plantation site was gently rolling, partially wooded pasture land on a dirt road a few miles due north of Downing. All traces of the home once occupied by Benjamin and his three sons had disappeared."

Flygare said at that time (we have no new information on the property) an elderly couple owned and lived on a half section of the land and had lived there since 1944. They grew a little hay and corn on the land and lived in a very old house that was not in existence in 1857 when Benjamin died. He said the existing farm was located on the 80 acres that Benjamin willed to his widow, Elizabeth. Across the dirt road, on a high spot in a hay meadow was a small thicket where Benjamin Tompkins was buried. There were stone markers for Benjamin and several other family members. Out of respect for the first pioneer to settle the land, the elderly farmer had mowed around the small cemetery for over 30 years. He had often wondered what happened to the Tompkins family and if someday, one of Benjamin's families might come to visit the lonely graves.

Benjamin and Elizabeth Tompkin's children were:
1. Nancy, Married a Whitlow
2. Elizabeth. Married a whitlow
3. Eunice, Married H.H. Cox
4. James married 1st, Nancy Mills, 2nd. Mahala Brooks Children by Nancy: William, Benjamin by Nancy. Children by Mahala; Elizabeth, Louisa, George, Nancy, Martha, James K.P.
5. Eli
6. Rebecca
7. ***Matilda. Married John Sisney.**
8. Maragaret. Married Hayse
9. Benjamin J.

10. George W.
11. John B.
12. Fanny D.

* Matilda Tompkins, Dazerine's maternal great-grandmother was born May 18, 1810 in Carter County, Tennessee. She married John Sisney on Nov.30, 1827. She was 17 and John was 31.

The Sisney Family

John Sisney's ancestral line is partially proven at this point. However, the correct spelling of the surname Sisney is still in question in genealogical circles. A variation in the spelling of surnames for early American immigrants is not uncommon. Whether the Sisney name was correctly spelled Cisney, Sesne, or other variations, has not been proven beyond a doubt.

John was the son of Dolly Holton and William Stephen Sisney or Cesna.

Stephen was the son of Thomas and Margaret Sisney. Baptismal records from the Church of St. James Episcopal Church in Lancaster County, Pennsylvania, record that Stephen was baptized at the church in 1755, and shows his mother and father to be Thomas and Margaret. (Record ID 312409) Further research on Thomas Sisney has been unproductive, but some record that Thomas Sisney's father was Stephen.

Several dedicated genealogists who researched the family for years, are convinced that John Sisney born 1796, in Guilford County, North Carolina, is the descendant of Count Jean De Cessna, a Huguenot refugee, from Normandy, France who arrived in America in the early 1700's. However, other research indicates that John Sisney's great-grandfather came from Scotland. While the Scotland theory seems to be the plausible one, there are no proven records beyond Stephen Sisney or Cesna

Records show that John Scot Sisney was born in North Carolina in 1796. He was the son of Stephen Cisney and Dolly Holton. Rockingham County, North Carolina records show that this Stephen Cisney was one of about 29 Tories captured on Fe.27,1776 during the Revolutionary War with the British, in the Battle of Moore's Creek Bridge in North Carolina. One record shows that his wife Dolly petitioned for his release after the war ended. "Scotch Highlanders In America" describes the Battle at Moore's Creek as a fight between Highlanders Settlement, numbering between 1500 and 3000 (including 200 regulars) and Revolutionary Patriots numbering 9000. The Battle reportedly lasted about 10 minutes with the Highlanders soundly defeated.

Highlanders, according to records, had taken up arms in support of King George not so much for political inspiration but because of a loyalty oath, they had taken with the governor of North Carolina. The Highlanders of North Carolina were Scottish and spoke Gaelic, not English. They had been told the revolution was an attempt to usurp their civil rights. After the Battle at Moores Creek, the Highlanders reportedly went to their homes and never again took up arms.

What some genealogical researchers question is whether Stephen was a Highlander who settled in North Carolina or was he a Regular who may have been christened in Pennsylvania? Did he migrate from North Carolina to Christian County, Kentucky? One report states that Stephen Sisney was captured as a Tory with the British Army 26th Regiment on his way to Moores Creek. He never got there, but was taken, as a prisoner of war, to a camp by way of Halifax, North Carolina.

Researchers found it interesting that Stephen's son John was called by his middle name, Scot.

Stephen and Dolly Sisney's children were:
1. *John Scot** who married Matilda Tompkins
2. Robert who married May
3. Mary who married a Mr. Grace
4. Rachel who married a Mr. Taylor
5. Elizabeth who married a Mr. Ray

The following reports on the Sisneys are also from proven records. By 1829, the family had moved to Christian County, Kentucky. Other Sisney families in that area date back to 1810. It was in Christian County, Kentucky that John and Matilda Tompkins were married.

One record shows that they had 12 children and raised seven. Nine children are listed in family records researched by Jean Fisher who did extensive research on the Sisney, Petty, Tompkins, Fisher, Meffords and other family ancestors of Louisa Dazerine Petty McIntyre. The Sisney and Tompkins families may have known each other in North Carolina. Records show the Tompkins family also came from that state and moved to Tennessee then to Kentucky. The Sisneys may also have lived in Tennessee because the families stayed close together from the time they lived in Kentucky to the time they arrived in Missouri. What was John and Matilda's part in the family strife that took place between the Tompkins family and the Matilda's brother, James and sister, Eunice? We can only guess, but they lived close to the Tompkins' plantation, if not on it while much of the strife was taking place, and it seems logical that they were involved.

In support of that theory, is the fact that it was about 1847 before John and Matilda, and their younger children, moved from Schuyler County to Green County, Missouri.

John and Matilda's daughter, Mary Jane married William Bisswell on Sept.1, 1847. Their first child was born 1849. The Tompkins stayed in Schuyler County with Mary Jane and her husband.

The couple's next daughter, Elizabeth T. married William E. McGlaughlin in Green County. McGlaughlin is believed to have died in the War Between The States. Elizabeth later married a widower named Solomon Petty. His son, Caleb, married their younger daughter, Martha Amanda; Solomon was Dazerine Petty McIntyre's grandfather and Caleb was her father.

John and Matilda moved with the other children to Douglas County, Missouri where five of their children married. By 1860, two of their children, Benjamin and Andrew were missing from the family. Benjamin is believed to have died since he was only 12 years old, but Andrew was thought to have married a girl named Lucinda. He died shortly after that.

By 1870 or before, John and Matilda moved to Ozark County, Missouri. John died Sept.4, 1880 at the age of 83 years, 10 months and 21 days old. He was buried in the Sisney Cemetery.

After John's death, Matilda moved to Arkansas to live with her son, William, and his family until her death in 1904 at the age of 94. She was taken back to Missouri to be buried next to the grave of her husband John.

One of William's descendants recalled that Matilda told her grandchildren how she and John came to Ozark County, Missouri by covered wagon pulled by oxen.

Sisney/Petty line

As previously stated, it was in Ozark County that two of the Sisney daughters married into the Petty family. Caleb Weden Petty, Dazerine's father, married Martha Amanda, John and Matilda's youngest daughter. Caleb's widowed father, Solomon Petty, married Amanda's sister, a widow named, Elizabeth. Elizabeth, more often known as Liz was 17 years older than Martha Amanda. Liz was 44 when she married Solomon. He was 59. After she married Solomon, his family referred to her, affectionately, as Aunt Liz. Liz's first husband had died in the Civil War. Both Solomon and Liz were country doctors and both were credited with curing skin cancers, and for saving premature babies, as well as other medical healing. Liz was also a faith healer.

Their individual and combined medical skills were well known and well respected throughout the countryside where they lived.

John and Matilda Sisney's Children:
1. Mary Jane b. 1832, Macon County, Illinois
2. Elizabeth T. b.1833
3. William Jefferson b 1834
4. Eli Blane b. 1838
5. Andrew J. b. 1840
6. Louisa F. b.1842
7. Nancy Ann b. 1846, Schuyler County, Missouri
8. Benjamin F. b. 1848
9. ***Martha Amanda** b. 1850, Schuyler County, Missouri, died Jan. 1900. m.1st James Huffman, 2nd Caleb Petty, 3rd. Robert Scott

The Meffords

Sophronia Mefford, the daughter of Nathan Mefford, was Solomon Petty's first wife, and mother of all his children. They were married in 1841. She was 18 and he was 23. They had eight children. How Sophronia and her son, Samuel, died has not been verified, but one family story has it that she and Samuel, 15, both died at the same time about 1870, on their journey to their new home in the Ozark Country of Missouri. The wagon they were in is believed to have turned over, and they were crushed. This legend is based on the fact that Sophronia's daughter, Dazerine, regularly visited two unmarked gravesites with her children, along a lonely roadway in the Ozarks and put flowers on the graves. She told her children, who were with her but still very young at the time, that the graves were for people in her family who had died when their covered wagon, pulled by oxen overturned and crushed them years before. Solomon and Sophronia reportedly moved their family to the Ozarks in 1870. While census counts in 1870 and beyond show Solomon and the rest of the family in Missouri, they do not show Sophronia or Samuel. Samuel would have been 15 in 1870. Several years later in 1877, Solomon married Elizabeth Sisney.

Sophronia's grandparents, George Conrad Mefford and his wife, Anna Magdelina Meffert (the name has been spelled more than one way) came to America from Frankfort, Germany in or about 1757 to escape the oppression and religious persecution in the Palatine region of Germany. Genealogical research indicates that the Meffords were German and came in-mass from the Palatines. The Palatines are actually two different adjoining regions in what is today, west-central Germany. It covered the area from roughly Stuttgart in the south, north to Coblenz and west to France. The Roman Catholic Church gave support to the King of the Palatinate in 945 AD, but later, in 1517, when Martin Luther gave momentum to the Protestant Reformation in Worms, the Palatinate embraced Protestantism and the Palatines became a haven for Protestant believers. They came from all over Europe to band together for safety. The Catholic Church saw its influence deteriorating and began to wage wars and persecution against the Palatines as well as Protestants all throughout Europe.

Leaving their home country and coming to America was not an easy decision for the Palatinates. It meant a long, dreadful ocean voyage and an uncertain future in a new land that they knew very little about. However, after Louis the XIV of France, decided to take the region for his own and the invasion by France in to their homeland with the devastation that followed the war brought them to the breaking point that helped them to decide that leaving their homeland was their only reasonable choice.

The French armies pillaged and burned the area from 1687 to 1697. After nearly 100 years of oppression and persecution, almost all of the inhabitants began to leave in mass for their own safety. Queen Anne of England either took pity or recognized a political advantage, and offered safe haven for the refugees. She then arranged to have them sent to Ireland or America thus allowing the Protestants to establish a stronger presence in Ireland and speed up the colonization of America. Most of the immigrants to America were resettled in either Carolina or Pennsylvania. Those who settled in Philadelphia were known as the Pennsylvania Deutsch (German).

Before they were allowed to leave the boat and settle in America, all the males over 16 had to swear allegiance to the King of England. There are immigration records that list the passenger who swore allegiance. The Meffords are on these lists.

Anna Magdalena, heavy with child during the difficult ocean voyage endured great hardships aboard the ship "Brothers." Some genealogical records report that her son, George, was born aboard ship. However, more recent findings indicate, George was born on September 25, 1751, shortly after arriving in America on Sept. 16.

George and Anna Magdalena's son, George, is on record as having served during the Revolutionary War from Washington Co, Pa. He served in the same company with Lot Masters, Nathan Masters, John Riggs and Thomas Riggs. We see these names again later when George ventured in to the wild Kentucky frontiers.

*George and Malinda Masters Mefford were reportedly married on July 27, 1779 at Redstone, Fayette Co. Pennsylvania, but to date, no record has been found of the marriage. Malinda was born January 18, 1763

George's first recorded visit into Kentucky was in the spring of 1783. In part of the deposition by John Riggs, taken in Mason County, Ky., July 3, 1797 (Will Book A-pg. 323) Riggs states, "Came down the Ohio River to the district of Kentucky in company with John Drinden, Thomas Mills, Lot Masters and George Mefford in May 1783. We made locations on the east fork of Cabin Creek at one place cutting the initials of George Mefford's name on a honey locust. He returned in 1785, reportedly floating from the area known as Brownsville, Pa., down the Ohio River on a "flatboat" with his family and settled near the present town of Maysville, He was appointed one of the six trustees for that town, the third established in Mason Co. by the Virginia Legislature. The others were Daniel Boone, Daniel's cousin Jacob Boone, Henry Lee, Arthur Fox and Thos. Brooks.

The Mefford family is recorded in Kentucky history as the first family of settlers near Maysville and outside a blockhouse. George built his cabin in 1787 with timbers from the old flatboat that he steered down the Ohio River. The spot was known as Mefford Station in 1787. George and Malinda's third son was the first child born in Mason County, born December 4, 1787.

George Mefford, frontiersman

Mefford's Station near Maysfield, Kentucky is a historic landmark on the Maple Leaf River a half mile from its junction U.S. 68, it is the only original fort of the Revolutionary War left standing in Mason County.

George Mefford built the flatboat that he used to come down the Ohio River into Kentucky territory. He later used the timbers to build his home.

George Mefford was a gun maker and is believed to have made guns for the American Army during the Revolutionary War.

George died Oct. 18, 1814. His widow, Malinda, remarried Sept. 25, 1816 to Ennis Duncan. She was deceased by September 1848.

George and Malinda's Children were:
All born in Mason co. Kentucky
1. Andrew, b. Jan.8, 1781
2. Samuel, b. May 21, 1785
3. John, b.Dec.4, 1787
4. Nancy Ann, b. Feb.6, 1788
5. *Nathan, b. Feb. 17, 1790
6. Mary, b. June 2, 1792
7. Elizabeth, b. March 15, 1795
8. George, b. Sept.23, 1797
9. Sarah, b. Jan. 27, 1799
10. Lydia, b. Nov. 14, 1800
11. Thomas, b.Feb.25, 1803
12. Joshua, b. March 10, 1805
13. Caleb, Weden, b.Feb.16, 1808

The Masters family

We know very little about the Malinda Masters family. Her parents were Mister Masters and Mary Masters. Mister Masters died sometime before 1804. Mary remarried to Jacob Mills. The Masters were from Mason County, Kentucky. They moved to Missouri about the same time the Meffords did, probably at the same time.

Mister Masters and Mary had six children:
1. Nathan
2. ? married John Riggs
3. ? Married Jeremiah Riggs
4. *Malinda Masters married George Mefford

5. Mary Ann married Thomas McGinnis
6. Lot died in 1790, killed by Indians at Mefford's Station

* Nathan Mefford was the fifth child of George and Malinda Masters. He was born Feb. 17, 1790. He married Mary (Polly) Tevis, January 29, 1808, in Lewis County, Kentucky. Polly was born about 1789. They moved to Frankford, Pike County, Missouri sometime before 1820. Nathan died July 1859 in Frankford and was buried in Frankford Cemetery

Nathan and Polly Tevis Mefford had eight children:
1. Noah, b. 1809 in Kentucky
2. John, b. 1810, Kentucky
3. Julia, b. 1814
4. Mary Ann, b. 1815
5. ***Sophronia**, b. 1823, Pike County, Missouri. Married Solomon Petty 1841
6. Caleb Weden, b. 1825. Married Cinderella Jane Petty, Solomon Petty's sister.
7. Wallace, b. 1826, Pike Co., Missouri m. Elizabeth Jane Myers, Feb.15, 1851
8. Tevis, b.1829 Pike County, Missouri, m. Nancy C. Myers, Dec.2, 1848

* Sophronia Mefford was born 1823. She married Solomon Petty (as previously
   mentioned in the Sisney/Petty part of this book) Solomon was the son of
   Absolom and Louisa Petty. He was born in Ohio in 1818.

The Boones, the Coffees, the Knights
The Paternal side of the family

The Boones:

The Knight/ Coffee family ties are through Israel Boone. Israel was the oldest brother to the famous American frontiersman, Daniel Boone. Daniel's heroic trail blazing, exploits across the early frontiers of American frontiers were of great historical value.

The Boone family came into America in the mid 1700s from England. There are few records in our family tree before our first proven ties to George Boone I. He was born, lived and died in England. There is only scant information on him, or his son, George II.

George II was born near the city of Exeter in Devonshire. His wife's name was Sarah Uppey. George II was a blacksmith by trade. He died at the age of 60. Sarah lived to be 80 and reportedly "never had an aching bone or decayed tooth."

It was George Boone III, the son of George II and Sarah Uppey who took the first known emigration steps toward America about 1712 or 13 when he sent his three oldest children; George IV, 23; Sarah 22, and *Squire,17, to investigate conditions in the new land. Their report must have been favorable because on August 17,1717, George III, his wife , Mary and their remaining six children set sail from Bristol, England and followed the older children to land in Philadelphia, Pennsylvania Sept.20 (old style calendar), or Oct. 10(new style calendar).

George III was a weaver by trade. He was born at Stoak, England (near Exeter) in 1666. He married Mary Maugridge. She was born 1669, in Bradninch the daughter of John and Mary (Milton) Maugridge. George and Mary had nine children. All married and had several children with the exception of John who never married.

When they first arrived in America, the Boone family lived with George IV who was married by then and had a home in Abington. They next moved to North Wales and two years later, moved to Oley Township, in the same county. The township was later renamed to Exeter Township for their old home in England. George established his permanent home there in 1720, building a log home on his land. Thirteen years later, he built a larger log house so that any of his children who might wish to, could live there. The Historical Society of Berks Co., Pennsylvania now owns the house and grounds where the second house was built.

While in England, the Boone family had traditionally been members of the Episcopalian Church. However, after George Fox founded a sect known as Quakers, or the Society of Friends, George and Mary joined them. That decision may have influenced their decision to immigrate to America and become a part of the Quaker settlement in Pennsylvania.

George Boone III was 78 years old when he died, about 8 a.m. on July 2, 1744. His wife, Mary died Feb.2, 1740-41 at the age of 72. They left 8 children, 52 grandchildren, and 10 great grandchildren.

In keeping with the tradition of the Friend's Society, no stone markers were placed on their graves.

In addition to the three oldest children of George III and Mary Boone's children:
1. George IV
2. Sarah
3. * Squire

The remaining six children are listed here:
4. Mary, b. Sept.23, 1699, m John Webb, d. 1774
5. John, b. Jan3, 1701-02, never married but he was a man of some learning, kept the record of the births, deaths, and passed them on to his nephew, James, after his death in 1785. James (the son of James and Mary) compiled the records into the genealogy that has been handed down through the family.
6. Joseph, b. April 5, 1704, m. Catherine
7. Benjamin, b. July 16, 1706, m. Ann Farmer, 2nd. Susannah
8. James, b. July 1709, m. Mary Foulke; 2nd. Anne Griffith
9. Samuel, b. about 1711, m. Elizabeth Cassel

Note: Information on the ancestors of Israel Boone was taken from Spraker's book, The Boone Family.

*Squire Boone, b.1695, Devon shire, England, died Jan.2, 1765 in Rowan County, North Carolina. He accompanied his brother George IV and his sister Sarah to America in 1712-13. His parents and the remaining six children followed them to America about five years later.

Squire married Sarah Morgan Sept.23, 1720 in Berks County, Pennsylvania. Sarah's father was Edward Morgan, an earlier settler of the Welsh Colony of Gwynedd, in Berks Co. Pa.

Following their marriage Sarah and Squire lived in Bucks County. New Britain Twp. for several years, and at least three of their children were born there. In 1730, he received a grant of land in Berks co. near the site of what later became the town of Reading, Pa., not far from his parent's home in Berks Co., and he moved his family there.

The Boones in Berks County were among the more prominent families in the community. Squire was a trustee in the 1736 Oley meeting in the Friends' Society; and was overseer in 1739.

However, Squire fell out of good standing with the church when two of his children married out of the church. Sarah, his oldest daughter, married George Wilcox who was not a Quaker in 1742. Then, in 1747, Israel, his oldest son, also married out of the church. Squire was reprimanded by the meeting when Sarah married out of the church and according to church minutes, he apologized for permitting that marriage to take place. He promised, at that time, to take care to prevent further infractions. Therefore, when five years later, the 21-year-old Israel also married out of the church, the church reaction was even more severe. Both Squire and Israel were seriously censured.

Southeastern Pennsylvania was fairly well settled by the mid 1700's with family groups from various countries of Western Europe, England, Wales, Scotland, Holland, Germany and other countries. While the colonist's lives revolved largely around their particular churches and religions, there was nothing to prevent the groups from commingling socially. However, the Quaker church was very strict in the belief that their members should marry only within the Quaker church. The monthly church minutes, usually very thorough in keeping records on marriages, births and death of its members, was unusually brief in recording Israel's marriage, stating only that he 'married out' on Dec.31, 1747. Some historians interpret the very brevity of the record as a measure of the church's intense disapproval of Israel's marriage.

However, by the time Israel married, Squire's attitudes about the marriage requirements of the church had changed. He had reached the opinion that his children should have the right to marry the person of their choice. To take such a stand, at that time, took strong moral fortitude on Squire's part. It could not have been an easy choice for Squire to make. The church, at that time, was a vital force in the lives of the early colonists and being a non-conformist could result in serious repercussions.

Squire was not comfortable living with the harsh feelings created by the friction between his family and the church after Israel married out of the church. After careful thought, he decided it was not a wholesome atmosphere to raise his family. He thought it was best for the family to move away from the critical eye of the church. In 1750, they moved to North Carolina.

In North Carolina, Squire, Sarah, and part of the family became Baptists and two of their sons were occasional preachers. Several members of the family signed the petition to establish the town of Louisville, and according to reports, Squire Jr. preached the first sermon in Louisville.

Children of Squire and Sarah Boone:
All the children were born in Pennsylvania.
1. Sarah, b. June 1724; m. John Wilcox in 1742
2. *Israel. b. May 9, 1726, Bucks County, Pennsylvania
3. Samuel, b. May 20, 1728; m. Sarah Day
4. Jonathan, b. Dec.6, 1730; m. Mary Carter
5. Elizabeth, b. Feb.5, 1732; m. William Grant
6. Daniel, b.Oct.22, 1734, or Nov.2. d. Sept.26, 1820, St.Charles Co., Mo; m Rebecca Bryan, Aug. 1756
7. Mary, b. Nov.3, 1736, m. William Bryan
8. George, b. Jan2, 1739; m. Ann (or Nancy) Linville.
9. Edward, b. Nov.16, 1740, m. Martha Bryan
10. Squire Jr., b. Oct.5, 1744 m. Jane Van Cleave.
11. Hannah, b. Aug. 1746; m. 1st. John Stewart; 2nd. Richard Pennington.

* Israel was the oldest brother of the famous Daniel Boone. Daniel, who was a boy of 13 when Israel married, reportedly spent a large part of his formative years in the care of Israel and his wife.

While still a young man, probably about 30, Israel died in North Carolina of consumption that he caught from his wife who died of the disease before him. The couple left four children, two sons and two daughters.

Israel's children were:
1. *Jesse, b.1748
2. Jonathan, b. Nov.21, 1750
3. Elizabeth, b.Nov.28, 1752-53
4. Sarah (Sallie), b. 1754

It is of some interest that according to a Dr. Draper, recorded to be of Jesse Boone's ancestry, who wrote a book on the Boone family, verifies the cause of Israel's' early demise. Dr. Draper said, "Evidence is contained in the Moravian Records as to the cause of Israel Boone's early death. The Moravians made their first settlement near Winston-Salem in 1753. This was only about twenty miles from the Boone and Bryan settlements on the Yadkin. In the first group of settlers was a young doctor, Hans Martin Kalberlahn, who obtained all the medical education available at that period and was actually fifty or seventy five years ahead of his time. These Moravians kept careful diaries, recording the happenings of each day. The diary for 1755 contains the following entry:

'August 26. A consumptive came with his mother and asked to remain two weeks for treatment and we could not refuse.

'September 1. The consumptive was taken home by his brother, who came for him last evening. He--Mr. Boone-- returned on the 6th. accompanied by his father, who remained overnight. On the 15th. his brother came for him and he left, there being small hope for his recovery."

In further notes, Dr. Hodges states that Israel died the following year in 1756.

*Jesse Boone:

Jesse was the oldest child of Israel and his wife (unknown). He was born 1748 in Pennsylvania. Dr. Hodges, along with a Dr. Draper researched the Boone family in depth and much of the information here came from their research. They recorded Jesse to be a man of about 5ft.8 to10 inches tall. He married Sarah McMahan, the daughter of James McMahan of Rowan County, in 1772 in Rowan County, Tenn. They had eight children. Jesse died about 1830 in McMinn, Tennessee. He was buried in the family graveyard at the old homestead where he lived near Athens, Tenn.

Historical records, gathered by Dr. Draper, report that Daniel Boone, Jesse's uncle, and Daniel's wife, Rebecca, raised Jesse after both of his parents died from consumption. Daniel had married two month after Israel died.

Jesse is known to have gone into Kentucky with his famous uncle on more than one occasion, along with Daniel's brother Squire Jr., to help with supplies.

According to Dr. Hodges research, Jesse first entered land in the initial formation of Burkes County. It was a common practice at that time for some frontiersmen to go into a new unsettled territory a year or two in advance of its establishment and "squat" on the portion of land they wanted to occupy as a home site.

Jesse and Sarah raised their children in Burkes County until 1810 when they moved to Watauga territory in North Carolina. They settled near what was called Coffee's Gap of the Blue Ridge but later was known as Watauga County. A creek that flowed through that section into the Watauga River was known as Boone's Fork.

The church was always an important part of Jesse's life and he was an active church member in the old Yadkin Baptist Church in Burke County, having been chosen clerk and deacon at different times.

However, his experience with the Three Forks Baptist church, founded in 1790 in Watauga section apparently did not go so well. The church minutes, still preserved, include a number of entries involving the Boones. Several controversies occurred between Jesse and the church leaders and at some point Jesse reportedly said something that angered church leaders and resulted in Jesse being excommunicated from the church. Some researchers believe that experience may have been what prompted him to move once again, even though he was an old man at that time.

He sold his farm in 1823 and moved to McMinn, Tennessee. In McMinn, Jesse built his last home with his own two hands. It was a large house for those days, twenty by twenty foot with a lean to and a large stone fireplace that would accommodate a six-foot-log. The fireplace was equipped with pot hangers and all the extras it took to make a good fireplace. A small cabin was built behind the house for Dinah, the family's "faithful old Negro woman." Dinah lived to be 100 years old. She was like a member of the family. She had joined the Three Forks Church with them.

By 1828, Jesse was seeking membership in a new church. The church, organized in 1822 by a group of pioneers in McMinn was called the Zion Hill Baptist Church. A group of pioneers standing on the banks of Chester Creek organized the church and cut logs to construct the first church building. Zion Hill Baptist church is the oldest church in McMinn County and is still active with a well-kept cemetery.

When Jesse, then 80 years old, came forward to the Zion Hill Church, he explained his difficulties he had experienced with the Three Forks Church. After hearing his story, Zion Hill Church members thought that Jesse's exclusion from that church seemed unjust. They wrote the Three Forks Church requesting a letter but the former church refused to send one. The Zion Hill Church then decided to override receiving the letter and voted to accept Jesse as a member anyway.

These minutes, taken from the old Zion Hill Church records note that, on Saturday Feb. 1828, "Old Father Boone came forward to the church and stated that he had been a member in the Baptist church, and was excluded from the church, and told us the circumstances, and we concluded to write the church where it was done, for a bill of charges, and appointed brethren John Byler and James Sewell to write the church concerning the matter."

Church minutes Feb.1829 states, "Received an answer from the New River Church concerning Old Father Boone's case and laid the matter over until the old man could be present." The church referred to Jesse as "Old Boone," because his grandson was also named Jesse. Jesse Boone died in 1829.

Jesse and Sarah's children were:
1. Jonathan, b.1775, Osage Co., Missouri
2. Daniel, b. 1776-77
3. Israel b.Feb.7, 1780
4. Sarah, m. Jonathan Wilson
5. Hannah, b. about 178
6. Anna, b. July 26, 1785
7. Celia, b. 1790
8. ***Rachel**, b. early 1793-4

The Coffees

*Rachel Boone;

Rachel Boone married Marvel Coffee Feb. 2, 1813. Marvel was the son of Asbury M. Coffee. He was apparently named for his father because Marvels' first name was also Asbury. The Coffee ancestral line is not easily traced, and has not yet been recorded in depth. The surname Coffee shows up intermittently in several of the Daisy Chain ancestry searches from early frontiers days. It shows up in the Petty, Mefford, Sisney, and other family lines. It is of interest why more is not known about the Coffee family because the name is found in records back in the 1700s. Records indicate that Rachel and Marvel Coffee moved to Kentucky soon after they married. Census records of 1850, Osage County, Missouri show that their fifth child,*Irvin, was born in Kentucky in 1822-23, probably in Wayne County where Rachel's brother, Daniel, lived.

After Rachel's father, Jesse, died, Rachel and Marvel lived on the old Jesse Boone homestead for about six years. In 1835, they moved to Central Missouri where Rachel's brother, Jonathan and his family, had moved a year earlier.

When Rachel moved to Missouri, she brought her 2-year-old grandchild with her. Her son-in-law, William Moss, the child's father, also accompanied the family. The child's mother, whose name is not known, was Rachel's daughter. She and her infant baby both died before the rest of the family moved to Missouri. Circumstances involved in their deaths may have delayed the Coffee's earlier move in 1834

Rachel and Marvel Coffee's children were:
1. A daughter (name unknown) married William Moss, in Tennessee. Probably died in 1834-35.
2. Lavinia Coffee
3. Elizabeth, m. William Petty; they lived in Maries county, Missouri until his death, After his death, Elizabeth and children moved to Howell County, Mo.
4. Temperance, m. James Orr
5. ***Irvin** b.1822, Wayne County, Kentucky
6. William Brazeal
7. Squire, b. May 3, 1828
8. Campbell, b. 1831 in Tennessee

Irvin Coffee was born in 1822-23, in Wayne County, Kentucky. He moved with his parents to Missouri in 1835. He married Nancy Hughes, who had a twin sister, Jane. He died in Maries County, Missouri in the early 1860s.Irvin and Nancy had nine children.

Children of Irvin and Nancy Coffee:
1. John, b. Dec.1844
2. *** Alexander Campbell**, b. Dec.20, 1846

3. William, m Belle Whitton
4. Squire, m. Sarah Gibson
5. Martha, m. E.P. Mahaney
6. Samuel, m. Sarah Vaughn
7. James, m. Maggie Crafton
8. A son died in infancy
9. A daughter died in infancy

*Alexander Campbell Coffee was born Dec.20, 1846 in Vista, Mo. He married Martha Ann Doyal Oct.11, 1866. He died Sept.6, 1912 and was buried in Doyal Cemetery, Vista, Missouri. They had nine children.

Martha Ann Doyal Coffee was born September 11, 1850. She was the daughter of William Lewis and Electra Leah (Fayling) Doyal. They were married the same day as Alex's brother John, in a double ceremony. Martha Ann died in Florence, Colorado. She was buried in Doyal Cemetery, Vista, Mo.

Alexander Campbell and Martha Ann Coffee's children:
1. William Marion, b. July24, 1867
2. Nancy Catherine (Katy) b., Dec. 25, 1869.
   m. Fernando Mahaney, d. a young mother in Texas, Nov.21, 1921
3. James Hugh, b., March 27, 1871, lived in Osceola, Mo. No children
4. Mary Ellen b.,Dec.10, 1872, Vista, Mo.
5. ***Lillie Evalina** b.Dec.26, 1876, d.1955, K.C. Mo.
6. Martha Rebecca, b., June 13, 1881
7. Arthur Bunker b., July 14, 1883
8. Estle Perry b., July13, 1886
9. Irvin Earl (twin to Estle) b, June 1886, died at four and a half months.

Lillie Evalina Coffee was born December 26, 1876. She first married Jason Moreland Knight of Weaubleau, Missouri when she was about 20. The Knight family was mostly local well-established business owners in that area. Jason Moreland was a carpenter contractor and "jack of all trades." They later moved to Kansas and then to Kansas City, Missouri. They were divorced about 1914. She married Frank Gaines. In later years, she married a Mr. Culver. She died in Kansas City, Missouri in 1955. Lillie Evalina and Frank Gaines had one daughter, Jean Ruth Gaines

Lillie and Jason Knight's children are shown in the Knight section of this book

The Knight Family:

Ephriam Knight is the first Knight of proven ancestry to the Homer Knight family. Very little is known about him except that he was of Scot-Irish descent. Family genealogists believe he was one of three brothers who settled near Baltimore, Maryland early in the history of this country in the 1700s. The brothers had a joint partnership in an import and export, mercantile business, but after a family disagreement, they parted ways. One went to Pennsylvania, the other stayed in Maryland and Ephriam went to Stafford County, Virginia where he died. Any Knights who trace their ancestry to Stafford Count, Va. are presumed to be related because Ephriam was reportedly the only Knight in that county.

There is some disagreement among researchers as to the origin of the surname Knight. Some researchers believe the name Knight may have been MacKnight or MacNaughten at one time. However, other researchers state that the Knights were a sept (branch of) of the McNaughten clan or the Knights of the McNaughten clan.

Ephriam's wife is unknown but a son, named ***James Valentine** is recorded in the family genealogy. Family researchers believe there were probably other children. However, they were not recorded.

* James married a Miss Kendal, first name unknown, in Virginia. A native of the Old Dominion State, James migrated to Ross County, Ohio at an early date. He was a soldier in the War of 1812.

Children of James Valentine Knight
1. ***John** b. Oct.20, 1802, d. 1888, Stafford County, Va.
2. Dan
3. Isaac
4. James
5. A daughter who married a Campbell
6. A daughter who married Little
7. A daughter who married Baker

*John Knight married Candacy or Candocia Mitchell, the daughter of Frederick Mitchell. Mitchell was a native of Ohio. The couple married in Ohio but moved to Indiana in 1834 and settled in Howard County. He served four terms as County Commissioner. He was a Baptist Minister and practiced medicine. He and his wife are buried in Albright Cemetery, Howard County, Indiana.

John and Candacy, s children were:
1. Mathiew b.
2. James Valentine, b. June 26, 1831, Howard, Co. Indiana
3. Henrietta, died at age 12.
4. ***John**, b. Sept.12, 1837, Howard County, Indiana
5. Elizabeth, b. Jan.25, 1839, Howard County, Ind.
6. PriscillaAnna, b. Aug.15, 1844, Howard Co. Ind.
7. Martha J., b 1845, Howard Co., Ind.
8. Lewis, b. 1848, Howard Co. Ind.
9. Isaac Newton, b. 1853, Howard Co., Ind.

* John Knight married Elizabeth Moreland, June 4, 1857. She was born Jan.17, 1843, the daughter of Jason Moreland and sister to Darius Moreland. Darius married John's sister, Priscilla.

John and Elizabeth Knight about 1870

John and Darius Moreland were probably childhood friends. Family records show that he and Darius made a trip with others to South Dakota by way of Cheyenne about 1851. John would have been about 14 and Darius about the same age. They also made another trip through the West after they were married but did not take their wives.

At one point John established a successful Hardware and Implement Business in Weaubleau, Missouri. The business handled a wide variety of inventory including carriages, wood cook stove, etc. and hardware.

Knight's Hardware and Implement Store
Weaubleau, Missouri

John and Elizabeth Knight's children were:

1. George A., b. Feb 22, 1863
2. William S. b.Sept.15, 1865, d. April 17, 1940
3. ***Jason Moreland**, b. Nov.26, 1867. d.Jan.29, 1923
4. John Knight III, b. Dec.3, 1869.d. Sept. 25, 1870
5. Ida Anne, b. July 7, 1871
6. Iven Robert, b. Aug.15, 1875
7. James Valentine, b. March 19, 1873
8. Ora Lucretia, b. March 1, 1878.D. May23, 1939. She taught at Indian Schools at Carlisle., Pa. andValentine Reservation, Arizona.

Knight Siblings: Bk.Row: Edith, George, Ida. Front Row: Ora, Jason, Maud

* **Jason Moreland Knight** married **Lillie Evalina Coffee** March 28, 1894 at Weaubleau, Missouri. She was born Dec.26, 1876. They lived in Kansas for at one time and later moved to Kansas City, Missouri. He was a carpenter-contractor. After Jason and Lillie were divorced about 1914, Lillie married Frank Gaines. That marriage didn't last and she married a Mr.Flanders, and later married.Mr. Culver.

Jason died Jan 29, 1923. Lillie died Jan.9, 1955. Both Lillie and Jason are buried in Mount Washington Cemetery, Kansas City, Missouri.

Jason, and Lillie Knight and son, John

Jason and Lillie Knight's children were:
1. John Alexander, b. Aug. 20, 1896,Weaubleau, Missouri,. m. Eva Scott, 2nd. Louise 3rd. remarried Eva d.April 9, 1976.
2. Vera Elsa, b. July 29, 1898.Weaubleau, Missouri m. Sim Brasher of Miss.; 2nd.Bert Eldon Irish March 28, 1932
3. Okla Marion, b. April 16, 1900, Weaubleau, Missouri. m. Erma Higgs. d. June 21, 1989 in Oregon
4. Oliver Bunker, b. April 16, 1900. A twin to Okla, d. Jan.1901
5. ***William Homer**, b.Feb.9, 1904, Weaubleau, Missouri. m. Iva Lillian McIntyre July 15, 1922. d. Sept.17, 1982
6. Noel Valentine, b. Feb.14, 1906.Weableau, Missouri m. Elnora Mamie Harkins, d. Nov. 10,1994San Antonio, Texas
7. James Morris, b. July 4, 1909. d. July 4, 1909
8. Juel Marie, b. July 4, 1909. d. July 4, 1909 James and Juel were twins
9. Leuzeaneth Edna, b. Jan21, 1910.d. July 21, 1910

John, Homer, Vera, Noel Knight about 1945 Vera and friend 1916

Vera and friend 1916

W. Homer Knight was born in Weaubleau, Missouri. The family moved to Kansas City, Kansas. Homer's parents were divorced about 1915 and he moved with his father, Jason Knight to Kansas City, Missouri. More on his life is included in the first section of this book, "They Called Her Daisy."

Homer and Lillian's Children were:

1. Jean Marie, b. July 29,1924 in Kansas city, Missouri, m. Paul Hale 2nd. James Fisher later lived in Channelview, Texas. 2009
2. Edna Muril, b. July 10,1926, Kansas City, Missouri, m. Troy H. Hart of Channelview, Texas. They lived in Channelview, Texas from 1953 to 1982. Now lives in Rosanky, Texas 1982-2009.
3. Audrey Joyce, b. Nov. 3, 1928, d. June 4, 1933 from Diphtheria, buried in Mount Washington Cemetery, Kansas City, Mo.
4. Judith Elaine (adopted) b. April 21, 1943 in Kansas City, Mo. m. Buddy McFarland d. June 16, 2007 in Channelview, Texas of emphysema

 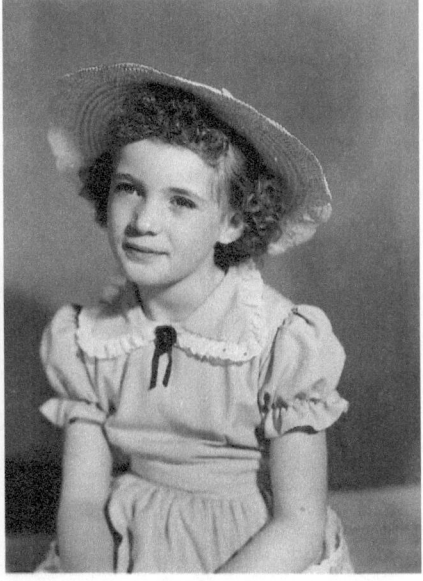

Muril Audrey and Jean Knight, 1929 Judith Elaine Knight, 1952